Symbolic Computation and Education

Symbolic Computation and Education

editors

Shangzhi Li

Beihang University, China

Dongming Wang

Beihang University, China & UPMC—CNRS, France

Jing-Zhong Zhang

Huazhong Normal University, Guangzhou University &
Chinese Academy of Sciences, China

World Scientific

NEW JERSEY · LONDON · SINGAPORE · BEIJING · SHANGHAI · HONG KONG · TAIPEI · CHENNAI

Published by

World Scientific Publishing Co. Pte. Ltd.

5 Toh Tuck Link, Singapore 596224

USA office: 27 Warren Street, Suite 401-402, Hackensack, NJ 07601

UK office: 57 Shelton Street, Covent Garden, London WC2H 9HE

British Library Cataloguing-in-Publication Data
A catalogue record for this book is available from the British Library.

SYMBOLIC COMPUTATION AND EDUCATION

ISBN-13 978-981-277-599-3
ISBN-10 981-277-599-4

Printed in Singapore by World Scientific Printers (S) Pte Ltd

PREFACE

Symbolic computation is one of the most fundamental areas of research in computational science that produces powerful software systems for exact computation and formal reasoning with expressions in symbolic form. Such systems provide a revolutionary way of presenting scientific knowledge and principles to the current generation of students. They have been widely used for education in many disciplines at different levels. How to make the use of symbolic computation systems more effective for education, how to create curricula and dynamic teaching and learning environments into which symbolic computation is integrated, how to design innovative pedagogical methodologies, techniques, and materials based on symbolic computation, how to evaluate the impact of symbolic computation in education, and what type of new methods and tools should be developed for educational purposes? These are some of the questions that have to be considered and studied but cannot be skirted round in today's world where computing technologies play an increasingly important role. Answers to these questions have profound implications for the formulation and implementation of educational policies and programs.

To address the above questions, to exchange ideas and views, and to present research and experiments, more than 40 foreign and Chinese researchers, educators, and other experts actively involved or interested in developing, using, and practicing methods and software tools of symbolic computation for education met at the International Seminar on Symbolic Computation in Education (SCE 2006 — http://www.cc4cm.org/sce2006), held at Beihang University, Beijing, China from the 12th to 14th April 2006. This book has evolved from the invited and contributed talks given at the seminar SCE 2006. It presents a collection of articles on current studies and concerns of mathematics education and the use and development of software systems and technologies of symbolic computation for education. The 14 formally refereed articles contained in the book are written mostly by leading experts and educators and cover a wide range of topics from teaching philosophy and curriculum development to symbolic and algebraic manipulation and automated geometric reasoning, and to the design and implementation of educational software and integrated teaching and learning environments.

The book consists of three related parts: the first part is concerned with the use of technologies for mathematics education at the secondary and undergraduate levels, the second part is devoted mainly to presenting dynamic geometry software and its integration and combination with computer algebra systems for educational purpose, and the third part describes several methods and techniques of symbolic and algebraic computation that have potential applications in mathematics education. The book is worth reading and may serve as a useful reference for researchers, educators, and other professionals interested in symbolic computation and education.

The editors thank all the authors for their valuable contributions and the referees for their expertise and timely help. The seminar SCE 2006 and the preparation of this book have been supported by the Key Laboratory of Mathematics, Informatics and Behavioral Semantics of the Ministry of Education of China and the School of Science, Beihang University.

Shangzhi Li

Dongming Wang

Jing-Zhong Zhang

Beijing and Wuhan

July 2007

CONTENTS

THE CRISIS WE FACE AND HOW TO TRY TO DEAL WITH IT

J. JERRY UHL[†] and DEBRA WOODS[‡]

Department of Mathematics
University of Illinois at Urbana-Champaign
Urbana, IL 61801, USA
E-mail: juhl@cm.math.uiuc.edu[†]
dwoods2@uiuc.edu[‡]
www.uiuc.edu

Math education in the United States is in crisis. Student performance and desire to learn is declining. Some groups feel that the cure is to drive math education back and increase rote memorization and teaching to the test. The fact is that the math taught 50 years ago will not prepare today's students for today's world.

Keywords: Math education.

The Failure of Math Education in Our Schools

One crisis of American education is the dramatic drop out rate of high school students from college-intending mathematics programs. Typically a full half of a high school freshman class will drop out of the college-mathematics preparation sequence before their sophomore year. Half of the remaining students are likely to drop out by the next year; and half of those remaining students are likely out during the following year. Only about 12% of the students who started will actually complete the sequence. Math eduction has failed to capture the interests and imaginations of today's high school students.[1]

This is a crisis for students in the schools because math permeates more of university education and life outside the university than ever before. In almost every field of study, math is strikingly more important than it was even twenty years ago. Many fields of study place demands on math that were not even thought about twenty years ago. Today's culture is both math-needy and math-hungry. But school math is failing to keep up with modern demands.

Meanwhile, a mathematical organization known as "Mathematically Correct" or "HOLD," whose goal is to drive math education back 50 years, has risen to dangerous political power in the United States. Their message seems to be that math is a bitter pill, which must be swallowed, and that progress in math education is somehow evil. For them, standardized high-stakes tests justify the importance of their courses (and the test makers are not accountable to anyone).

The result is a continuing crisis in math education. As Sherri Fraser testified at a November 6, 2006 hearing of the American National Chicago:

> This crisis in mathematics education is at least 25 years old. I remember in the 1980's when the crisis in school mathematics became part of the national agenda with such publications as An Agenda For Action (NCTM, 1980), A Nation at Risk (National Commission of Excellence in Education, 1983), and Everybody Counts: A Report to the Nation on the Future of Mathematics Education (NRC, 1989). Those of you on the board who have been involved with mathematics education should remember these documents as well. Our country was in trouble. We were not preparing students for their future.

And we have yet to start. Recently William Wulf, President of the National Academy of Engineering, gave a speech called "The Urgency of Engineering Education Reform." His main points were that academia has not kept pace with changes in the professions and is failing to educate students to be technologically literate.

About 15 years ago, Peter Lax, then president of the American Mathematics Society, complained that calculus, as taught then, was full of "inert material" and "parlor tricks" and was not paying enough attention to approximate numerical methods. Though the situation remains unchanged, Mathematically Correct seems to be happy with the state of mathematical education, but thinking citizens are not.

There is not much in American school math that captures the imagination of the students. Students seem to recognize that they are being fed very little information that they will ever need or use. As Alfred North Whitehead warned: "There can be nothing more destructive of true education than to spend long hours in the acquirement of ideas and methods that lead nowhere." The students know that the only people in modern life who regularly use pencil-and-paper algebra and calculus are those who teach pencil-and-paper algebra and calculus. Modern American students are turned off by math courses that seem to play no role in students' futures. This is a real shame.

Right now, thanks to the abundance of inexpensive computers, we have the opportunity to improve math instruction on a vastly broader, more interesting front, which will improve the importance of the math learned by students. For instance, with the help of the Monte Carlo method, and programs such as *Mathematica*, probability can ascend to the top of school mathematics. The stranglehold difficult combinatorics has on school probability disappears. Important measurements related to normal (Gaussian) and exponential distributions can be handled by the Monte Carlo method thereby making that portion of mathematics no more complicated than counting.

Another example is area-of-growth models coming from $y' = f[x, y]$. By simply plotting the region where $f[x, y] > 0$ and the region where $f[x, y] < 0$, the general long term behavior of solutions can by found by visually inspecting the plot. Popular media such as Jurassic Park and Numb3rs have made students crave an understanding of chaos theory. Mathematical educators can satisfy this craving by introducing discrete dynamical systems, such as predator-prey models, where extra prey are added or harvested.

In fact the course MBC (Math before calculus) is full of such examples and may be downloaded and run on Mathematica-equipped computers. See http://calcand.math.uiuc.edu/courseware/math016/ for download and http://mtl.math.uiuc.edu/cpm/ for a description of the lessons. The material in this courseware places students in a virtual sandbox where they can play with the ideas leading up to calculus.

References

1. Mathematical Sciences Education Board, & National Research Council (1989). Everybody counts: A report to the nation on the future of mathematics education. Washington, D. C.: National Academy Press.

MATHEMATICS TOPICS FOUNDATIONAL TO CALCULUS AT THE SECONDARY LEVEL

ANTONIO R. QUESADA

Department of Theoretical & Applied Mathematics
The University of Akron, Akron, Ohio 44325-4002, USA
E-mail: aquesada@uakron.edu

In the last decade, the integration of technology in the teaching and learning of mathematics has increased substantially. As a result, many graphical ideas, some numerical ones, and some good modeling problems have found their way into the precalculus literature. At the same time, relevant concepts, methods, and approaches, now available via technology, are being ignored. In this article, we review examples of accessible concepts, approaches and applications, not yet present in most precalculus books, that illustrate how the numerical and graphical capabilities of graphing calculators together with the variety of data types that they provide, can further be used to enhance the teaching and learning of key calculus concepts.

1. Introduction

The integration of technology in the teaching and learning of mathematics is having an impact in every aspect of instruction. According to Tooke, more than a quarter of the mathematics content taught before the arrival of the scientific calculator is not being taught today.[1] Indeed, the effect of technology can nowadays be observed from changes in content and assessment, to more hands-on inquiry teaching methods and classroom activities. Thus, a simple comparison among current precalculus books and those written 15 years ago, before technology started to be integrated, reveals that visualization is playing an increasing role not only in the scope of the content, but also in the way that many concepts are introduced, and in the type of questions that students are asked. After 10–15 years of using graphing calculators, it is appropriate to ask: Are we taking full advantage of the main capabilities that this technology offers in order to provide secondary students with the best possible preparation for calculus? Before we proceed to address this question, it is convenient to review and contrast very briefly the main tendencies found in the mathematics classroom before and after the integration of technology started.

We remark that in this article, unless otherwise specified, that by technology we mean any technology with the capabilities of modern graphing calculators without symbolic manipulations. In fact, the syntax used in the commands and the screens provided corresponds to the Texas Instruments TI-83. The screens included, sometimes in excess, will remove any doubts in reproducing the solutions provided.

2. Mathematics Instruction Before the Integration of Technology

Prior to the integration of technology, the accessibility of various topics in secondary mathematics was fairly linear, since it depended on the analytical capabilities of the students. In the United States, problems were typically categorized as belonging to algebra I, algebra II, geometry, precalculus or calculus. Thus, optimization problems, for instance, were first studied in calculus, since the calculation of local extrema typically requires differential calculus. Similarly, given that without technology most graphs could not be properly drawn without calculus, some properties of functions like the range were introduced, but only very simple examples were considered; other properties such as the extrema, or the local behavior of functions were not considered. Moreover, the topics studied were also limited by constraints imposed by the extent of the calculations needed and length of time they required. Hence, even after the scientific calculator appeared, very little was done numerically with these topics and secondary students.

In addition, mastering calculations was essential to finish problems. Hence, the teaching of algorithms often took precedence over conceptual understanding and the study of relevant applications. Furthermore, the time required for exploration and discovery without the use of technology did not contribute to make these regular classroom activities. Finally, teaching tended to be more teacher-centered rather than student-centered.

3. Mathematics Instruction After the Integration of Technology

After the integration of technology started, the distinction between activities appropriate to students at various courses and ability levels becomes less clear. The ability to bridge over cumbersome calculations via technology allows students at various levels to i) use technology to meaningfully

6

explore concepts and problems previously proposed to the most advanced mathematics students, and to ii) extend the breadth and depth treatment of these concepts. Teaching with technology provides new insight into concepts and helps build connections.[2] Also, "when students can see the connections across different mathematical content areas, they develop a view of mathematics as an integrated whole".[3] Technology facilitates changing the focus to a more conceptual one, while including more relevant applications and increasing classroom exploration and discovery. Teaching is becoming more student-centered, with inquiry playing an increasingly bigger role on the delivery, and on the activities proposed. It should not come as a surprise that assumptions about mathematics curricula made in a time prior to the integration of technology in the classroom are, in some cases, no longer valid. Thus topics such as optimization, different matrix applications,[4] linear and nonlinear regression,[5] recursion[6] etc. are now accessible to students prior to calculus in secondary and introductory college levels.

4. Goals of This Article

In this article we present a selection of examples and applications, some of them not yet present in most precalculus books, which illustrate:

(1) How the numerical and graphical capabilities of graphing calculators can be used to enhance the teaching and learning of key calculus concepts (functions, approximation, optimization...) at the secondary level.
(2) How some of these concepts (for example local and end behavior) can be presented, using different representations, in the way they were originally developed and are better understood, i.e., via approximations.
(3) How it is possible to introduce at this level relevant concepts, traditionally reserved for upper levels, which now are accessible via technology.
(4) How the data types available in graphing calculators help to introduce new approaches to problem solving.
(5) Since technology enables students to revisit problems from different perspectives based upon the depth of their mathematical knowledge, it is possible to use a spiral approach to some of these concepts, like optimization, through different courses preceding calculus.[7]

Before we start presenting examples that illustrate other topics that can be introduced to strengthen students' conceptual understanding and overall preparation for calculus, it is important to decide on what criteria we shall use to select the concepts, mathematical models, or tools that we include.

We believe that any new topic should be assessed based on the relevance of the concepts that it addresses and/or facilitates as evidenced by, i) its usefulness, as defined by the variety and importance of applications that the topic can be used for, and ii) its accessibility, with an appropriate degree of complexity of the concepts and calculations needed for the level that it is proposed.[8] Unless otherwise mentioned, the examples we have included have been tested with precalculus students.

We remark that since this paper is written for math educators with some familiarity with graphing technology, what we denote as the solution of each example refers to comments we deem relevant on the exploratory process of solving the problem, rather than to a detailed explanation of all the steps involved in obtaining the solution.

5. How the Integration of Technology Expands the Study of Functions in Precalculus

We list next major possible changes that technology facilitates on the traditional coverage of functions.[9]

(I) The learning of basic transformations, such as $f(x) + a, f(x + a), -f(x), a \cdot f(x), f(ax), |f(x)|$, and $f|x|$ facilitates the study of families of functions, each with a root or parent function.

(II) The simultaneous introduction of the analytical, graphical, and numerical aspects of functions makes possible that students can: i) support graphically and/or numerically analytical solutions of equations, ii) support analytically graphical and numerical solutions, whenever possible, iii) moreover, they can find some irrational solutions that would not be available analytically at this level.[10]

(III) In addition to the properties traditionally considered for every family of continuous functions, the integration of technology allows one to include:

(a) finding the range of all functions studied,
(b) determining irrational zeros, hence all the real zeros,
(c) finding local extrema, with intervals where the function is increasing or decreasing,
(d) using sequences to explore the local and end behavior,
(e) comparing relative growth of functions or families of functions,
(f) considering relevant examples of data that can be modeled via regression by the family of functions studied,
(g) optimization problems.

(IV) The toolbox that we provide to the students can now include the use of nontraditional tools such as lists, sequences, and recursion to solve different problems.

One cannot ignore the fact that with every new technology a new set of misconceptions and students errors begin to appear. We will try to address in the examples some of the common misunderstandings associated with the graphing technology, namely that "every function seems continuous," "exceeding the precision of the machine," "use of inadequate window," etc.

6. On the Role of Transformations with all Families of Functions

Traditionally, students have been taught to complete the square of a quadratic expression. However, the emphasis generally was placed on justifying the quadratic formula or in other algebraic lessons derived from this process. Often, the graphical connection between the functions $y = (x - a)^2 + b$ and $y = x^2$ was omitted. Similarly, one rarely finds in the basic books any reference to the transformations needed to obtain, for example, a logarithmic function, such as $y = \ln[2(x - 1)^3]$ from the parent function $y = \ln x$, or a rational function like

$$f(x) = \frac{5x - 11}{x - 2} \text{ from the "root" function } g(x) = \frac{1}{x}.$$

With the exception of trigonometric functions, very little attention seems to be paid to the role of transformations on the basic families of continuous functions studied. As the next example illustrates, graphing technologies facilitate the study of these transformations and their implications.

Example 6.1. What transformations are needed to obtain

$$\text{a) } f(x) = \frac{5x - 11}{x - 2} \text{ from } g(x) = \frac{1}{x} ?$$

$$\text{b) } y = \ln[2(x - 1)^3] \text{ from } y = \ln x ?$$

a) By simple division we can express $f(x) = 5 - 1/(x - 2)$, and follow the changes of the graph of $g(x)$ via the horizontal shifting and the reflection (y_3) as seen in Figs. 1a and 1b, and after the vertical shifting (y_4) as seen in Fig. 1c. Hence, we can understand the effect of the transformations on the original function's properties, such as the asymptotes of $g(x)$, as compared with the resulting function $f(x)$.

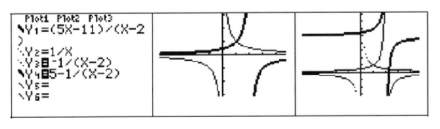

Figure 1a   Figure 1b   Figure 1c

b) Similarly, using basic properties of logarithms, students can re-express the given function as $y = \ln 2 + 3\ln(x-1)$. From this expression, it is easy to see the

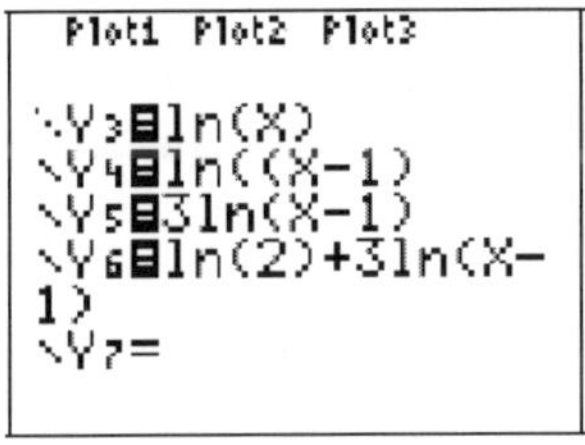

Figure 1d 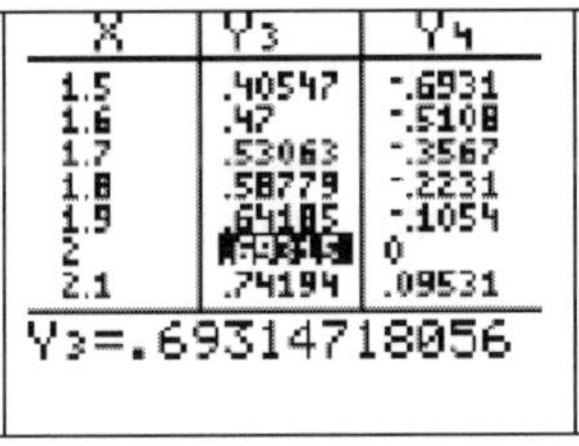   Figure 1e 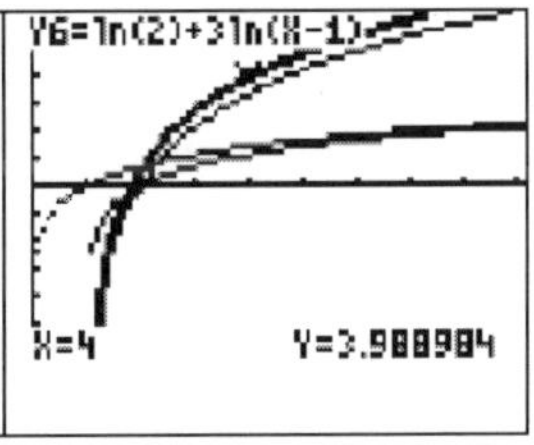   Figure 1f

transformations needed (Fig. 1d) to obtain the given function from the root function $y = \ln x$.

As in the previous example, the student may choose to confirm his answer by tracing on the graphs of the sequence of functions obtained after each transformation (Fig. 1f). He may also want to track down the effect of each transformation on a value of x, using the table as shown in Fig. 1e.

When studying transformations, we have found that to deepen students' understanding, it is convenient to ask questions to either find the transformations used to obtain one graph from another, or to apply some transformations to a given graph of a function rather than to the algebraic expression of the function. Thus, in Fig. 1g we can ask for the transformations needed to obtain $G(x)$ from $F(x)$; or we can provide the graph of a function, say $H(X)$, as in Fig. 1h and ask the students to draw the graph resulting from applying a sequence of transformations to it, say $K(X) = 2 - 3H(x+1)$.

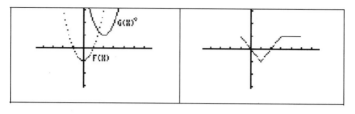

Figure 1g   Figure 1h

7. On Solving Equations and Inequalities

The interplay among the different representations now available is particularly helpful when solving equations and inequalities. We present two
examples, the first, involving a quadratic inequality, illustrates how the old
algebraic approach becomes obsolete when the students can visualize the
graph. Our second example aims to show the students that graphs can be
misleading, and that they need to corroborate what "seems" to be true. To
that end, we show a transcendental equation whose graph seems to show
that there are two solutions when it only has one.

Example 7.1. Find the closed form or exact solution of the inequality

$$2x^2 - 2x - 1 \geq 0.$$

Solution. Asking for the exact solution is the easiest way of forcing the
student to use an algebraic approach.[11] Once the exact solution of the
equation involved is obtained via the quadratic formula, namely $(1 \pm \sqrt{3})/2$,
students can confirm its correctness as well as the sign of the function on the
intervals that the zeros create by testing values in *Homescreen* (Fig. 2a) or
in the table (Fig. 2c). They can also solve the equation graphically (Fig. 2b),
and compare its decimal expressions of the graphical solution with those of
the exact solutions found.

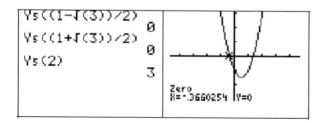

Figure 2a   Figure 2b

Clearly, simply by observing the graph (Fig. 2b), the students can identify the intervals where the function is non negative as:

$$(-\infty, (1 - \sqrt{3})/2] \cup [(1 + \sqrt{3})/2, \infty)$$

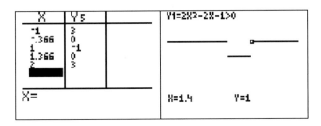

| Figure 2c | Figure 2d |

Finally, one may graph the given inequality using the fact that these calculators evaluate a true comparison as one and a false comparison as zero. Tracing in the graph obtained (Fig. 2d) we can confirm the intervals where the inequality is true and where it is false.

In the past, students were taught to solve algebraic inequalities involving polynomial or rational functions by factoring the associated equation, and then creating a table to test each factor and their product or quotient, to determine the sign of the function on each of the subintervals that the zeros create on the domain. Indeed, looking at the graph makes this approach obsolete.

In our opinion, when graphing calculators are available, students should be asked to solve more inequalities than equations, since they force the students to think graphically. Hence, the fact that most textbooks that include the use of graphing calculators do not ask the students to solve inequalities with every family of functions studied, is perhaps an indicator of the constraints that the old curriculum still brings to bear on us.

We remark that research has consistently shown that the ability to double check the solutions obtained, consistently ranks in the top of the list of things that students, at different levels, like about using graphing calculators.[11,12]

Our next example illustrates a transcendental equation that can not be solved without technology at this level. It shows that, in contrast with the traditional analytical approach, the numerical and graphical approaches for solving equations are the same no matter what continuous functions are involved. In addition, this is a good example to warn students of the risks of over–relying on what the graphs seem to show us.

Example 7.2. Solve $x^3 - 2x = 2\cos x$.

Solution. Students can either find the intersections of the functions representing either side of the equation $f(x) = x^3 - 2x$ and $g(x) = 2\cos(x)$, or the zeros of the difference function $h(x) = x^3 - 2x - 2\cos x$. In general, using the latter seems to prevent more students' mistakes when finding all the solutions. This may be due to the fact that students are more familiar with obtaining the zeros of the graph of a continuous function, than with considering the relative growth of two functions to determine hidden solutions, a topic that typically is not part of the curriculum.

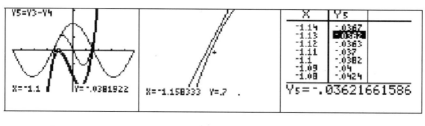

Figure 3a   Figure 3b   Figure 3c

Figure 3a shows the graphs of $f(x)$, $g(x)$, and $f(x) - g(x)$, the last with a thick line. Initially, there seems to be two intersections, however, by zooming in a small neighborhood of the leftmost portion of the graph, we see (Fig. 3b) that this is not the case. Students using the table can see that the function does not change signs on the interval that seems visually to contain the zero. Figures 3d and 3e illustrate how to get the only existing intersection using the difference function. We remark that, as the table illustrates, the change of sign facilitates using the "numerical zoom in." This process consists in successively locating nested intervals containing the zero until the precision sought is found. In every step, once an interval containing the zero is found, we redefine the table setup by letting *TblStart* be the left hand side of the interval and ΔTbl be one tenth the length of the interval (see Figs. 3e and 3f).

8. On the Relative Growth of Functions

The need for introducing the relative growth of different families of functions is essential if we are going to use the graphical approach. Otherwise,

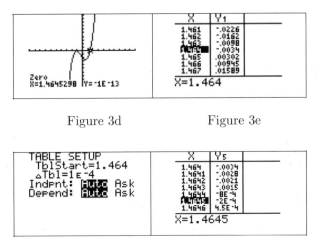

Figure 3d   Figure 3e

Figure 3f   Figure 3g

students will not be able to know when they may expect the existence of intersects not shown in the window in use. We have been able to introduce this idea without investing much time, by simply asking the students a few problems like the example that follows.

Example 8.1. Organize the given functions

$$f_1(x) = 10x^2, \ f_2(x) = \sqrt{x}, \ f_3(x) = 2^x, \ f_4(x) = 2\ln x$$

from slowest to fastest increasing.

Solution. A look at the graphs (Fig. 4a) shows that the power and the exponential functions grow faster than the other two, thus it is easier to analyze them in pairs. Students learn quickly that trying to find the right window to solve the problem graphically can be time consuming, while using the table in this case is easier and faster (Figs. 4b–4c).

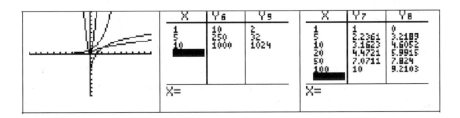

Figure 4a   Figure 4b   Figure 4c

Example 8.2. Solve $x^4 = 2^x$.

The graph of this example (Fig. 5a) illustrates how understanding that the exponential function grows faster than the power function is essential to guess the existence of a third root in this equation.

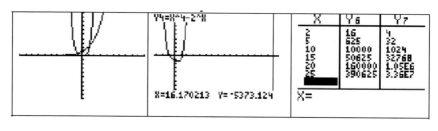

Figure 5a   Figure 5b   Figure 5c

As mentioned before, it is usually easier to find a hidden solution when treated as a zero (Fig. 5b), i.e., when working with the difference function. Otherwise, as seen in Fig. 5c, simply by using the table, secondary students can easily decide which function grows faster and guess the existence of a hidden intersection. Our next example considers the relative growth of functions from the same family.

Example 8.3. Where do the graphs of the given functions

$$f(x) = -x^3 + 3x^2 + x - 3 \text{ and } g(x) = 5 - 2x^2$$

intersect?

Solution. If students are familiar with the fundamental theorem of algebra and using the zeros of the difference function to find intersections, they can easily guess the existence of a hidden solution, since the overall degree of $f(x) - g(x)$ is three and there are two visible intersections. However, many students are satisfied with the graph shown in Fig. 6a, and since they have not been exposed to the relative growth of functions, they miss one solution. Hence, this exercise provides another example of how knowing that the cubic function grows faster than the quadratic function, makes one expect to find another intersection on the fourth quadrant (Fig. 6b). Again Fig. 6c shows the advantage of working with the difference function as it displays the third zero in the default window.

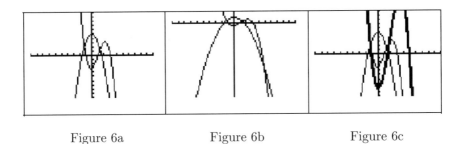

Figure 6a   Figure 6b   Figure 6c

9. On the Range and Local Extrema of Functions

Next we look at the concept of range when technology is available. Determining the range of most continuous functions used to be beyond the scope of precalculus, but since technology readily allows us to obtain the graph and, in most cases, the local extrema of these functions, it is possible now to obtain a good approximation of their ranges without calculus. In a later section we will consider optimization problems as an immediate consequence of the ability of determining local extrema. We remark that in order to solve these problems without calculus, students must become familiarized with some facts that can be "discovered" by exploration. Thus knowledge of the end behavior of basic continuous functions and the possible number of turning points of polynomial functions is essential to solve the following example.

Example 9.1. Find the range, the local extrema, and the interval where the given functions

$$\text{a) } f(x) = 2\sqrt{x} - x, \text{ and b) } g(x) = x^4 - x^3 - x^2 - 1$$

are increasing.

Solution. Since the values of x are larger than those of $2\sqrt{x}$ for $x > 4$, the graph of $f(x)$ will continue decreasing after $x = 4$, hence once the local maximum is determined from the graph via $CALC$ (Fig. 7a) or using the $TABLE$ (Fig. 7b) we can establish that the range of this function is $(-\infty, 1]$. In the second function the graph in Fig. 7c denotes the presence of three turning points, the maximum possible for a polynomial of degree four, hence $[-2.096735, \infty)$ provides a good approximation for the range. The intervals where the function is increasing do not pose any conceptual problem, since they can be immediately read from the graph once the local extrema are calculated.

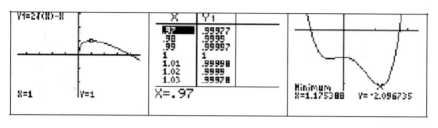

Figure 7a   Figure 7b   Figure 7c

10. On Factoring Real Polynomials

In our next example, we revisit a traditional problem using technology to illustrate three key points. First, we will see how the usual way to factor real polynomials over the rational numbers becomes simplified. At the same time, we see that this approach calls into question the need, at this level, for some of the theorems traditionally taught with this topic, like Descartes' Rule of Signs. Second, it is possible now to find *all* the real roots of real polynomials. Finally, we will illustrate the versatility that the variety of data types provides, by finding the quadratic factor of a cubic with only one real irrational root, using two different approaches. We have not used this last part of the problem in precalculus.

Example 10.1. Factor $p(x) = x^5 - 19x^3 + 6x^2 + 48x - 96$ over $\mathbb{Q}$ and $\mathbb{R}$.

Solution. Let $\mathcal{S} = \pm\{1, 2, 3, 4, 6, 8, 16, 24, 48, 96\}$ be the set of possible rational zeros.

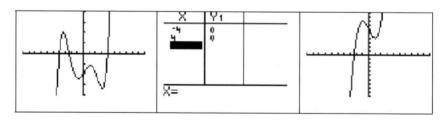

Figure 8a   Figure 8b   Figure 8c

By simple observation of the graph intercepts (Fig. 8a), the set $\mathcal{S}$ can be reduced to $\mathcal{S}' = \{\pm 4\}$. Using the table (Fig. 8b), we immediately confirm that -4 and 4 are the only rational zeros of $p(x)$ hence we can write the factorization of $p(x)$ over $\mathbb{Q}$ as $p(x) = (x + 4)(x - 4)(x^3 - 3x + 6)$.

Let $q(x) = x^3 - 3x + 6$. Its graph (Fig. 8c) shows that there is only one irrational root. This root is obtained first numerically (Figs. 8d–8e) using the Intermediate Value theorem (also referred to, as mentioned before, as a "numerical zoom-in"), and then graphically (Fig. 8f).

We remark that the value of x displayed in the graph does not show the precision of the calculation. This can be seen in Fig. 8g, where this value is stored in R and then manipulated numerically to display the entire decimal expression obtained, namely $x = -2.3553013976081$.

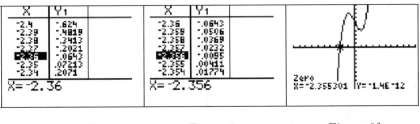

Figure 8d	Figure 8e	Figure 8f

At this point we know that the cubic $q(x)$ has two imaginary roots, but can we determine the quadratic factor that they determine? We answer the question in two different ways. First, as seen in Figs. 8h–8i, we divide the cubic by the linear factor determined by the irrational root, obtaining a quadratic function that we graph (Fig. 8.i). Then we find the vertex (H, K) of the parabola and store the coordinate values (Figs. 8j–8k), that yields the quadratic factor $y = (x - H)^2 + K$ sought.

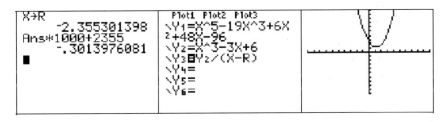

Figure 8g	Figure 8h	Figure 8i

To see how close the quadratic expressions y_3 and y_4 are, we may either move the cursor vertically from one graph to the other (Figs. 8m–8n) observing the y-values, or simply look at the table of values (Fig. 8o) of the

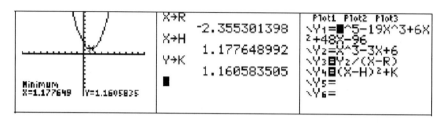

Figure 8j   Figure 8k   Figure 8l

difference function

$$y_5 = \frac{x^3 - 3x + 6}{x - R} - [(x - H)^2 + K].$$

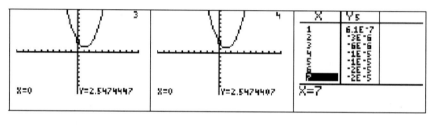

Figure 8m   Figure 8n   Figure 8o

A second approach to obtain the quadratic factor consists in generating a sequence of points for y_3 (Figs. 8p–8q), and then running a quadratic regression on them. Figure 8p displays how to generate a list L_1, containing 300 x-values, and how the list L_2 of corresponding y-values is obtained by evaluating $y_3(L_1)$.

Figure 8r shows the result of running the command $QuadReg L_1, L_2, y_6$ on them. The coefficient $R^2 = 1$ indicates that the regression smoothes out all the noise of the first approach, yielding an excellent approximation, as the table of values for $y_5 = y_3 - y_6$ that follows (Fig. 8s) confirms. The factorization of $p(x)$ over R is

$$p(x) = (x+4)(x-4)(x+2.3553013976081)(x^2+2.355301398x-2.547444674).$$

Consider now the following extension to this problem: Can we find points on the real plane whose coordinates are the real and imaginary parts of the complex solutions of the quadratic equation?

The interesting thing about this problem is that the solution was found by Shaun Pieper, a 12-grade student from St. Paul's School, Concord, New

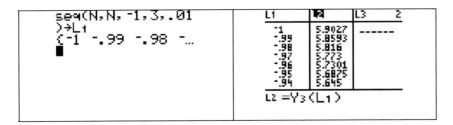

Figure 8p   Figure 8q

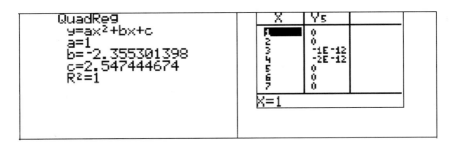

Figure 8r   Figure 8s

Hampshire.[13]

We remark that, in fact, one of the remarkable facts about the integration of technology into secondary school, is that there seems to be an increasing number of mathematical discoveries obtained by students at this level.[14] Shaun proposed the following approach that we have mimicked in Fig. 8t using Cabri Geometre software.

(1) Reflect the parabola upon $y = k$, to obtain $y = -(x - h)^2 + k$.
(2) Find the zeros of the new parabola, $A = (h - \sqrt{k}, 0)$ and $B = (h + \sqrt{k}, 0)$.
(3) Rotate 90° the segment $\overline{AB}$ determined by these zeros,
(4) The endpoints of the segment obtained are $C(h, \sqrt{k})$ and $D(h, -\sqrt{k})$.

11. On the Local and Global Behavior of a Function

When using a graphing calculator to investigate local and global behavior, topics such as scale and error become more important. For example, when graphing a function, a root might not appear in the graphing window. This can be caused by too small of a graphing window or too large of a scale, among other things. Therefore, for local or global behavior, selecting the correct viewing window becomes an essential skill.[15] Local behavior allows

20

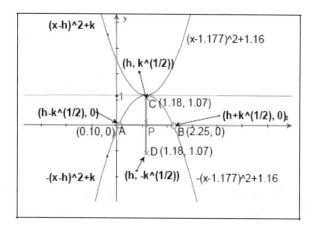

Figure 8t

one to introduce the concept of local discontinuities.

Our next example deals with the local behavior of a function. Purposely, we have chosen an example which cannot be easily solved using the traditional techniques seen in calculus. Yet we will see that technology facilitates the study of this topic numerically. This method is far more intuitive, can be used for any type of functions, is independent of ready-made formulas, and can be implemented using different approaches from elementary types (table), to a more sophisticated one such as recursion.

Example 11.1. How does the given function

$$f(x) = \frac{|x+2|}{|1 - \sqrt{x+3}|}$$

behaves as $x \to -2$?

Solution. To determine the values that the function takes in a neighborhood of -2, we generate two sequences converging to this number from either side. For simplicity we use $\{-2 \pm 10^{-n}\}$ as $n \to \infty$. The simplest way of creating these sequences is to input the x-values one by one into a table (Fig. 9a). Students familiarized with the use of the command seq may select this command to generate the sequences, and see the lists generated in the list editor as depicted in Figs. 9b and 9c. In either approach, the calculator may round up the value displayed, but as seen in Figs. 9a and 9c, placing the cursor on a particular value allows one to see its full decimal part at the bottom. As seen in Figs. 9a–9c the function approaches 2 as x approaches -2 from either side.

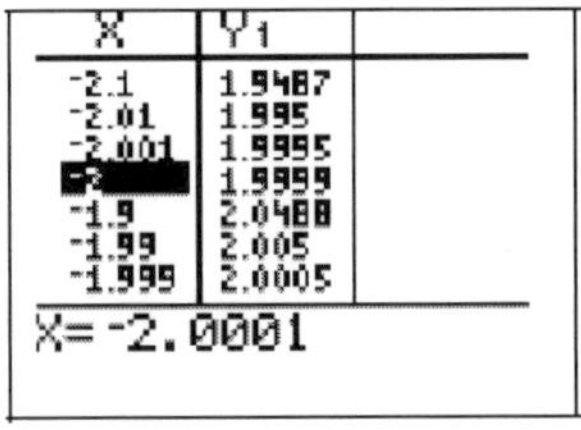

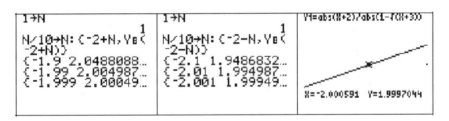

Figure 9a 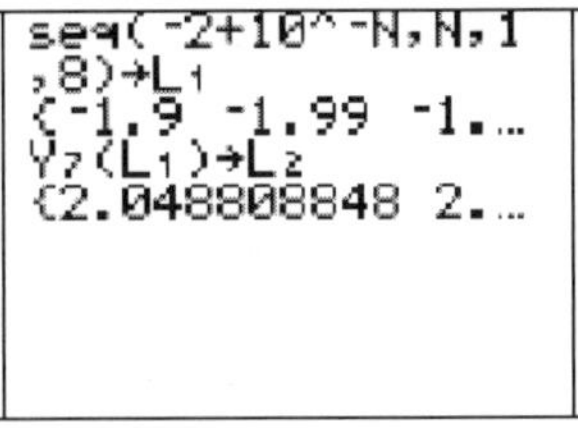   Figure 9b 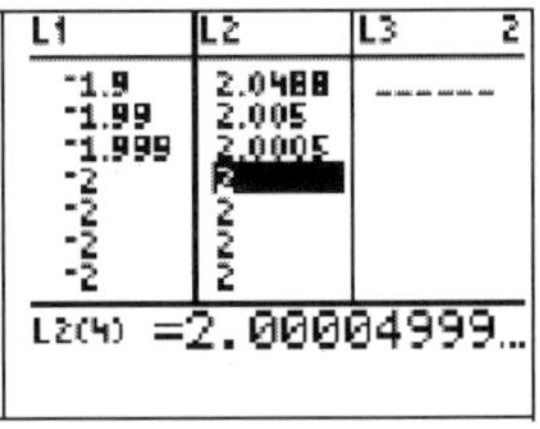   Figure 9c

We believe that, once this technology is introduced in the classroom, recursion shall become a vital part of the secondary student's toolbox.[6]

In Figs. 9d and 9e we use lists generated recursively in the *Homescreen*. Asking students to confirm graphically their numerical results reinforces the interplay of both representations. Figures 9f and 9g confirm our previous result via zoom-in. Moreover, "the zooming capabilities of graphing calculators, both graphically and numerically, allow a good intuitive sense of the difficult concepts of limits to be explored by students".[16]

Figure 9d   Figure 9e   Figure 9f

Let us now consider global behavior, i.e., the behavior of a function as the independent variable grows unbounded. For this topic, students must be acquainted with the concept of a *complete graph*, i.e., the graph or portion of the graph that contains all the relevant elements of the function such as zeros, local extrema, discontinuities, and asymptotes.

According to Demana and Waits, "the key is to build an intuitive understanding of what is considered important (intercepts, high and low points, increasing, decreasing, and end behavior) about different classes of functions. One modern role of calculus is to prove analytically when a graph is complete".[15]

Example 11.2. How do the given functions

$$\text{a) } y = \frac{3x-1}{x+1}; \quad \text{b) } f(x) = \left(1 + \frac{1}{x}\right)^x$$

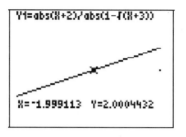

Figure 9g

behave as $x \to \pm\infty$?

Solution. In the case of the global behavior, we evaluate the function at divergent sequences like $\{\pm 10^n\}$ and observe if it seems to approach a value from either side as seen in Fig. 10a; or choose an appropriately large window to trace on the graph (Fig. 10b).

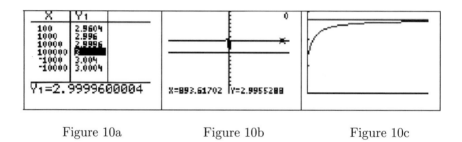

Figure 10a   Figure 10b   Figure 10c

Our second example can be used to introduce the number e in precalculus. By exploring the global behavior of this function, and then comparing the resulting values with $y = e$, as shown both graphically and numerically in Figs. 10c and 10d, students give some context to this irrational number by learning that:

$$\left(1 + \frac{1}{x}\right)^x \to e \text{ as } x \to \infty.$$

We caution that some students, while pursuing graphical convergence, may choose a window whose dimensions exceed the precision of the calculator, obtaining the chaotic behavior shown in Fig. 10e, due to the round up error. This kind of situation provides an excellent opportunity to demystify this or any other technology in use by underlining its limitations.

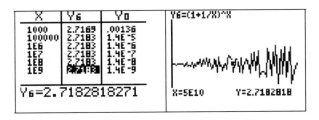

| Figure 10d | Figure 10e |

12. On Continuity

A continuous function can be intuitively defined before calculus as one whose graph can be drawn without lifting the pencil from the paper. Students understand that holes or jumps break continuity. The problem stems from the fact that graphing technology is discrete in nature (since a finite number of pixels get to be connected and shown), therefore irrational discontinuities cannot be displayed, and rational discontinuities may or may not show, depending on the window chosen and the precision of the calculator used. As a result, students tend to think that a function whose graph "seems" continuous is continuous. To fight this type of error, one should make an effort to present examples of where this happens, and guide the student to discover the discontinuity.

Example 12.1. Are the given functions

$$\text{a) } y = \frac{\sin(x - 1)}{x - 1}; \quad \text{b) } \sqrt{\frac{(|36000x| - 1)^2 - 1}{36000}}$$

continuous?

Solution. Our first example does not shows the discontinuity on the default or the trigonometric windows; however, as seen in Fig. 11a, the "zoom decimal" clearly displays it. The window dimensions are $[-4.7, 4.7] \times [-3.1, 3.1]$, and the tracing step is 0.1 in this case. From this information, we learn that the screen of this calculator has 95 horizontal and 63 vertical pixels. Hence, when trying to show a rational discontinuity, say at $x = a$, one may center the window about this value by choosing $[a - 4.7k, a + 4.7k]$, where $k \in \mathbb{N}$.

In the second example, it is time consuming to find a window that displays the intervals where the function is discontinuous. A more sensible approach is to recognize that the given function will be undefined when the function in the numerator of the radicand becomes negative, and work with that function as shown in Fig. 11c.

24

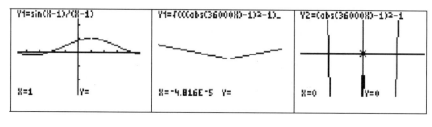

| Figure 11a | Figure 11b | Figure 11c |

Before a formal proof of the continuity of exponential functions is presented in advanced calculus, the reader of basic algebra textbooks is asked to accept that the value of the function for an irrational exponent can be approximated by evaluating the function at a sequence of rational numbers approaching the exponent. Graphing calculators allow for a hands–on approach that may help to develop students' numerical understanding of this concept, while using the same idea needed for a formal proof.

We have used the next example with honor students, providing them some guidance in the process.

Example 12.2. Explore the continuity of $y = 5^x$ at $x = \sqrt{2}$.

Solution. Students can be asked to obtain the decimal expansion of the exponent, $\sqrt{2} = 1.4142135623731\ldots$, and then asked to generate an increasing sequence that converges to the value from the left, namely $L_1 = \{1.4, 1.41, 1.414, \ldots\} \to \sqrt{2}$. Next, we ask them to obtain a decreasing sequence that converges to the value from the right, i.e., $L_3 = \{1.5, 1.42, 1.415, \ldots\} \to \sqrt{2}$. Depending on the group, it may be convenient to provide a guiding first step. Thus, one may provide the students with the starting values of the sequences (Fig. 12d), and then ask them to evaluate the given function at the values of these two sequences, comparing their results. The compatibility of the data types in these calculators allows us to evaluate a function on an entire list, and to generate the list of differences $L_5 = L_4 - L_3$ as seen in Figs. 12e–12f, which illustrates that $5^{L_2} - 5^{L_1} \to 0$. Figures 12g–12i illustrate the power of these calculators, by solving this problem using converging sequences on the *Homescreen*.

13. On Modeling

Modern precalculus textbooks using technology are giving an increasing importance to applications problems using real data. Thus, taking advantage

L1	L2	L3	2
1	2	------	
1.1	1.2		
1.14	1.15		

L2(4) =

L2	L3	**L4**	4
2	5	25	
1.5	9.5183	11.18	
1.42	9.6727	9.8296	
1.415	9.7352	9.7509	
1.4143	9.7383	9.7399	
1.4142	9.7385	9.7386	
1.4142	9.7385	9.7385	

L4 =Y1(L3)■

L3	L4	L5	5
9.7385	9.7386	**1.6E-4**	
9.7385	9.7385	1.6E-5	
9.7385	9.7385	1.6E-6	
9.7385	9.7385	1.6E-7	
9.7385	9.7385	1.6E-8	
9.7385	9.7385	1.6E-9	
9.7385	9.7385	2E-10	

L5(6) =1.56735759...

Figure 12d	Figure 12e	Figure 12f

```
seq(iPart(√(2)*1
0^N)/10^N,N,0,13
,1)→L1
{1 1.4 1.41 1.4...
■
```

```
seq(iPart(√(2)*1
0^N+1)/10^N,N,0,
13,1)→L2
{2 1.5 1.42 1.4...
■
```

```
5^L1→L3
{5 9.518269694 ...
5^L2→L4
{25 11.18033989...
L4-L3
...57E-11 1.6E-12}
```

Figure 12g	Figure 12h	Figure 12i

of the linear and nonlinear regression features available in graphing calculators, one finds excellent problems connecting the new family of functions studied with real life situations. Students input the data and learn about modeling, the goodness of fit, and forecasting. Not only do these problems provide the students with concrete evidence of the importance of the functions studied, but we believe that in a time when data is so readily available in the Internet, these skills are essential.

In addition, graphing calculators automatically generate the residuals of the regression model obtained; this provides the possibility for introducing at this level the fact that an excellent regression coefficient does not necessarily precludes the existence of a better model.[5]

Our first problem[17] shows how an old optimization problem, typically found in calculus, can be presented earlier when technology is available.

Example 13.1. An open box is to be made from a rectangular piece of sheet metal 20"x15" by cutting equal square pieces from the corners and folding the sides up. Find:

(i) The algebraic representation for the volume of the box with the appropriate domain.

(ii) What size square must be cut to form a box of 250 in^3? Of at least 250 in^3?

(iii) What size square must be cut to form a box of maximum volume?

Solution. The first question calls for the student to restrict the domain of the function to truly represent the problem situation, a fact often ignored. The second question encourages the student to think graphically, by asking for answers involving inequalities. Finally, the last question asks for the maximum volume found in Fig. 13b.

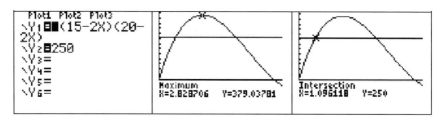

| Figure 13a | Figure 13b | Figure 13c |

In the second example taken from a classical book,[18] we point out that it is possible to introduce optimization at different levels of secondary school. The figures displayed are obtained with a TI Voyage200.

Example 13.2. A person in a rowboat 4 miles from the nearest point on a straight shoreline wishes to reach a house 12 miles farther down the shore. If the person can row at a rate of 3 mi/hr and walk at a rate of 5 mi/hr, find the least amount of time required to reach the house.

Solution. Some modern calculators have dynamic geometry software capabilities. This allows creating diagrams that model problem situations like the one above (Fig. 14a). The measurements in the figure are created taking into consideration the relations established in the problem, thus $rd = \sqrt{40^2 + x^2}$ and $CD = 120 - x$ where $BC = x$. We have used 40 and 120 in lieu of 4 and 12 for convenience when doing the graph. Then, a student can solve the problem by grabbing and moving the point C, where the rowboat will touch the shore along the shoreline. Since the variable values are dynamically modified, all that is needed is to stop moving the point when the total time seems visually to be the minimum, as shown in Fig. 14b.

Alternatively, the point C can be animated so that it moves on its own on BD while the values of the variables selected are collected in a table at every position of C (Fig. 14c). After selecting variables, the data can then be

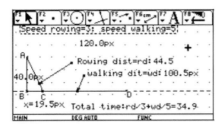

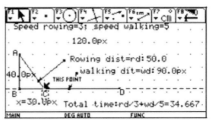

Figure 14a   Figure 14b

plotted as shown in Fig. 14d. A student familiar with the use of regression can then guess the model that best fits the data by comparing the regression coefficient of different models, or by observing how the graph of the model selected fits the plot when the regression coefficient is not available.

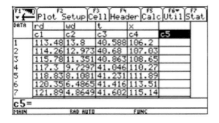

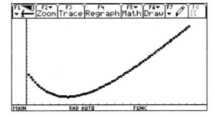

Figure 14c   Figure 14d

A student experimenting with different models may end up using the quartic (Figs. 14e–14f), which has an excellent coefficient of auto-determination.

Figure 14e   Figure 14f

In Figs. 14g–14h we have drawn the quartic obtained and the exact function

$$f(x) = \frac{\sqrt{40^2 + x^2}}{3} + \frac{120 - x}{5}.$$

No graphical differences can be perceived; however, after obtaining the minimum using both functions, we can observe a difference in the order of thousandths.

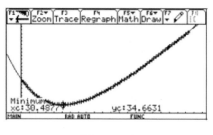 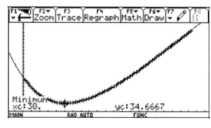

Figure 14g   Figure 14h

Although symbolic capabilities go beyond the boundaries we set for this article, we remark that this calculator has them, so the problem could have been solved using calculus. In addition the calculator even has a function *fmin* which calculates the minimum of a continuous function. It is clear that technology has opened the door to solve optimization problems once the students can create the model, hence given the importance of this topic, should we consider its introduction at different levels? Students would tackle the problems using different methods learned in each course, and this spiral approach is bound to give them a better understanding of modeling and of optimization before studying calculus.

14. Conclusion

To answer our initial question, we cannot say that we are taking full advantage of the capabilities that graphing calculators provide. We agree with Manoucherhri when she says "... the relevance of a topic for a particular grade level is no longer determined based upon its historical value in school mathematics. Relevance is, however, determined based upon the extent to which the topic empowers students to understand related concepts in greater depth and detail".[19] The selection of examples presented included many relevant and accessible ideas such as using transformations, or finding the range or the local extrema of functions, that are being, at least, partially ignored. The same can be said about some of the different tools and problem solving approaches introduced in these examples. But even when some topic may be mentioned in a textbook involving a particular family of functions, we noticed that often, no further reference is made to it when dealing with other families of functions. That is, *there does not seem to be a uniform approach, including these ideas, to the study of the different families of continuous functions studied.* It seems like textbooks are supplementing the traditional approach rather than developing a cohesive new one, which is research-based. Is this based on a conscious decision?

Numerical ideas are rarely used in most precalculus textbooks; in fact, there is hardly any reference to approximations. Yet, the fact that the main concepts of calculus were developed using approximations, suggests that exposing students to this approach may have a positive impact on their conceptual understanding of them.

How can we expect students to know if they have a proper graphical representation of a function, if we do not pay much attention to the concept of the complete graph of a function? On a similar note, when solving equations graphically, how can our students recognize the existence of hidden solutions if we do not expose them to the relative growth of functions?

Optimization is perhaps one of the most widely used mathematics topics in business and industry, yet we typically expend one week in the first semester of calculus addressing this concept, often for the first time, therefore excluding everyone who does not take calculus. Since technology facilitates the introduction of this topic earlier, do we still need to wait until students study calculus to introduce it?

Clearly, the conflict remains between the increasing number of new relevant mathematical ideas being added to the curriculum, and the need for eliminating some of the traditional material. Do the topics we teach respond to a conscious decision based on their relevance and accessibility, or are we still teaching topics because traditionally they have been taught at this level?

Symbolic calculators have been in the market for ten years, and they bring their own set of curricular and pedagogical questions. Should we not agree on most of the questions raised here before moving forward?

References

1. J. Tooke. Mathematics, the Computer and the Impact on Mathematics Education. *Computers in the Schools*, Vol. 17, 1–7. The Haworth Press Inc., Nevada (2001).
2. D. Tall, D. Smith, and C. Piez. Technology and Calculus. *Research on Technology and the Teaching and Learning of Mathematics*, edited by Kathy Heid and Glen Blume, Information Age Publishing, Inc. (2006).
3. National Council of Teachers of Mathematics. *Curriculum and Standards for School Mathematics*, Reston, VA: NCTM (2000).

30

4. A. Quesada. The Impact of Graphics Calculators on Teaching Matrix Applications at Secondary and Introductory College Levels. *Proc. of the Seventh Ann. Int. Conf. on Techn. in Colleg. Math.*, 382–386, Reading, Ma: Addison-Wesley (1995).

5. A. R. Quesada and N. Rosillo. Nonlinear Models of Data Fitting. *Epsilon*, No. 46–47, Vol. 16 (1–2), 81–96, Spain (2000).

6. A. Quesada. Should Recursion be Part of the Secondary Student's Mathematics Toolbox? *The Intern. Journal of Computer Algebra in Math. Ed.*, Vol. 6, No. 2, 103–116, UK (1999).

7. A. Quesada and M. T. Edwards. A Framework of Technology Rich Exploration. *The Mathematical Association of America, MathDL, Journal of Online Mathematics Applications (JOMA)* (2005).

8. A. Quesada. Generating Number Sense Via Numerical Ideas. *Proc. of the Eigth Ann. Int. Conf. on Techn. in Colleg. Math.*, 314–318, Reading, Ma: Addison-Wesley (1996).

9. A. Quesada. Using Technology to Teach Mathematics Topics Foundational to Calculus. *Proc. of the 19th Ann. Int. Conf. on Techn. in Colleg. Math, In Press.*

10. F. Demana and B. Waits. *The Role of Graphing Calculators in Mathematics Reform.* ERIC: ED458108 (1998).

11. A. Quesada and M. Maxwell. The Effects of Using Graphing Calculators to Enhance College Student's Performance in Precalculus. *Educational Studies in Mathematics*, 27, 205–215. Netherlands: Kluwer Academic Publishers (1994).

12. A. Quesada. On the Effects of Using Graphing Calculators in Calculus. *Proc. of the Sixth Ann. Int. Conf. on Techn. in Colleg. Math.* 296–300, Reading, Ma: Addison-Wesley (1994).

13. S. Pieper. Visualizing the Complex Roots of Quadratics (Proof Without Words). *American Mathematical Monthly*, 28:5, 359 (1997).

14. A. Quesada. New Geometrical Findings by Secondary Students. *Universitas Scientiarum*, Pontificia Universidad Javeriana, Vol. 6, No. 2, 11–16, Bogotá, Colombia (2001).

15. F. Demana and B. Waits. The Calculator and Computer Precalculus Project: What Have we learned in Ten Years? *Impact of Calculators on Mathematics Instruction.* University Press of America, Blue Ridge Summit, PA (1994).

16. B. Kissane. *Personal Technology and the Calculus.* Reflections, 23:28–31. http://wwwstaff.murdoch.edu.au/~kissane/calculus/calculus.htm.

17. F. Demana and B. Waits. *Precalculus, Functions and Graphs.* Reading, Massachusetts. Addison Wesley Publishing Company, Inc. (1990).

18. E. Swokowski. *Calculus.* PWS-Kent Publishing Company, Boston, MA (1991).

19. A. Manoucherhri. Computers and School Mathematics Reform: Implications for Mathematics Teacher Education. *The Journal of Computers in Mathematics and Science Teaching*, Vol. 18, 31–48 (1999).

HAND-HELD TECHNOLOGY IN SECONDARY MATHEMATICS EDUCATION

BARRY KISSANE

School of Education, Murdoch University
Murdoch, WA 6150, Australia
E-mail: B.Kissane@murdoch.edu.au

While extraordinary gains have been made in the capabilities of and access to symbolic computation in many educational settings, there are still many secondary school mathematics classrooms in many countries in which student access to such facilities is either very limited or non-existent, either at home or at school. This paper focuses on secondary mathematics education for students and teachers who are without reliable and regular access to computers or to the Internet. While the arguments and analysis are of general relevance, the particular focus of this paper is on Asian contexts. The place of hand-held technologies, including scientific calculators, graphics calculators and integrated devices such as the *ClassPad 300* will be considered, using examples from Casio, one of three major manufacturers. The computational support offered to students by such devices will be described and evaluated. Opportunities presented by hand-held technologies for students to learn mathematics in different ways than in the past and for teachers to teach differently will be described. The significance of hand-held technologies for the mathematics curriculum, its evolution and its assessment will be outlined and some issues associated with effective integration of symbolic computation into the secondary school curriculum will be explored.

1. Introduction

While extraordinary gains have been made in the capabilities of and access to symbolic computation for mathematics in many educational settings, especially universities and especially in more affluent countries, there are still many secondary school mathematics classrooms in many countries in which student access to such facilities is either very limited or non-existent, either at home or at school. This paper focuses on secondary mathematics education for students and teachers who are without reliable and regular access to computers or to the Internet.

The paper suggests that there substantial reasons for using hand-held technologies to meet the needs of students, mostly deriving from the accessibility and affordability of the technology to a wide group of students. In addition, and importantly, hand-held technologies have been developed with the particular needs of secondary school mathematics education in mind, unlike more sophisticated technologies, which have been developed for quite different purposes. A four-level hierarchy of available hand-held technologies is described, identifying the particular mathematical advantages (and limitations) of each for educational purposes.

While those less experienced with technology in schools frequently regard the main purpose as completing arithmetical calculations, in fact more important roles are at stake. Three key roles concerned with computation, the learning experience and curriculum influence are identified and exemplified with a range of technologies. While hand-held technologies might serve these roles, the paper recognises some key implementation issues, and addresses these briefly. Of prime importance is the capability of mathematics teachers and the nature of the school mathematics curriculum, both of which need to be taken into account if secondary school mathematics is to be improved through the use of technology.

The arguments in the paper apply to a range of settings, and draw in part on experiences in developed countries, such as Australia and the United States. In developing countries, where resources for education are more modest both at school and at home, the arguments for hand-held technologies are more compelling, as they may represent the only realistic means to make progress connecting the mathematics curriculum to a modern world, laden with technology.

2. Technology for Education

Technology of many kinds is now widely available to most people throughout the industrialized world and in many parts of the developing world, especially in commerce and industry. It has now become a familiar part of the everyday world of citizens, parents and teachers. In addition, many technologies of potential interest to secondary school mathematics are manufactured in East Asia. Despite the widespread presence of technology, it seems that technology is not yet widely used in secondary mathematics teaching and learning in East Asian countries, such as China, Japan and Korea.

When considering 'technology' for educational purposes, it seems that many people interpret the term to refer to 'computer technology' of various kinds, and recently also to include the Internet. In this regard, the term

IT (information technology) is nowadays commonly expanded to be ICT (information and communications technology). Official statements about IT or ICT in education usually focus on ways in which computers can be used in various parts of the curriculum. Very recently, the term 'technology' has been extended to include devices such as digital cameras and mobile telephones, generally with some connection to computers as well.

It is much rarer for discourses regarding technology to refer to hand-held technologies, such as calculators and similar devices, although these are arguably of more importance to some parts of the school curriculum than computers. It is common practices for IT departments of school systems, IT policies, IT budgets in schools and elsewhere to make no reference to calculators and similar hand-held technology devices in education.

The enthusiastic promotion and discussion of technology in mathematics education by both official sources and by commercial companies seems to take place under the assumption of an ideal education world. In the extreme, such an ideal world would be characterized by the following: (i) all students have unlimited access to modern high-speed computers; (ii) all software is free, or budgets for software are essentially unlimited; (iii) students and teachers have unlimited access to high-speed Internet lines; (iv) facilities in students' homes match those in their schools; (v) teachers are well-educated enthusiasts in mathematics and pedagogy, with unlimited free time; (vi) curriculum constraints, including externally imposed and administered examinations, do not exist.

Idealistic assumptions of these kinds certainly have an important place in thinking about technology in mathematics education, despite being apparently unrealistic. Proceeding on the basis of such assumptions, teams of professionals can develop good uses of technology, free of the constraints of the present reality. These professionals include mathematicians, computer scientists, software developers, mathematics teachers, and others.

Few contexts today match these idealistic assumptions, however. The virtual world that has no constraints is not the same as the present world inhabited by most students in most classrooms in most schools, in most countries (including the more affluent countries).The present paper is concerned with the real educational world in which many students, teachers and curriculum developers find themselves, in these early years of the twenty-first century. In the real world inhabited by most people today, calculators are of more significance than computers, and hence are the focus of this paper.

3. Hand-held Technologies

Although computer technologies are very powerful, there are some very good reasons for using hand-held technologies for education, which provide significant opportunities for learning mathematics. In this section, these reasons are briefly outlined with a brief description of different manifestations of hand-held technologies.

3.1. *Advantages of Hand-Held Technology*

Hand-held technologies have some inherent advantages for secondary education. Five important advantages include the following:

(1) They are easily portable, and can be comfortably carried in a school bag along with other materials students need to carry with them. A consequence of this portability is that they can be used both at home and at school, and that they can be easily taken from one school classroom to another.

(2) They are less expensive than computers[a], especially when all the software needs are taken into account (since calculators have their own software built in). This cost issue has important implications for accessibility.

(3) They are potentially more accessible to a wider range of students than are other forms of technology, as a consequence of the first two advantages. Curriculum developers can design curricula on the assumption that students can use technology while learning, only when it is accessible on a wide scale.

(4) They can be used in formal examinations, of considerable importance in many educational settings. This advantage is mostly a consequence of the preceding reasons, since it is realistic to design curricula and associated examinations only for technologies that are potentially available to all relevant students; to do otherwise is likely to be regarded as unfair.

(5) Most of them have been designed, and continue to be modified, for the express purpose of school mathematics education. Unlike other forms of technology, which have been designed for other purposes, today's calculators are developed for the purposes of education, and so can be expected to be sensitive to the needs and interests of those involved,

---

[a]In recent years, there has been discussion about an internationally available $100 computer for educational purposes, but this has not yet become a reality. Software costs are likely to be necessary, in addition to hardware costs.

such as students and teachers.

A possibly surprising consequence of this last advantage is that, un-like other more sophisticated forms of technology, hand-held technologies are less likely to be used by mathematics professionals than by secondary students and their teachers. At least in the developed world, the present generation of professionals in the mathematical sciences are comfortable users of computers and computer software, but have often had little expe-rience with the comparatively recent technologies of interest to this paper.

3.2. *A Hierarchy of Hand-Held Technologies*

In this section, a four-level hierarchy of sophistication of hand-held tech-nologies, in which each member includes the characteristics of the previous member, is described. This hierarchy is also a hierarchy of prices, too, as the more sophisticated devices are more expensive to purchase, with a consider-able jump between the prices of scientific and graphics calculators in most countries, depending on a variety of market forces and local conditions.

3.2.1. *Arithmetic Calculators*

Sometimes described as 'four-function' or 'basic' calculators, arithmetic cal-culators are in common use in commercial contexts. These include shops and street markets, where the main function is sometimes to communicate prices. Arithmetic calculators essentially provide a means of completing nu-merical calculations of an everyday kind, using decimals, and are very inex-pensive. They are generally restricted in capabilities to the four operations of addition, subtraction, multiplication and division[b]. More sophisticated versions have been developed for educational use. One embellishment is to use appropriate priority order for arithmetic calculations, so that $2 + 3 \times 4$ gives the correct result of 14 instead of 20. Another is to include operations with fractions as well as decimals.

Arithmetic calculators have been available to elementary (primary) schools for many years now, although the extent to which they have been adopted has varied between teachers and even between countries. Despite the concerns of some teachers and parents, research has established that these are educationally useful, and not harmful.[1,2] However, they provide

---

[b]This explains the use of the common term, 'four-function'. In fact, very few arithmetic calculators are restricted to only these functions: most have a square root key and a percentage key and various memory storage and retrieval capabilities as well.

insufficient capabilities for secondary school students, whose mathematical needs extend considerably beyond mere computation.

3.2.2. *Scientific Calculators*

Scientific calculators provide little more for students than numerical calculation. Typically, a scientific calculator provides students with the same facilities as an arithmetic calculator, and extends with some more sophisticated calculations, such as powers and roots. Table functions are also provided: values of functions previously obtained from mathematical tables are available directly from the keyboard. These include logarithmic, exponential, trigonometric and inverse trigonometric functions. Statistical calculations are available, so that means and standard deviations are calculated for data entered, and for many calculators, bivariate statistical calculations (such as correlation coefficients and linear regression coefficients) are also included. Recently, sophisticated versions have included higher level calculations of interest to secondary schools, such as those involving complex numbers, probability distributions and combinatorics. In essence, scientific calculators provide students with the capacity to undertake numerical calculations relevant to the mathematics of the secondary school.

Scientific calculators have been routinely used by secondary school students in industrialized countries for more than twenty years. They are generally regarded as inexpensive items of equipment, essential for computation in mathematics and science, and are usually permitted for examination use. They reduce the need for extensive by-hand calculation and consulting of tables of values of functions, characteristic of secondary school calculations of the previous generation.

3.2.3. *Graphics Calculators*

Graphics calculators are distinguishable by their relatively large graphics screen, which accommodates several lines of display or a visual image of some kind. As well as including the capabilities of scientific calculators, graphics calculators include their own software for a range of mathematical purposes, including the representation of functions in tables and graphs, statistical displays and two-dimensional drawings. The range of mathematical capabilities varies between models, but can include numerical calculus, complex numbers, matrices, spreadsheets, probability simulation, sequences and series, numerical equation solving, statistical analysis and hypothesis testing, financial analysis and geometry. Some more advanced (and thus more expensive) graphics calculators also include Computer Algebra Systems (CAS). A distinguishing difference between scientific and graphics calculators is the possibility of students using the latter for mathematical explorations, rather than just calculations, either spontaneously or under the direction of the teacher.

In most industrialized countries, graphics calculators have been well-received in schools over the past twenty years, and are now routinely used by many students in the senior secondary school years as well as the early years of post-secondary study. As an illustration of the reception of this technology by teachers, the Australian Association of Mathematics Teachers' graphics calculator communiqué[5] recently described several ways in which this technology is being used in Australian schools to good effect. In many places, graphics calculators are permitted for use in formal external examinations, such as those for selective entrance to universities.

3.2.4. *ClassPad 300*

The *ClassPad 300*, manufactured by Casio[c], is a recent addition to the hierarchy of hand-held devices for school mathematics. In some respects, it is similar to a graphics calculator, with in-built CAS, and includes the capabilities of most graphics calculators within its software suite. It is distinguished from graphics calculators in two important ways. In the first place, it contains more significant mathematical software, dealing with a wider range of mathematical concepts, including powerful computer algebra systems with exact solution of differential equations, three-dimensional graphing and vectors. In the second place, it provides significant interactivity between the various software applications, using a touch-sensitive screen and mechanisms for dragging and dropping objects between screens. In these respects, it enables both more sophisticated mathematical ideas to be handled (in addition to less sophisticated ideas) and offers extensive opportunities for student manipulation and exploration.

The *ClassPad 300* is a relatively recent machine, and is described here to make it clear that the hierarchy does not end with graphics calculators. Although it has been available for only a short time, it has already attracted

---

[c]In this paper, examples of the capabilities and uses of hand-held technologies manufactured by Casio are used, mostly for convenience and consistency. Broadly similar examples with models from other manufacturers (such as Hewlett Packard and Texas Instruments) might have been used. The Casio *ClassPad 300* is an exception to this, as there is not an equivalent device available from other manufacturers, at the time of writing.

considerable attention, and is permitted for formal examinations use in some locations (such as Melbourne, Australia).

4. Three Roles for Hand-held Technologies

It is important to recognize the different roles for technology in secondary mathematics education. For example, the *Technology Principle* of the National Council of Teachers of Mathematics, widely quoted, asserts that "Technology is essential in teaching and learning mathematics; it influences the mathematics that is taught and enhances students' learning."[3] In elaborating this principle, the NCTM observes:

"Calculators and computers are reshaping the mathematical landscape, and school mathematics should reflect those changes. Students can learn more mathematics more deeply with the appropriate and responsible use of technology. They can make and test conjectures. They can work at higher levels of generalization or abstraction. In the mathematics classrooms envisioned in *Principles and Standards*, every student has access to technology to facilitate his or her mathematics learning."[3]

In this section, three important and different roles for hand-held technologies in secondary mathematics education are identified and illustrated. These roles concern computation, the provision of different educational experiences and influence on the school mathematics curriculum. These roles are elaborated in an earlier paper.[8]

4.1. *Computational Role*

An important role concerns mathematical computation. Hand-held technologies can meet all of the computational needs for secondary education, providing a means to obtain reliable answers to numerical questions. This role is significant, since it potentially allows more time to be devoted to developing mathematical concepts, where previously a great deal of time was required to do computations. The centrality of calculation in mathematics was emphasized by Wong's observation that mathematics is a "subject of calculables."[6]

For younger students, an arithmetic calculator allows students to undertake everyday calculations with any measurements that are meaningful to them, an important consideration if realistic problem solving is to be included in the curriculum. The scientific calculator extends this capacity to large and small numbers, including those expressed in scientific notation.[d] This is an important consideration for any mathematical modelling undertaken by students, whether in a mathematics class, a science class, or elsewhere. When confronted with calculation needs that could not be handled mentally, or for which reasonable approximations were insufficient, previous generations of students have been reliant on less efficient means of calculation, such as by-hand methods, or in secondary schools, logarithms and tables. A scientific calculator provides values for functions that were previously tabulated (such as trigonometric and logarithmic functions, as well as squares and square roots), and thus offers the opportunity to avoid long and tedious calculations. Historically speaking, in many mathematics curricula, calculations have frequently became ends in themselves, distracting from the important mathematical features of the work, and rarely offering much insight to students.

As well as handling arithmetic calculations, scientific calculators also provide a means for efficiently dealing with easy, but lengthy computations, such as those associated with combinatorics (such as determining $^{52}C_{13}$, the number of bridge hands possible from a standard deck of cards) or with elementary statistics (such as finding the mean and variance of a sample of 30 measurements). It is interesting that such calculations were not routinely available on early scientific calculators, but were added to later models, designed for education, almost certainly to accommodate the computational needs of secondary school students rather than 'scientists', for whom the original scientific calculators were designed.

The scientific calculator now has a history of more than thirty years in secondary schools, and has continued to undergo developments, partly fuelled by competition between rival manufacturers, and partly as a consequence of advice from mathematics teachers themselves. Over the last thirty years, scientific calculators have become much easier for students to use, with more informative screens and a broader range of capabilities, which have together improved their capacity to fulfill the computational role for students. It is noteworthy that recent scientific calculators also provide some exact answers as well as numerical approximations, consistent with the continuing support of computational needs. Figure 1 shows two examples from a recent scientific calculator model.

As well as providing reliable answers to computational questions, such capabilities might support student thinking and even curiosity about the

---

[d]This is one of the many reasons that an arithmetic calculator is inadequate for secondary school use.

mathematical ideas involved.

Figure 1: Exact computation on an entry-level scientific calculator

The computational role of the scientific calculator is also available on graphics calculators: for the most part, modern graphics calculators provide at least the same suite of capabilities as scientific calculators (so that it is not necessary for students to have access to both kinds of devices.) A difference between graphics calculators and scientific calculators is that more extensive computations can be undertaken with relative ease. Space precludes a complete listing of these, which vary a bit from model to model and from manufacturer to manufacturer, but Figure 2 shows some examples of calculating a logarithm, evaluating an expression involving complex numbers and inverting a matrix.

Figure 2: Computations with a Casio fx-9860G graphics

The examples in Figure 2 illustrate routine numerical calculations that, by hand, occupy a good deal of student time. Although evaluating the logarithm involves conceptual thinking about the nature of logarithms, neither the inversion of a matrix nor the expansion of a complex power involve anything other than routine processes, which some would argue are better left to a machine.

The further examples of computations shown in Figure 3 all demonstrate how significant numerical work can be completed on a graphics calculator. The examples of series evaluation, numerical integration and numerical solution of an equation are significant, as they each raise issues regarding the balance of mathematical concepts and skills in the curriculum, as elaborated further later in this paper. Similarly, the final example in Figure 3, showing some statistical calculations related to a sample of size 50, is suggestive of a deeper issue regarding the appropriate balance of human and machine work in statistics.

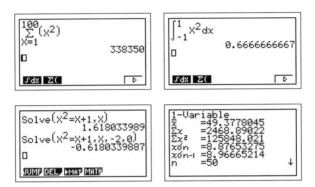

Figure 3: Further computations with a Casio fx-9860G graphics calculator

Finally, Figure 4 shows some examples of computations available on one of the most sophisticated hand-held technology currently available for secondary school mathematics, Casio's *ClassPad 300*. The nine examples chosen for this purpose illustrate the powerful capabilities for exact computation and symbolic computation routinely available on this device. In each case, a computation has been entered on a single line, with the result displayed on the following line.

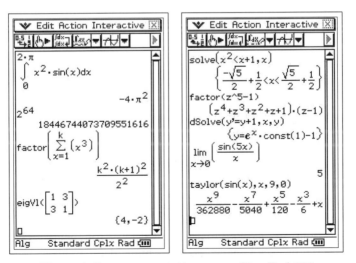

Figure 4: Some computations on a ClassPad 300

Several of the examples chosen make direct use of the computer algebra system built into the *ClassPad 300* software; these show integration by parts, the solution of a quadratic inequality, factoring of simple and complicated expressions, a Taylor series expansion and the determination of eigenvalues of a matrix. While secondary school students have previously undertaken computations of these kinds by hand, since the necessary results could not be obtained in any other way, the algebraic processes involved have generally been routine in nature and have not added greatly to the quality of their mathematical thinking. It is important to recognise that routine activities of this kind can now be accomplished by a few keystrokes on a hand-held device.

The fact that exact computations are available is also of significance, both for numerical work and for symbolic work. Some of the results shown in Figure 4 can be obtained numerically (although not exactly) on graphics calculators, while others can be obtained only on a CAS-capable device.

The examples in Figure 4 have been chosen from many possibilities, to illustrate and support the claim that any of the routine computational needs of secondary school mathematics can be readily obtained on a device like a *ClassPad 300*.

4.2. *Experiential Role*

While computation is important, it is not the main contribution of hand-held technology to teaching and learning mathematics. The experiential role, describing the possibility of students encountering different experience, is arguably of greater significance. In this section, some examples of the ways in which technology can offer students fresh opportunities for learning and teachers new ways of teaching are briefly described, with reference to different kinds of hand-held technology. A major element is the opportunity for students to explore mathematical ideas for themselves, supported by a technology that is responsive to their actions.

In the case of the scientific calculator, opportunities for fresh experiences are relatively limited, which possibly accounts for the fact that the calculators are mostly regarded as devices to produce numerical answers. A source of the limitation is the lack of a graphics screen, allowing for various representations of mathematical objects. Despite this limitation, scientific calculators can be used to help students experience important mathematical connections and explore mathematical ideas for themselves. A recent example is the project,[10] which contains many detailed ideas, mostly for a sophisticated scientific calculator, ranging across several areas of mathematics, including algebra, functions, trigonometry, geometry, statistics, calculus and business mathematics. Some of the examples derive from the ability of the calculator to show different representations of numbers, such as fractions and decimals, powers and logarithms. Others derive from alternative approaches to mathematical topics, such as numerical solution of equations or evaluation of integrals. Still others derive from the capacity of a scientific calculator to implement iterative schemes efficiently, allowing compound interest or chaos to be examined by students informally.

For graphics calculators, experiential opportunities are much more plentiful, as the availability of a graphics screen offers students ways of interacting with mathematical ideas that were not available to them prior to the advent of technology. There are very many examples in Kissane & Kemp,[12] but space here to include only a few.

Perhaps the most common ways in which graphics calculators offer students new experiential opportunities are those related to the representation of functions. A graphics calculator allows for both graphical[e] and tabular representation of a function, in addition to symbolic representations, as Figure 5 illustrates.

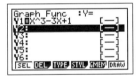 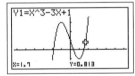 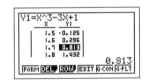

Figure 5: Three representations of a function
on a Casio fx-9860G graphics calculator

Students can readily manipulate and explore these representations, in order to understand each one better. There are many opportunities for learning brought about by this. For example, students can modify the symbolic function and see almost immediately the consequences for the graph, compare the graphs of several functions at once to understand the impact of the coefficients, and can learn about functional forms (such as linear, quadratic, cubic) interactively. They can zoom in or out on the graph to

---

[e]The possibility of representing a function graphically probably gave rise to the description of graphics calculators as 'graphing' calculators. While this is not an inaccurate description, it has given rise to interpretations of graphics calculators as important *only* for graphing functions, which is a very limited view, not taking account of their numerical capabilities nor the suites of mathematical software they usually contain, unrelated to graphing.

44

study its shape and characteristics in detail. They can examine at close quarters the numerical values of the function, connecting this to equations or roots or both. They can study the intersections of graphs and connect these to the solutions of equations. They can examine the shape of a graph in detail to encounter ideas of rates of change informally. The experiences offered by these three representations provide both teachers and students with new ways of thinking about the mathematical ideas involved.

A powerful way of using these sorts of capabilities involves the derivative of a function. The idea of a derivative at a point (rather than the slope of a tangent to a function at the point) is well illustrated on the graphics screen shown in Figure 6, using an automatic derivative tracing facility built in to the Casio *fx-9860G* calculator.

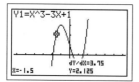 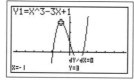 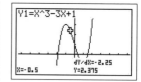

Figure 6: Using a derivative trace to explore the idea
of a derivative at a point

The calculator can also be used to represent a derivative function, by evaluating the derivative at each point of a function and graphing the result, as shown in Figure 7. Since both the function and its derivative are represented on the same screen, important connections between these are readily examined by students. In this case, the characteristic parabolic shape of the derivative function is important; so too are the observations that the derivative function has a value of zero when the original cubic function has a turning point.

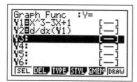 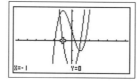 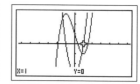

Figure 7: Simultaneous graphical representation
of a function and its derivative function

As another example, recent graphics calculators provide substantially more opportunities for students to undertake data analysis than would be the case with a scientific calculator. The distinctly different contributions of a graphics calculator are that data are stored in the calculator once entered, and then can be manipulated in a variety of ways. For example, data can be edited to correct errors or omissions, can be transformed (e.g. with a log-arithmic transformation, in order to linearise an exponential relationship), can be represented in graphical displays (such as scatter plots, histograms or box plots), can be compared with ideal mathematical models and can be used to undertake standard statistical tests. Figure 8 shows representative screens for some of these sorts of operations.

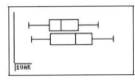 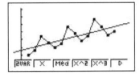 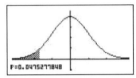

Figure 8: Examples of data analysis activities on a graphics calculator

Taken together, these sorts of capabilities suggest that a graphics calculator can be regarded as device for exploratory data analysis in a range of flexible ways, supporting both descriptive statistics and inferential statistics, and allowing students an opportunity to develop important data analytic skills and understandings.

Figure 9 shows examples of the kinds of interactions with which students can engage in exploring the behaviour of a series. In this case, the series converges quite quickly to $e = 2.71828...$, as can be seen from both the graph and the table of values. Again, the experience of series behaviour, in this case resulting in apparent convergence, is qualitatively changed by use of the graphics calculator.

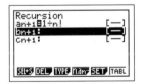 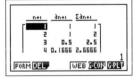 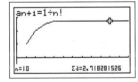

Figure 9: Exploring a series with a graphics calculator

As a geometric example of offering a different experience to students, Figure 10 shows some Casio *fx-9860G* graphics calculator screens concerned with different aspects of plane geometry. The first screen shows a geometric construction of the circle containing three points A, B and C, which can be executed with calculator commands. The properties of the figure (such as the two perpendicular bisectors intersecting in the circumcentre) are invariant under changes to the location of points A, B and C, a result which students can find out for themselves as a result of directly manipulating the points.

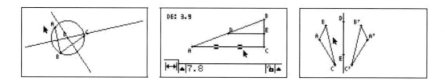

Figure 10: Experiencing geometry with a graphics calculator

The second screen in Figure 10 depicts a triangle ABC, with D and E midpoints of AB and BC respectively. Students can move point B, and observe that the length of DE remains half the length of AC, and is parallel to it. Students can move point B, and observe that the length of DE remains half the length of AC, and is parallel to it. Such observations offer students an opportunity to find geometric properties, and some motivation to seek ways of understanding why the properties hold. Experiences of this kind are not available easily without the support of technology. The third screen depicts a similar situation, in which the plane has been reflected about line DE, and the triangle ABC has a mirror image shown under this reflection. Properties of the reflection can be explored directly in this environment, again providing fresh opportunities for both students and their teachers to engage with the mathematical ideas involved.

Another kind of opportunity made available through a calculator is simulation, a powerful tool for both understanding probabilistic situations and for modelling contexts. The sample screens shown in Figure 11 contain histograms of simulated tosses of two dice. Students can readily perform the simulations on a calculator and then graph the results.

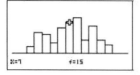 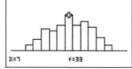 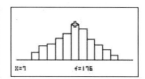

Figure 11: Simulations of the total of two dice thrown 50, 200 and 999 times

While some practical work of this kind can, and should, be undertaken by students in class with real pairs of dice, efficiency suggests that technology is needed to provide a good environment for learning about the regularities involved. In this particular case, a larger number of simulations results in a more symmetrical distribution, and a closer match to the theoretical result obtained on the basis of a probabilistic analysis. In a school classroom, the potential for students to compare their simulations with each other offers extra opportunities for learning about the nature of randomness.

Opportunities for new learning experiences are even more plentiful on a more sophisticated device such as a *ClassPad 300*. To give an illustration, Figure 12 shows the reflection of the plane about line DE, with the triangle ABC and its image $A'B'C'$, both shown.

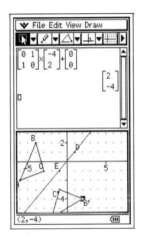

Figure 12: Reflections on a ClassPad 300

In this case, the student is able to manipulate the elements directly and see the results: moving line DE and changing the triangle ABC will both result in interesting effects. In addition, and very powerfully, students can also drag a point and its reflection from the lower (geometric) window to the upper (algebraic) window to produce automatically the relevant transformation matrix, indicating that the image of $B(-4, 2)$ is $B'(2, -4)$. This kind of environment offers opportunities for student learning (about reflections and about linear transformations in this case) that are not available otherwise.

In summary, this section has provided some examples, from a potentially much larger set, to elaborate the notion that hand-held technology can significantly alter the experience of learning mathematics for students, by providing them with access to tasks and opportunities not otherwise available to them. For the same reason, the opportunities for teachers to provide a different experience for students are also significantly changed.

4.3. *Influential Role*

The availability of hand-held technologies raises important curriculum questions for secondary school mathematics, arising from the execution of the previous two roles concerning computation and experience. In this sense, the technology has become an important source of curriculum influence. There are at least three dimensions of this influence, concerned with the place of computation, the mathematical ideas included in the curriculum, and the sequence in which material is presented to students, as elaborated below.

4.3.1. *Computation*

One set of questions arises from the fact that routine computational procedures can be conducted efficiently on a calculator. Curriculum developers need to decide the extent to which it is necessary, or desirable, for students to develop expertise at doing by hand, less efficiently and less reliably, the procedures available on their calculators. Few would suggest that all procedures ought to be mastered by all students, partly because there is insufficient time likely to be available for this. Alternatively, few would suggest that hand-held technology be relied upon too heavily for computational purposes, since the development of a level of personal computational expertise is widely regarded as an important outcome of mathematics education. The issue instead is one of finding a suitable balance between these opposing views, which is not an easy matter.

The situation might be illustrated by considering the solution of systems of linear equations, universally included in the secondary school mathematics curriculum. An example of such a system is the following:

$$x + 4y + z = 5$$
$$2z - 2x = 7$$
$$2x - y + 6z = 3$$

Algebraic procedures involving Gaussian elimination have been available to handle this task, and students have routinely been taught how to use them in secondary school. Such procedures are powerful, relatively efficient, generalizable and should always produce the correct solution; in addition, refined versions of the procedures using matrix representation and arithmetic are available, rendering the tasks even more efficient, as attention is paid only to the coefficients. On the other hand, the procedures are complicated, heavily laden with elementary arithmetic and hence fundamentally error-prone when completed by hand. Furthermore, the execution of the procedures offers very little insight into the solution, in most cases. Developing student expertise at this sort of task requires considerable time in class and time for practice, possibly at home. Using curriculum time for such tasks means that the time is not available for other tasks, since the total time available to students is always constrained.

On a graphics calculator, the matrices of coefficients are readily entered, and readily manipulated to produce a solution, as shown in Figure 13 on the Casio *fx-9860G*. To do this, students need to both know how a linear system can be represented by a matrix and how to use their calculator to do this. They also need to know how the matrix formulation can be used to represent the solution[f], and how to obtain this, using the inverse of the matrix of coefficients.

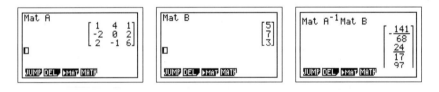

Figure 13: Matrix solution of the system of equations

The computations involved can be streamlined even further, however, on this graphics calculator, as shown in Figure 14, in which the augmented matrix of coefficients is shown and the student needs merely to execute a solve command to see the result, available as both a decimal and a fraction in this case, after scrolling the solution vector. While the same procedures are employed internally in this case and for the matrix formulation, this version of the calculator solution does not require that students know anything about matrices or their manipulations. They merely need to recognize the problem as one that involves the solution of a system of simultaneous equations and know how to enter the coefficients faithfully.

---

[f]The final screen in Figure 13 shows the result, which needs to be scrolled down a little in order to see $z = 97/68$.

50

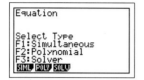 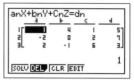 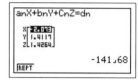

Figure 14: Direct calculator solution of the system of equations

In each of these cases, students need to both know about the idea of a system of linear equations and how to both represent and solve it in the calculator. As for developing by-hand algebraic procedures, this also requires the use of curriculum time, although the amounts of time needed are likely to be substantially different with and without the technology.

It might be argued that the regular use of a calculator to solve a system of linear equations might render students powerless when confronted with a more significant system, such as one that could not be solved numerically, in fact similar procedures are available on more sophisticated devices, using a computer algebra system. To illustrate this, see Figure 15, which shows the solution of the linear system above, but with the first equation replaced with $x + ky + z = 5$, the variable k replacing the 4. (The result on the *ClassPad 300* occupies more then a single line, so a second screen is shown to display the result after horizontal scrolling.)

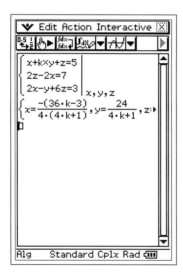 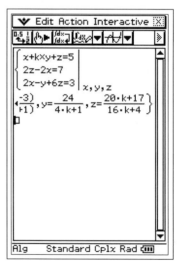

Figure 15: Solving a linear system of equations on the ClassPad 300

This example, chosen from many possibilities, illustrates the influence that hand-held technologies might exert on thinking about the secondary school mathematics curriculum, at least as far as computation is concerned. The fundamental question that needs to be addressed concerns the extent to which students ought to be taught to imitate by hand the vast range of procedures that can be quickly, efficiently and reliably undertaken by a machine. While the answer to such a question is necessarily one of finding the appropriate balance, it seems inevitable that the balance will be shifted somewhat as a result of the influence of the technology.

4.3.2. *Content*

A second aspect of potential influence concerns the content of the curriculum, which represents an answer to the fundamental question: which aspects of mathematics are of sufficient importance to be included in the curriculum, and which can be safely left until later, or even excluded altogether?

The answers to such a question have always varied between countries and over time within a country. The answers depend to some extent of course on the amount of time that can be devoted to school mathematics in the wider school curriculum and the aspirations and interests of the students concerned. Thus, many countries have a range of courses to suit students of different kinds, with varying emphases on various aspects of mathematics, such as algebra, calculus, trigonometry, geometry, statistics, probability, and so on. In addition, there is varying emphasis given to mathematical processes, such as proof, problem solving, mathematical modelling, inductive and deductive reasoning.

Hand-held technologies influence the answers to this sort of question, since they potentially provide access to different aspects of mathematics in a variety of ways. To continue the example of equations explored briefly in the previous section, access to hand-held technologies provides an opportunity to reduce the emphasis on some algebraic manipulations associated with solving equations, and at the same time extend the repertoire of equations and solution methods to which students are exposed. As argued by Kissane,[9] more attention might be paid in secondary school mathematics to numerical methods of solution of a wide range of elementary equations and less attention to exact algebraic methods of solutions of a very small range of elementary equations (mostly linear and quadratic).

In a similar way, the calculus curriculum has always required that students develop substantial competence with essentially algebraic procedures, such as differentiation and integration, because progress in using calculus to solve problems requires such expertise. Although students in the past have developed the necessary expertise, for too many students this has taken so much time and energy that the (arguably more important) conceptual development has been less well developed. A good example involves integration, where students have been taught a suite of methods to handle various situations, such as integration by substitution, by parts and by partial factions. While there is some conceptual value in such procedures, their main place in the curriculum is as a means to an end, rather than because of intrinsic mathematical interest. A hand-held device can provide integrals without focusing on the methods of integration employed, offering opportunities to reconsider the balance between the idea of integration and its many uses and the routines associated with evaluating them.

In other cases, the nature of school mathematics can be reconsidered because of the availability of hand-held technology. In the statistics curriculum, attention can be directed to statistical thinking and choices by students to represent data in various ways, rather than on the tedium of calculation or construction of graphical representations. A graphics calculator essentially provides students with a suite of data analysis techniques, so that attention might shift towards how, when and why to make use of these, and more attention can be directed at previously neglected aspects such as designing the collection of data to answer questions of interest and interpretation of statistical results.

In addition to reconsidering the existing curriculum, the availability of hand-held technologies might offer opportunities to augment the curriculum with new material. This might be done either to refresh the content, providing students with an opportunity to engage with mathematical ideas of current interest outside school, or to provide some access to ideas recognized as having intrinsic interest.

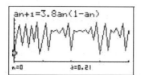 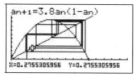 

Figure 16: Images of chaos and the Mandelbrot set on a graphics calculator

The screens in Figure 16 show examples of this kind, taken from the reference,[12] where the corresponding ideas are discussed in a little more detail. To date, it has not been possible to include material of this kind in the school curriculum, without sufficient technological support.

4.3.3. *Sequence*

Another form of curriculum influence involves the sequence of ideas in the curriculum, which is also potentially influenced by the availability of hand-held technology. When thinking about the curriculum, under the assumption that technological support is available, some concepts appear earlier than might have been previously expected.

There are elementary examples of this on a scientific calculator of a kind that might be used by students early in secondary school, as shown in Figure 17. In the two cases illustrated, the calculator has represented a result as a negative number and in scientific notation, either of which may arise before students have been formally taught about these representations in their mathematics classroom.

Figure 17: Unexpected appearances of mathematical ideas
on a scientific calculator

Similarly, a graphics calculator may produce results which suggest that some mathematical ideas may be introduced into the curriculum earlier than might otherwise have been the case. Two examples are shown in Figure 18. Both the evaluation of the square root of a negative number and the solution of the cubic equation $x^3 + x^2 + x + 1 = 0$ result in complex numbers.

Figure 18: Unexpected appearance of complex numbers
on a graphics calculator

More significantly, other aspects of the sequence of the mathematics curriculum may be affected by the availability of hand-held technology. Some of these are concerned with the capacity of a graphics calculator to display graphs of functions and allow them to be interrogated by the person using the calculator. The shapes of various families of functions (such as linear, quadratic, cubic and exponential) will be accessible to students at an earlier stage than previously, and without the necessity of tedious and extensive plotting of points. This might be expected to lead to a consideration of the nature of different kinds of functions earlier than previously.

In a similar vein, having ready access to a graph of a function changes some of the rationale for traditional approaches to the calculus. Before the technology was accessible, early approaches to the calculus focused attention on sketching curves in order to understand their shape, including their asymptotic shape, and also to identify key aspects such as local extrema. Some understanding of differential calculus and some expertise at finding and using derivatives was needed in order to consider such mathematical ideas. Similarly, the concept of the area under a curve was not introduced before the study of integration. However, as the screens in Figure 19 suggest, the mathematical ideas can be extracted from calculator graphs, which are accessible to students long before the study of calculus is introduced.

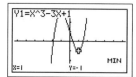  

Figure 19: Early graphical introduction to local extrema, asymptotic behaviour and integration

Changes of this kind may serve to help us reconsider the role of the calculus in school: not merely as a means to answering questions about functions, but a means of doing so *exactly*, rather than with numerical approximations. Excellent numerical approximations are available to students well before the formal study of calculus, thus influencing the way in which we regard the calculus itself later in the sequence.

5. Some Key Issues

In this section of the paper, some key issues associated with the use of hand-held technologies are identified and briefly explored.

5.1. *Integration of Technology*

A major advantage of hand-held technology over other forms of technology for secondary school mathematics is the possibility of it being integrated into the curriculum, rather than being regarded as an addition of some kind. It is important that there be coherence in the place of technology for each of teaching, learning and assessment; hand-held technology offers the best prospects for this.

In many contexts, such as those in Australia,[4] a key aspect of the integration of technology concerns its role in external examinations, especially those used at the end of secondary school for selection into universities. When technology is permitted for use in examinations, it is much more likely to be a part of the teaching and learning practices of schools, for obvious reasons. In the same vein, when technology is not sanctioned for use in examinations, schools and teachers are understandably reluctant to make good use of it in their teaching and learning activities. The small size, portability, relatively low cost and (perhaps ironically) limited mathematical power together render hand-held technologies much more likely to be permitted into formal assessment programs than, say, computers or the Internet. All of these characteristics enhance the likelihood of coherence and integration.

If technology is integrated into the curriculum, both curriculum developers and textbook manufacturers can develop materials that make sound use of it. Without widespread integration, it seems unlikely that the necessary curriculum changes (some of which were suggested in the previous section) can be seriously undertaken.

An additional aspect of integration concerns teachers, most of whom are unlikely to have extensive experience themselves with hand-held technologies. As noted earlier, graphics calculators are much more likely to be found in secondary schools than universities, so that even recent graduates may not have a lot of experience with them as learning tools. Integration of technology requires that teachers be supported adequately, as elaborated later in this section.

5.2. *Supporting Learning*

Hand-held technologies of the kinds considered in this paper are frequently misunderstood as having *only* a computational role, especially it seems by people who do not make much use of them.[g] Such a view is understandable, particularly when 'calculators' are naturally interpreted as devices whose main purpose is to 'calculate'. However, this is a limited view of the many

---

[g]Indeed, a major purpose of this paper is to identify and elaborate *other* significant characteristics of hand-held technology.

ways in which learning can be supported, some of which are described earlier and others are described elsewhere (e.g. the references[4,5,12]).

A fundamental issue at stake in this respect concerns the nature of sound learning in mathematics, and the significance of formal algorithms and procedures. While none would doubt the importance of these, educators are increasingly questioning the balance of concepts and skills in curricula. Extensive memorization and development of by-hand algebraic and arithmetical skills would seem to be of less importance in the opening years of the 21st century than they were a few decades ago, before technologies of the kinds discussed here were first developed.

In a similar way, formal assessment mechanisms, such as external examinations, seem now more likely to encourage conceptual development and careful mathematical thinking than smooth repetition of memorized procedures, so that the roles of the calculator to foster learning need to be considered in such a context.

5.3. *Motivating Learning*

Reference has already been made to the role of external examinations as a source of influence, widely recognized in many countries (both East and West) as a key agent in directing the activities of both teachers and their students. When hand-held technologies are integrated into examinations, the motivation to use them thoughtfully and efficiently is considerable.

In addition, hand-held technologies can be intrinsically motivating, as they offer students a responsive environment in which to experiment with mathematical ideas and explore connections between them. As noted earlier, calculator display screens can themselves provoke students to explore new aspects of mathematics, when surprising results are given (such as the new kinds of numbers shown in Figure 17). The powerful range of software built into devices such as Casio's *ClassPad 300* and fx-9860G graphics calculator offers a platform upon which many interesting learning ideas can be developed to motivate learning (e.g., see the reference[12]).

5.4. *The Role of the Teacher*

Effective use of hand-held technology requires teachers who are themselves competent and confident users of the technologies concerned. This is of critical importance: nothing important changes in mathematics classrooms without the teacher changing in some way.[7]

Supporting the professional development of teachers for this task takes both time and effort. While publications[12] and websites[11] are important components of the professional development involved, experience in Australia suggests that hands-on time in workshops, together with the support of colleagues in a school are also key elements.[4,5]

5.5. *Pedagogical Effects*

By their very nature, hand-held technologies are personal devices that lend themselves to individual work or shared work among two or three students. Their use thus has some implications for pedagogy, with more emphasis on individual and small group work in a classroom than on whole-of-class instruction.

Of course, there continues to be a place for whole class instruction, well supported by recent technological advances in projection of calculators onto screens for this purpose. Some classroom time needs to be devoted to making sure that students can use their technology well, including thoughtfully deciding when not to use it at all, and a means of projecting a calculator for the whole class to see is useful; both overhead projection panels and emulators displayed via a computer projector can be used productively in classrooms. Similarly, productive discussions can be provoked by a calculator display visible to all members of a secondary school classroom.

Interesting and recent developments include opportunities to creatively mix both individual and collective work, through the connection of individual student graphics calculators to a computer projector, so that the work of one student can be the subject of discussion by many students in a class, and the use of calculator networks within a classroom, to enhance productive communications among learners and the teacher.

5.6. *Changing the Curriculum*

Finally, it has often been recognized that it is very difficult to bring about deep change in mathematical curricula. There are many understandable reasons for this: a natural conservatism of teachers, especially older teachers; a reluctance to remove from the curriculum anything that the current generation of university and high school teachers themselves learned as students; the difficulties of adjusting well-developed and well-understood practice, and reluctance to risk existing practices for new alternatives that have not yet stood the test of time; the extreme difficulty many teachers have to find any time to acquire new skills and take on new challenges, in the context of doing a job that is already very demanding. In such circum-

58

stances, and with the history of curriculum development in mind, we should be cautious about expecting too much curriculum change too quickly.

Alternatively, if curricula do not undergo a process of gradual change, they risk a process of having to make very large changes periodically, which is much more difficult. Hand-held technologies offer an opportunity for teachers themselves to explore some new opportunities for teaching and learning in their classrooms, rather than relying entirely on external influences, such as curriculum and assessment authorities. It is clear that many teachers have found this opportunity valuable [e.g. 4], laying important groundwork for others to change and for larger-scale changes to be contemplated. From the perspective of curriculum developers, there seems to be more likelihood that technology can bring about curriculum change if it takes the form of hand-held technology than other variations, as these seem to have more prospects of being widely accessible. It seems most unlikely that large-scale curriculum change is possible, at least as far as technology is concerned, unless universal access to the technology can be contemplated. This probably explains why it is easier to change curricula on a local level (such as a single classroom, a single teacher, or a single school) than on a global level (such as a school district, a province or a country).

6. Conclusions

In this paper, we have surveyed the place of hand-held technologies in secondary mathematics education, relying on an analysis of the devices themselves from one of the major manufacturers, their mathematical capabilities and the educational consequences of using them. If secondary mathematics education is to be responsive to the changing technological world of the 21st century, there appear to be good prospects for using these kinds of devices to do so. While this is already the case in developed and affluent countries such as Australia and the USA, the arguments seem also to be relevant to less affluent and less developed communities, including many countries in Asia, Africa and South America.

References

1. Hembree, R. & Dessart, D.J., Research on calculators in mathematics education. In J.T. Fey (ed.) Calculators in Mathematics Education: 1992 Yearbook of the National Council of Teachers of Mathematics (pp. 22–31). Reston, VA: NCTM (1992).
2. Groves, S., The effect of long-term calculator use on children's understanding of number: Results from the Calculators in Primary Mathematics project. In

Scott, N. & Hollingsworth, H. (eds.) Mathematics: Creating the Future (pp. 150–158). Melbourne: The Australian Association of Mathematics Teachers (1997).

3. National Council of Teachers of Mathematics, The Technology Principle. http://standards.nctm.org/document/chapter2/techn.htm (2000).

4. Morony, W. & Stephens, M., Students, mathematics and graphics calculators into the new millennium. Adelaide: Australian Association of Mathematics Teachers (2000).

5. Australian Association of Mathematics Teachers, Graphics Calculators and School Mathematics: A communiqué to the education community. http://www.aamt.edu.au/projects/gc/#communique (2001).

6. Wong, N-Y., Conceptions of doing and learning mathematics among Chinese. Journal of Intercultural Studies. 23, 2, 211–229 (2002).

7. Kissane, B., Technology and the curriculum: The case of the graphics calculator. New Zealand Mathematics Magazine, 39(1), 64–84 (2002).

8. Kissane, B., Three roles for technology: Towards a humanistic renaissance in mathematics education. In Rogerson, A. (ed) The Humanistic Renaissance in Mathematics Education: Proceedings of the International Conference (pp. 191–199). Palermo, Sicily: The Mathematics Education into the 21st Century Project (2002).

9. Kissane, B., Equations and the graphics calculator, In D. Edge & Y.B. Har (eds.) Mathematics Education for a Knowledge-Based Era: Proceedings of Second EARCOME, Volume 2 (pp. 401–408). Singapore: Association of Mathematics Educators (2002).

10. Casio ES Series Scientific Calculator Project http://world.casio.com/edu/resources/activities/activity/index.html (2005).

11. Shriro Pty Ltd, Casio Teachers web site, http://www.casioed.net.au (2006).

12. Kissane, B. & Kemp, M., Mathematics with a graphics calculator: Casio fx-9860G, Perth, Mathematical Association of Western Australia (2006).

COLLEGE ALGEBRA CHANGE

ROBERT L. MAYES

Science and Mathematics Teaching Center
University of Wyoming, Laramie, WY 82071, USA
E-mail: rmayes2@uwyo.edu

VENNESSA L. WALKER and PHILIP N. CHASE

Department of Psychology, West Virginia University
Morgantown, WV 26506, USA

Reports nationwide have shown that success rates in college mathematics classes have been dismal, particularly those prior to Calculus (Lutzer, Maxwell & Rodi, 2002). The current paper evaluates the utility of providing Supplemental Practice (SP) as a means to facilitate learning in an Applied College Algebra course. A pilot study revealed that students who earned more attendance points for SP sessions also received higher course grades. Additionally, students who earned the same number of SP points performed equally well regardless of their incoming skill level. A more controlled study revealed similar results, indicating that students who attended more SP sessions performed better on exams and earned higher final course grades than those who attended fewer SP sessions. Pragmatically, however, the only students for whom SP effectively facilitated success were those who passed a Pre-assessment exam of basic skills.

The Business Higher Education Forum (2005) identifies a crisis in mathematics education that could have serious long-term effects on U.S. scientific and technical advancement. The American Diploma Project (Achieve, 2004) reports that the percentage of ninth grade students in the U.S. who graduate from high school is 68%, 40% of these same ninth graders start college, only 27% of them persist through the second year, and only 18% earn a degree. Twenty-two percent of college freshmen are not ready for the entry-level mathematics course and require remediation. This number is even more frightening than it appears, since the entry level mathematics course identified is College Algebra, not Precalculus or Calculus. The Statistical Abstract of Undergraduate Programs in the Mathematical Sciences in the United States (Lutzer, Maxwell & Rodi, 2002) reported that while college enrollments are increasing, calculus enrollments are stagnant, with only 9% of students matriculating into calculus. The majority of first year students' first college mathematics course is either remedial, liberal arts, or College Algebra. Failure and withdrawal rates in before calculus courses are often dismal, reaching between 40% and 60%.

In response to this crisis in mathematics education at the undergraduate level, West Virginia University established the Institute for Mathematics Learning (IML) in the summer of 2001. The IML has been implementing reform in before calculus courses over the past five years, including Liberal Arts Mathematics, Applied College Algebra, College Algebra, College Trigonometry, Precalculus, and Applied Calculus. Extensive data were collected and analyzed on student success in these and subsequent courses over the first four years. In the fall 2004 – spring 2005 academic year, students were successful in a subsequent course (received an A, B, or C) 80% of the time if the student received an A or B in the IML restructured course, providing evidence that the courses met an important criterion of validity. Success rates in the courses in the fourth year of the IML were also promising (Table 1), though the goal of 70% success rates was not achieved.

Over the fall 2004 – spring 2005 academic year a number of innovations were introduced in the Applied College Algebra course and a more in-depth study of outcomes was conducted. The remainder of this report will focus on the Applied College Algebra course reform and its impact, with a focus on the curricular aspect of Supplemental Practice. The Applied College Algebra course in this study began with an in-depth introduction to the function concept, followed by an introduction to mathematical modeling using the techniques of finite differences and least squares. The remainder of the course introduced the standard functions studied in a college algebra course as models for real world data: polynomial, rational, radical, absolute value, logarithmic, and exponential functions.

Theoretical Framework

One critical aspect of the reformation of the Applied College Algebra course is the integration of learning theories that has governed its evolution. Rather than give priority to a particular theoretical perspective, the work in this report has been governed by a focus on evidence that College Algebra has improved. The authors came from diverse backgrounds, but they shared an optimistic, pragmatic point of view: put in place multiple methods for evaluating whether the course is successful and then make systematic changes to achieve success.

The work began with a change in the goals of the curriculum that was based in the constructivist theory of learning and numerous calls from many fronts for a change in the teaching of algebra. Leaders in United States mathematics education, including Usiskin, Fey, and Hied, and the NCTM's Curriculum and Evaluation Standards (2001) called for algebra to shift from a focus on manipulative skills towards development of conceptual understanding, a functions based approach, multiple representations of function and methods of solving equations, real-world problems to contextualize theory and motivate students, and technology as a tool to actively engage students in discovering mathematics. The report Achieving Quantitative Literacy (2004) calls for an increase in quantitative reasoning with data in real world contexts. They define quantitative literacy as

- the reasoning capabilities required of citizens in the information age which provide for economic competitiveness both for the individual and society
- personal welfare in supporting decision making about budgets, health, and financial planning
- citizenship skills such as dissecting political arguments and economic discourse.

The Mathematical Association of America's Committee on the Undergraduate Program in Mathematics (CUPM) Curriculum Guide calls for alignment of courses with students needs. The CUPM recommends a focus on conceptual understanding of powerful mathematical ideas that motivate students and on students engaging in a variety of mathematical strategies. A Collective Vision: Voice of Partner Disciplines (Ganter & Barker, 2004) provides insight from other disciplines on appropriate outcomes for mathematics courses. The report reinforced the need for courses that stress mathematical modeling, conceptual understanding, and critical thinking strategies. They call for an increased emphasis on problem solving, communication, and real world applications.

Business groups are also weighing in on the need for change. Tapping America's Potential: The Education for Innovation Initiative (Business Round Table, 2005), A Commitment to America's Future: Responding to the Crisis in Mathematics and Science Education (Business Higher Education Forum, 2005), and the American Diploma Project (Achieve, Inc., 2004) all expound the need for improved mathematical ability among graduates as essential to the future strength of the economy.

The canons for implementing change in the Applied College Algebra course also were informed by examining the university's Liberal Studies Program goals. Most lower division mathematics courses are included as options in university Liberal Studies Programs. The Applied College Algebra course addresses liberal studies outcomes for the general college population, including:

- Introducing the great ideas and controversies in human thought and experience, in this case the function concept.
- Developing the ability to reason clearly, communicate effectively, and understand major influences of society.
- Developing critical thinking by requiring logical inquiry to evaluate decisions, question posing, problem formulation, and interpretation of results.
- Incorporating a writing component.

These outcomes of the WVU's Liberal Studies Program, now called the General Education Curriculum, were also incorporated into the goals for Applied College Algebra.

Although some of the sources also called for a reduction in computational skills, the authors' experiences with at-risk students suggested a review and integration of computational skills with critical thinking skills was needed. Thus, our attempts at reform accepted the challenges and goals set forth by constructivist critiques, but included components derived from cognitive and behavioral research to assure that the students had the prerequisite computational skills. Research from cognitive and behavioral science have provided insights into how the mind works and how to arrange learning environments that provide critical experiences for the student. For example, English (1997) views reasoning as embodied and imaginative. It is embodied in that students' reason with structures which emerge from their experiences as they interact with their environment. Reasoning is imaginative because it draws upon a number of powerful, illuminating devices that structure concrete level experiences and transform them into models for abstract thought. It is important to emphasize the interaction of teachers and students in a highly engaging setting. This idea is consistent with both good constructivist teaching concepts and good behavioral ones. For example mastery learning and PSP both focus on the active student. The goal of the Applied College Algebra course is for students to engage in critical thinking; that is, using algebra not just computing algorithms. This idea also is independent of the above broad theoretical perspectives. Precision teaching, a movement in behavioral education, has always focused on application and problem-solving. Programmed instruction has focused on a variety of advanced conceptual skills (concept formation, problem-solving, strategies, etc.). The Applied College Algebra course attempts to actively engage students in the learning of mathematics, both through laboratory experiences and in-class participation activities. The goal is to balance teacher-directed activities with student-directed activities.

This balance is closely related to the Learner Centered Instruction movement and behavioral education (Chase, 2003), which tout active participation by the learner. The Applied College Algebra course integrates behavioral and learner centered instruction tenets for engaging the student in two primary ways. First, the course has instituted weekly computer laboratories that stress conceptual understanding and modeling real world problems in cooperative groups. In labs, students explore open-ended questions that require critical thinking and reasoning. Second, classroom presentations each week engage students in participation activities through the use of Personal Response Systems (PRS) with a focus on skills, concepts, and applications.

The final tenet for change employed in the restructuring of the Applied College Algebra course was Treisman's Model. Treisman (1985) developed a model for teaching undergraduate calculus based on his work with African-American students at the University of California, Berkeley. Treisman (1992) was concerned about the high failure rates of these students and the blame for these rates being attributed to the students' deficits in motivation, lack of previous mathematics preparation, and lack of family emphasis on education. He replaced the traditional remedial approaches with an honors program that encouraged students to collaborate on challenging problems in an environment of high expectations. Treisman used weekly collaborative learning sessions in small groups with student mentors to provide a supportive atmosphere with high expectations for the student. Rather than focusing on remediation in these sessions, he required students to engage in challenging mathematics problems that were engaging and meaningful. Finally, he instituted faculty sponsorship in development and management of the courses. The program has been so successful that it has spread to other universities throughout the United States. The IML adopted Treisman's Model as a guide for the development and implementation of the computer laboratory component of all courses it sponsors. Applied College Algebra engages students in a weekly computer laboratory. In the lab, groups of 25 students are assigned a mentor who is an undergraduate mathematics or mathematics education major or a graduate mathematics student. Students work in groups of 2 or 3 on understanding a mathematical concept or modeling a real world problem, thus providing challenging, meaningful, and engaging problems. The IML Faculty include mathematicians and mathematics educators who provide faculty sponsorship. The IML Faculty coordinate the IML courses, developing curriculum and assessments, teaching a section of the course, and mentoring the instructors teaching other sections of the course.

Applied College Algebra Curricular Reform

The Institute for Mathematics Learning (IML) has instituted a common vision for restructuring six large enrollment lower division mathematics courses. First, the courses are computer enhanced, using Vista WebCT course management software, web sites, and interactive Java applets to provide access to course materials, implement assessment, communicate with students, engage students in exploring and discovering mathematics, and manage the course grades. The Applied College Algebra course has created a dynamic interactive Java based tool called the Grapher, which provides students a tool for exploring functions and modeling data. The course has 10 online quizzes, 4 on-line chapter reviews, 4 on-line exams, and an on-line gateway Pre-assessment to determine student mathematical deficiencies. Second, the courses incorporate a computer laboratory component, where students are peer mentored while they engage in explorations of mathematical concepts and apply mathematics to solve real world problems. Third, the courses focus on active student learning and student accountability, implementing teaching strategies that engage students and provide informal formative feedback on their progress. The Applied College Algebra course uses the PRS to implement 22 classroom participation activities. The PRS allows multiple choice problems to be presented within the PowerPoint slides. Students work through the problem either individually or collaboratively, log an answer on their PRS response pad, and then receive immediate feedback on their answers. Power point slides guide the course discussion, serve as student lecture outlines, and provide real world data problems as well as a guide to key concepts to be explored.

In the Applied College Algebra course an additional curricular component called Supplemental Practice (SP) was introduced. Supplemental Practice grew out of the IML effort to improve students' success rates. It began in the spring and fall of 2002 when a Pre-assessment was incorporated into the course to determine the basic algebra skills of students entering the course. Students were given one attempt at the Pre-assessment and advised to drop the course if their performance was sub par. These developments did little to improve retention in the course. In Spring 2003 the students were offered a retake of the Pre-assessment, with any student scoring less than 80% being provided access to the computer intelligent tutoring system ALEKS. Because the use of ALEKS was not part of the students' grades, however, participation in using the system to build skills also was negligible and no impact on retention was detected. In Fall 2003 a series of help sessions were required for students who scored below 80% on the Pre-assessment and in Spring 2004 these help sessions were formalized into Algebra Aid. Algebra Aid was offered weekly throughout the semester in the IML Computer Center. It consisted of answering students' questions about problems on the on-line homework quizzes or labs. Although attendance was reasonable, student engagement was very passive. At this point the decision was made to offer extra weekly class sessions where students were required to actively participate in solving mathematics problems. This was the start of Supplemental Practice. SP was first implemented in Fall 2004 via paper worksheets focusing on selected skills or applications. Two versions of SP sessions were created, an Algorithm based SP and an Application based SP. Both consisted of a one-hour interactive session each week, but Algorithm SP focused solely on basic skills without context, while Application SP used real world applications to motivate the need for learning basic skills. SP was then updated in Spring 2005 by selecting the questions asked of students from a programmed text with well documented success (McHale, Christenson, and Roberts, 1986) and implementing components of the program using a Personal Response System.

Students were assigned to SP based upon their performance on the Pre-assessment. If students scored below 80% on two attempts on the Pre-assessment, they were required to attend SP. The research analysis focuses on both the relations identified from the Pre-assessment and the effects of the SP component of the Applied College Algebra course.

The research questions addressed were:

(1) What are the plausible effects of an SP program targeted at students at risk of failure?
(2) Does Application SP or Algorithm SP have the greatest impact on student success in the course?
(3) What is the impact of the reformed Applied College Algebra course on student success in the course and attitude towards mathematics?

Analyses were conducted using quantitative methods, including univariate and repeated-measures analyses of variance (ANOVA) and correlations. Significant main effects were further analyzed with pairwise comparisons using a Bonferroni adjustment. A Nonequivalent Control Group quasi-experimental research design was employed (Figure 1).

Fall 2004

In Fall 2004 the first study of the impact of SP on student cognition and attitude was conducted. During the fall semester, SP sessions were implemented using paper-and-pencil tasks for review. The Algorithm SP and Application SP sections were held at the same late afternoon time in different sized classrooms with the two instructors switching sections every week. An unfortunate consequence of this was that students did not always attend their assigned session, selecting one instructor over the other instead, resulting in some students not consistently receiving either the Algorithm SP or Application SP treatment. Consequently the two treatments could not be compared during this study. The data from the first study, however, could be examined in terms of other variables, particularly the interactions between student performance on the Pre-assessment and attendance at the supplemental sessions.

Method

Participants

Participants in the study were 399 students enrolled across 3 sections of Applied College Algebra. To qualify for enrollment in the course, students must have scored at least a 20 on the math portion of the ACT, completed a pre-College Algebra workshop, or passed a math placement exam administered by the university.

Setting

Algorithm SP sessions were conducted in a large-lecture classroom (capacity 250) while the Application SP took place in a small-lecture classroom (capacity 50). Both forms of SP sessions were offered outside of regular class time on Wednesdays from 4:00–5:00 p.m. Students were not required to reserve this time and so some did have conflicts with other courses.

Materials

Students were given a Pre-assessment exam, which consisted of 25 items designed to test basic skills such as simple operations and basic expression manipulations. A retired version of the mathematics portion of the ACT was used as a standardized measure for pretest and posttest purposes. The ACT exam provided subscales for Pre-Algebra and Elementary Algebra (PAEA), Intermediate Algebra and Coordinate Geometry (IACG), and Plane Geometry and Trigonometry (PGTRG). The Mathematics Attitude Inventory (MAI), consisting of 30 Likert scale items, served as a pretest and posttest measure of students' attitudes and beliefs about mathematics. MAI was based on an attitude survey developed by the first author supplemented with items from other surveys of mathematics attitude. The MAI had five subscales:

- Utility — student's view of mathematics as useful in solving real-world problems
- Concept vs. Skill — student's view of mathematics as understanding concepts or as memorizing algorithms and performing skills
- Locus of Control — student's view of learning mathematics as internal, self-controlled versus external, provided by others
- Belief about Mathematics — student's view of mathematics as a subject versus other subjects
- Math Technology — student's view of technology as a tool in learning mathematics

Secondary dependent measures included performance on 9 labs, 10 homework quizzes, and 4 exams. Labs were computer-based activities designed to facilitate exploration of concepts and application through the use of technology. Homework quizzes were online quizzes designed to help students pinpoint areas of weakness primarily in mastering skills, though there were a small percentage of application and conceptually oriented questions. The 3 exams administered during the course of the semester covered the material presented during lectures and were not cumulative. The final was a cumulative exam over all chapters.

Procedure

During the first week of class, students took the MAI survey and the ACT pretest. After a week of reviewing College Algebra prerequisites, such as simplifying polynomial, rational, and radical expressions, students took the Pre-assessment exam. Students who scored below 80% on the first attempt were required to attend an SP review session and then retake the Pre-assessment within a week. If the student failed to attain an 80% or higher mark on the Pre-assessment on either attempt, they were required to attend SP for the remainder of the semester (Required). Students who scored above 80% were encouraged to attend SP, but their attendance was not required (Optional). Optional students who scored less than 70% on any of three subsequent tests, however, were then required to attend SP until they earned at least 70% on a later test. Two weeks prior to the end of the semester, the MAI survey and ACT posttest were administered.

Results

For purposes of the Fall 2004 analyses, the Required/Optional categorization for SP was based solely on Pre-assessment exam performance. Based on these categorizations, 7 Cohorts were created using the Required versus Optional categorization and the number of SP points earned. Students received SP participation points (maximum of 11) in one of two ways. Those in the Optional group could receive points for attending SP or by keeping their average on exams at 70% or above. For example, the Optional Earned 6–9 cohort involved students who had a Pre-assessment score of at least 80%, but scored below 70% on a subsequent exam and were required to attend SP for that chapter. They received a score of between 6–9 because they failed to attend SP when required between 2 and 5 times. The Optional 10–11 cohort, however, included students who did not attend any SP sessions, but they kept their exam grades above 70% throughout the semester. Students classified as Required had to attend SP to receive participation points regardless of their performance on subsequent tests.

To analyze performance on the ACT, a 7 x 2 repeated-measures ANOVA with a between-subject factor of Cohort (Required 0, Required 1–5, Required 6–9, Required 10–11, Optional 1–5, Optional 6–9, and Optional 10–11) and a within-subject factor of Test (ACT pretest and ACT posttest) was conducted. There was no significant interaction, nor was there a significant difference between the cohorts on overall ACT score. In fact, the post-test ACT means are remarkably consistent across all Optional and Required cohorts. There was a significant main effect of Test, $F(1, 283) = 335.695$, $p < .001$, with the posttest scaled scores ($M = 19.86$, $SD = 3.02$) exceeding the pretest scaled scores ($M = 15.71$, $SD = 3.11$). These data show that scores improved on a standardized assessment of mathematical skills regardless of cohort. Analyses for the Pre-Algebra and Elementary Algebra (PAEA) and Intermediate Algebra and Coordinate Geometry (IACG) subscales of the ACT revealed similar results; there were no significant differences between the cohorts, but there was significant improvement from pretest to posttest.

The final course average for Applied College Algebra was also analyzed to determine the impact of SP. Table 2 shows the final course averages for all students enrolled in the Applied College Algebra course. A univariate ANOVA indicated a significant effect of Cohort on final course average, $F(6, 398) = 6.970$, $p < .001$. Pairwise comparisons using a Bonferroni adjustment indicated that both the Required and Optional 6–9 cohorts outperformed the Required 0 cohort, $p < .05$. Additionally, both the Required and Optional 10–11 cohorts outperformed the Required 0 cohort, $p < .001$. No significant differences were found between Required and Optional students who earned the same number of points for SP. This suggests that SP has a positive impact on the Required cohorts, moving these students up to similar levels as those in the Optional cohorts. There is also overwhelming evidence that the more a student attended SP, the better they did in the course. The Required cohort course means increase with increased SP attendance. A Required student attending SP 6 to 9 times has a course mean equivalent to an Optional-Earned 6–9 student, while a Required student attending 10 to 11 times actually had a higher mean than an Optional-Earned 10–11 student.

The Mathematics Attitude Inventory (MAI) was also given to all students twice, as a pre-test and a post-test. The same 7 x 2 ANOVA using cohort and test as factors was used to analyze the data. Table 3 shows the means and standard deviations for both administrations of the attitude survey by cohort. There was a significant interaction between test and cohort, $F(6, 330) = 2.22$, $p = .041$. Simple effects analyses indicated that on the pretest, the Optional 10–11 cohort reported significantly higher attitude scores than the Required 0 cohort. Additionally, on the posttest, the Optional 10–11 group reported significantly higher attitude scores than the Required 0, Required 1–5, and Required 6–9 cohorts. All simple effects were significant to the 0.05 level.

Discussion

There was strong evidence that SP has a positive impact on student learning, based on students' performance on the ACT and their final course averages. However, student attitudes towards mathematics were not positively impacted. A number of variables, however, interfered with answering the questions of the study. Differences between Algorithm SP and Application SP could not be assessed due to a diffusion of treatment resulting from students attending both SP sections, the difference in group sizes resulting from room capacities (Algorithm SP had a capacity of 250, while Application SP had a capacity of 50), and instructor variables due to different instructors. In addition, different methods for tracking students' attendance weakened the analysis. The research from Spring 2005 addressed these issues. The detailed statistical analysis of this research is reported elsewhere and only a summary of results is given below.

Spring 2005

The inclusion in Spring 2005 of a Personal Response System (PRS) in Supplemental Practice and offering Algorithm SP and Application SP at different times in large lecture classrooms allowed more control over tracking students. The question of which type of SP was most effective could now be addressed. In addition, the general categories of Required SP and Optional SP could be broken down by exam, allowing tracking of students across exams. So students were no longer categorized as Optional or Required based only on the Pre-assessment, but on performance on the last exam taken.

Results

The Spring 2005 data confirmed that there was no significant difference in student performance on the ACT measure between the Algorithm SP and Application SP groups. There was an improvement in students' quantitative skills from the beginning to the end of the semester, so the overall course had a positive impact. For students who passed the pre-assessment at an 80% or above level, SP had little impact. Student outcomes on the ACT subscales of Pre-Algebra and Elementary Algebra, Intermediate Algebra and Coordinate Geometry, and Plane Geometry and Trigonometry where all significantly improved for both the required and optional SP groups, suggesting that the course curriculum and pedagogy had a positive impact on the quantitative skills of the students across the semester. However, unlike the fall study findings, SP did not raise the required SP students to the same level as the optional SP students.

Analysis of student outcomes on course measures, such as final course average, exam average, computer laboratory average, homework average, and attendance where also conducted to determine SP impact. Analyses of the final course average indicated that SP had an overall impact for students required to take it if they attended SP at least 50% of the time. Analysis of exam average showed that while optional SP students continue to outperform the required SP students, within the required SP group the SP sessions positively impacted student performance. Even student performance on computer laboratories was positively impacted by SP. This is surprising since SP addresses skill development and the laboratories focused on conceptual understanding and applying mathematics to solve real world problems. A more expected result was the positive impact of SP on students homework average, after all the skills focus of SP is directly related to homework targeting skill mastery. Finally an analysis of student attendance in lectures and laboratories provides evidence of an effort component, with those committed to SP attending both the labs and lectures at a significantly high rate.

A correlation analysis was conducted to further analyze the relations between SP, diagnostic assessment performance, attendance, and course components. Diagnostic assessment scores and SP attendance were both significantly correlated with final course average, exam average, and lab average. These correlations add to the evidence that SP had a positive impact. The only course component not strongly correlated to other course components and measures was the homework quiz average. Perhaps this indicates a disconnect between homework and course laboratories or exams, or it could be a lack of student engagement in completing homework.

To explore the evaluative capabilities of the pre-assessment, four cohorts where constructed based on the score on the pre-assessment: 0–39, 40–59, 60–79, and 80–100. ANOVAs indicated a significant difference between the cohorts on the final course average, exam average, lab average, and homework quiz average. In addition the cohorts showed a high correlation with ACT performance. These data strongly support the validation of the diagnostic assessment as a means for evaluating student quantitative skills.

Unfortunately student attitudes as measured by the Mathematics Attitude Inventory did not improve. In fact the subscales of Utility, Locus of Control, and Belief actually indicated a drop in student attitude. This is a disappointing outcome when the intent of basing the course on real world modeling was to improve student engagement and interest.

Discussion

Results from the 2004–2005 school year indicate that students are making gains in their mathematical skills, based on their performances on the ACT. This suggests that the course has a positive impact on student's performance. However, Supplemental Practice (SP) has had mixed results. Analyzing performances accounting for the different kinds of SP (Application and Algorithm) yielded no significant results, suggesting that neither approach is superior. The remaining analysis focused on the impact of SP regardless of type. The intent of SP was to improve student success in the course by improving mathematical skills, targeting students at risk of failure as measured by a score in the 60–79% range on the Pre-assessment. The Spring 2005 study indicated that SP has a linear effect in general, with higher scores being recorded for those students who attended more SP sessions. The variability within these cohorts is tremendous, however, leading to non-significant statistical results and clouding interpretations that might be made regarding the effectiveness of SP. On the other hand, the lack of significant difference on ACT posttest performance between Optional and Required cohorts indicates that students with a poorer mathematical background (Required) were performing as well as those with a stronger mathematical background (Optional).

Significant correlations between SP attendance and Exam Average and Final Course Grade suggest that SP is having a positive impact on student learning. Based on the results comparing cohorts, however, these correlations only seem to indicate that, for low performers, SP raises their grades from a low failing grade to a high failing grade or possibly a low passing grade. Regression analyses showed that using SP Attendance and Exam Average as predictors of Final Course Average and Exam Average accounted for a significant portion of the variance in scores on these two measures, and suggested that a closer inspection of the Pre-assessment Exam might be warranted.

The Pre-assessment Exam seems to be indicative of success in the course, based on its correlation with Final Course Grade and Exam Average. When the scores on the Pre-assessment were divided into cohorts, analyses comparing those students who passed the Pre-assessment with students who failed it revealed that those who passed were significantly outperforming those who failed on all course measures except for Homework Quiz Average. The failure to find differences between the highest cohorts and the lowest cohorts on Homework Quiz Average may be attributed to the similar means between cohorts and the high variability in the lower cohorts, however. Additionally, those who scored 80–100% on the Pre-assessment were consistently outperforming those who scored 60–79%, which is consistent with findings that SP Optional students outperformed SP Required students. These singular analyses of Pre-assessment performance suggest that the Pre-assessment Exam may be a useful gateway test that predicts success in the course. The 52% of students in Applied College Algebra who scored 80–100% on the Pre-assessment had a mean Final Course Average of 74.12, a solid C average. Those who scored 60–79% had a mean Final

74

Course Average of 60.05, which is a low passing grade, but it nonetheless suggests that some changes to the curriculum may be able to improve this cohort's grades to a C average. If the performance of students who pass the Pre-assessment with a 60% or better could be raised to at least a C average, success in the class would increase from 52% to nearly 80%. Those who fail the Pre-assessment, however, are consistently not performing up to standards, and alternatives to the class may need to be provided for these students.

The analyses of the Homework Quizzes suggest that the quizzes are not having a significant impact on student performance, since they are not correlated with performance in other components of the course, specifically exams. Thus, although the quizzes are intended to serve as reviews for the exam material, quiz performance is not indicative of exam performance. Thus, overhauling the Homework Quizzes may provide an avenue for increasing student performance.

Results on the MAI indicate that the course is not having the desired impact on student attitudes and beliefs about mathematics. Inclusion of modeling in an algebra course is meant to improve student engagement and confidence, but students' attitudes actually decreased in the subscales of utility, locus of control, and belief. Positive student affect is essential for student engagement in the course, which directly impacts success. More analysis is needed on the interaction of the course components and student affective outcomes.

References

1. Achieve Inc. (2004). *The Expectations Gap. Washington*, DC: Achieve.
2. Achieve Inc. (2004). *Creating a High School Diploma that Counts*. Washington, DC: American Diploma Project.
3. Business Higher Education Forum (2005). *A Commitment to America's Future: Responding to the Crisis in Mathematics and Science Education*. Washington, DC: Business Higher Education Forum.
4. Business Round Table (2005). *Tapping America's Potential: The Education for Innovation Initiative*. Washington, DC: Business Round Table.
5. Chase, P. N. (2003): Behavioral Education: Pragmatic answers to questions about novelty and efficiency. In: *Behavior Theory and Philosophy* (K. A. Lattal and P. N. Chase eds), pp. 347–367. New York: Plenum Press.
6. English, L. (1997): *Mathematical Reasoning: Analogies, Metaphors, and Images*. Mahwah, New Jersey: Lawrence, Erlbaum Associates.
7. Ganter, S., Barker, W. (2004): *A Collective Vision: Voice of Partner Disciplines*. Washington, DC: Mathematical Association of America.
8. Lutzer, D., Maxwell, J., Rodi, S.(2002): *Statistical Abstract of Undergraduate*

Programs in the Mathematical Sciences in the United States. Washington, DC: American Mathematical Society.

9. Mayes, R., Reitz, J. (2003): *ACT in Algebra: Applications, Concepts, and Technology in Learning Algebra.* Boston: McGraw-Hill.
10. McHale, T. J., Christensen, A. A., Roberts, K. J. (1986): *Intermediate algebra: Programmed.* Reading, MA: Addison-Wesley.
11. National Council of Teachers of Mathematics (2000). *Principles and Standards for School Mathematics.* Reston, Virginia: NCTM.
12. Steen, L. (2004): *Achieving Quantitative Literacy: An Urgent Challenge for Higher Education.* Washington, DC: Mathematics Association of America.
13. Treisman, U. (1985): A study of the mathematics performance of black students at the University of California, Berkeley. Unpublished doctoral dissertation, Univerisity of California, Berkeley.
14. Treisman, U. (1992): Studying students studying Calculus: A look at the lives of minority mathematics students in college. *The College Mathematics Journal* **23(5)**: 362–372.

Table 1.   Success Rates for Fall 2004 – Spring 2005

Course	Success Rates (A, B, or C grade)
Liberal Arts Mathematics	65.9%
Applied Algebra	63.3%
College Algebra	58.6%
College Trigonometry	63%
Precalculus	64%
Applied Calculus	68%

Table 2.   Final Course Average by Cohorts of Students (Fall 2004)

	Cohort	Number	Minimum	Maximum	Mean	SD
Optional						
	Earned 1–5	14	31.42	84.71	64.21	16.53
	Earned 6–9	57	1.84	91.79	61.07	21.07
	Earned 10–11	165	.08	98.26	70.35	21.53
Required						
	Earned 0	24	.00	89.67	44.08	29.86
	Earned 1–5	35	11.47	89.41	59.24	21.82
	Earned 6–9	52	.71	89.68	61.79	26.44
	Earned 10–11	52	16.91	93.92	72.53	13.63

Table 3.   Means and Standard Deviations for MAI by Cohort (Fall 2004)

Cohort	N	MAI 1		MAI 2	
		Mean	SD	Mean	SD
Optional Earned 1–5	21	3.02	.81	2.25	1.55
Optional Earned 6–9	59	2.99	.72	2.31	1.30
Optional Earned 10–11	113	3.10	.76	2.71	1.16
Required Earned 0	9	2.20	1.71	1.33	1.61
Required Earned 1–5	16	2.80	.80	1.63	1.51
Required Earned 6–9	43	3.06	.66	1.97	1.39
Required Earned 10–11	76	3.02	.84	2.57	1.13

Figure 1.   Research Design

$$O_1 \ O_2 \ O_3 \ X_1 \ O_4 \ O_5 \ O_6$$

$$O_1 \ O_2 \ O_3 \ X_2 \ O_4 \ O_5 \ O_6$$

O_1 and O_4: Pre- and Post-Mathematics Attitude Inventory (MAI)
O_2 and O_5: Pre- and Post-ACT Exam
O_3: Pre-assessment of Basic Skills
O_6: Final Exam
X_1: Algorithm SP
X_2: Application SP

MATHEMATICS EXPERIMENTS
— LEARNING AND INVESTIGATING MATHEMATICS
WITH THE HELP OF COMPUTERS

SHANGZHI LI

Department of Mathematics, Beihang University (BUAA)
Beijing 100083, P. R. China
E-mail: lisz@buaa.edu.cn

Some interesting examples are given in this article to show how one can learn and investigate mathematics through experiments with the help of computers. Each example begins with a problem. Trying to solve the problem one experiences exploration, invention and application of mathematics in the process.

Keywords: Experiment, mathematics, computer, learning, investigation, exploration.

Introduction

Mathematics has traditionally been regarded as a pure theoretical subject, only consisting of deduction and proofs, having no experiments at all.

The advent of computers changed this old picture. Now experiments are becoming an increasing important part of mathematics.

We have been teaching a course 'Mathematics Experiments', and we have written and published a textbook[1]. In this course the students try to learn and investigate mathematics with the help of computers. We hope to stimulate their interest in mathematics through examples and experiments.

Some examples are given here to show how we do this in our course. All these examples are selected from the textbook[1]. Each example begins with a problem. Trying to solve the problem you go further and further, and experience exploration, invention and application in the process.

1. The Graphs of Functions

We begin with drawing graphs of functions by using Mathematica.

1.1. *Taylor's Series*

Example 1.1. Construct the functions $y = \sin x$ and $y = kx$ for different values of k, e.g. $k = 0.8, 1.0, 1.2$.

The following is the Mathematica command for drawing the graphs of these functions in the interval $[-\pi, \pi]$.

```
Plot[{Sin[x],0.8x,x,1.2x},{x,-Pi,Pi}]
```

Run this command we get the graph

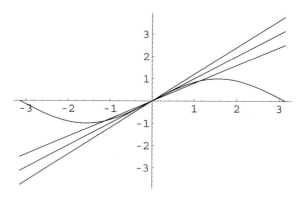

Fig. 1.   Approach $y = \sin x$ by a linear function

Compare the graphs of $y = \sin x$ and $y = kx$. They pass through the same point $(0,0)$. Find by observation for which value of k the straight line $y = kx$ approaches the sinusoid $y = \sin x$ most closely?

One can find that the line $y = x$ with slope $k = 1$ approaches the sinusoid $y = \sin x$ most closely. This slope can be viewed as the slope of $y = \sin x$ at $x = 0$, and is just the derivative of the function $y = \sin x$ at $x = 0$. $y = x$ is the best linear function approaching the sine function $y = \sin x$ for the values of x near 0.

Example 1.2. Calculate an approximation of $\sin 1°$.

Solution. We can use the linear function $y = x$ to approach $y = \sin x$ for the values of x near 0. In particular, $1°$ is a small angle, so its radian value $x = \frac{\pi}{180} \approx 0.01745$ can be used as a good approximation of $\sin 1°$. We have

$$\sin 1° \approx \frac{\pi}{180} \approx 0.01745.$$

Observe the sinusoid $y = \sin x$ and the line $y = x$ in Fig. 1. They pass through a same point $(0,0)$ when $x = 0$, and they go to a same direction when x increases from 0. They are very close when x is small, so for small x (such as $x = \frac{\pi}{180}$ in Example 1.2) we can use the formula $\sin x \approx x$ to get a good approximation of $\sin x$. But when x becomes larger and larger, the graphs of $y = \sin x$ and $y = x$ separate and go to different direction, we can no longer use a linear function as a good approximation of $y = \sin x$. But in such case we can consider polynomial $y = a_0 + a_1 x + \cdots + a_n x^n$ of degree n higher than 1 to approach $y = \sin x$. Since $y = \sin x$ is an odd function, we can only consider polynomial $y = a_1 x + a_3 x^3 + \cdots + a_{2n+1} x^{2n+1}$ consisting of terms of odd degrees.

Example 1.3. Construct the functions $y = \sin x$ and polynomials

$$y = x - \frac{x^3}{6}, \quad y = x - \frac{x^3}{6} + \frac{x^5}{120}, \quad y = x - \frac{x^3}{6} + \frac{x^5}{120} - \frac{x^7}{7!}$$

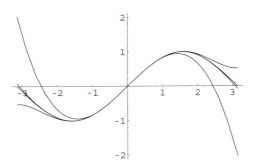

Fig. 2. Approach $y = \sin x$ by polynomials

Compare the graphs of polynomials $y = x - \frac{x^3}{3!} + \cdots + (-1)^k \frac{x^{2k+1}}{(2k+1)!}$ with the sinusoid $y = \sin x$. One finds that when the degree $n = 2k + 1$ becomes larger, the graph of such polynomial approaches the sinusoid better. In fact, the graphs of $y = x - \frac{x^3}{3!} + \cdots - \frac{x^9}{9!}$ of degree 9 and $y = \sin x$ coincide so well in interval $[-\pi, \pi]$ that we can hardly distinguish them by eyes. But in larger interval $[-4, 4]$, etc. we can observe their difference. This difference can be eliminated by using polynomial of higher degree to approach $y = \sin x$.

If a function $y = f(x)$ (such as $y = \sin x$) has n-th derivative $f^{(n)}(c)$ at a given value c of x for all integers $n \geq 0$, then $f(x)$ can be expanded as infinite series $T(x) = a_0 + a_1(x - c) + \cdots + a_n(x - c)^n + \cdots$ in certain interval of x around c, called Taylor's series of $f(x)$ at $x = c$. And thus $f(x)$ can be approached by polynomials $T_n(x) = a_0 + a_1(x - c) + \cdots + a_n(x - c)^n$ consisting of the first $n + 1$ terms of such series, for $n = 0, 1, 2, \ldots$. The Taylor's series $T(x)$ of $f(x)$ should have the same n-th derivative at $x = c$. This gives the formula $a_n = \frac{f^{(n)}(c)}{n!}$ for calculating the coefficients a_n of the Taylor's expansion.

1.2. *Fourier's Series*

Example 1.4. Construct the functions

$$y = \sin x + \frac{1}{3}\sin 3x + \cdots + \frac{1}{2m + 1}\sin(2m + 1)x$$

in the interval $[-2\pi, 2\pi]$ for different integers $m \geq 0$. Observe the tendency of the graphs when m increases infinitely.

For integers $2m + 1$ not too large, e.g. $2m + 1 = 7$, the Mathematica command can be as

```
Plot[Sin[x]+Sin[3x]/3+Sin[5x]/5+Sin[7x]/7,{x,-2Pi,2Pi}]
```

and the following graph is obtained .

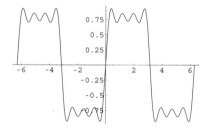

Fig. 3. $y = \sin x + \frac{1}{3}\sin 3x + \cdots + \frac{1}{7}\sin 7x$

But for a large $2m + 1$, such as $2m + 1 = 501$, it would be too difficult to write all the terms $\sin(2k + 1)x/(2k + 1)$ ($k = 0, 1, 2, \ldots, 250$) in the expression of $y = \sin x + \frac{1}{3}\sin 3x + \cdots + \frac{1}{501}\sin 501x$. The Mathematica permits write the sum $\sum_{k=0}^{250}\sin(2k + 1)x$ of all these terms as

```
Sum[Sin[n*x]/n,{n,1,501,2}]
```

And thus we can use the command

```
Plot[Sum[Sin[n*x]/n, {n, 1, 501, 2}], {x, -2Pi, 2Pi}]
```

to obtain the graph

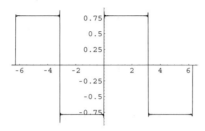

Fig. 4. $y = \sin x + \frac{1}{3}\sin 3x + \cdots + \frac{1}{501}\sin 501x$

One observes that for very large integers $2m + 1$ the graphs of $y = \sum_{k=0}^{m}\frac{1}{2k+1}\sin(2k + 1)x$ approach a 'square wave'. This seems strange: all the $y = \frac{1}{2k+1}\sin(2k + 1)x$ are continuous and smooth, their sum should also be continuous and smooth. But the sum of infinitely many such $y = \frac{1}{2k+1}\sin(2k+1)x$ is a 'square wave' which has infinitely many discontinuous points $x = k\pi$ (k ranges over all integers).

The above function is a linear combination

$$a_1 \sin x + a_2 \sin 2x + \cdots + a_n \sin nx$$

with the coefficients $a_k = \frac{1}{k}$ for odd integers k, while $a_k = 0$ for even integers k. Of course we can try other combinations with other choices of coefficients. Since all the $\sin kx$ are odd functions having common period 2π, all their linear combinations must be odd functions having period 2π. Try different choices of the coefficients a_k's. For example, construct the following functions

(i) $y = \sum_{k=1}^{n}\frac{1}{k}\sin kx = \sin x + \frac{1}{2}\sin 2x + \cdots + \frac{1}{n}\sin nx$;

(ii) $y = \sum_{k=1}^{n}\frac{1}{k+1}\sin kx$;

(iii) $y = \sum_{k=1}^{n}\frac{1}{k^2}\sin kx$.

Observing the graphs of the different combinations one can find that, the graphs of the different combinations have different shapes. Similarly, all the linear combinations of $\cos kx$ ($k = 0, 1, 2, \ldots$) are even functions with period 2π, but the graphs of different combinations have different shape. More generally, linear combinations of $\sin kx$ and $\cos kx$ ($k = 0, 1, 2, \ldots$)

are functions having period 2π, the graphs of different combinations have different shape .

Conversely, we may ask a question: for any given shape of a curve of period 2π, is it possible to find a linear combination of $\sin kx, \cos kx$ $(k = 0, 1, 2, \ldots)$ with suitable coefficients, such that its graph is exactly this curve?

French mathematician J. Fourier investigated this problem and gave a positive answer. He declared that a function $y = f(x)$ having period 2π (and satisfying certain condition of continuity) can be expanded as a combinations of $\sin kx, \cos kx$ $(k = 0, 1, 2, \ldots)$. Such a combination is called Fourier's series. For more detailed knowledge about this, please refer to a textbook of calculus.

1.3. *Graph of* $y = \sin \frac{1}{x}$ *near* $x = 0$.

We know that the function $y = \sin \frac{1}{x}$ has no definition at $x = 0$. Let us observe what happens when x closes to 0.

Example 1.5. Construct the function $y = \sin \frac{1}{x}$ in the interval $[-1, 1]$. Observe its trend when x closes to 0.

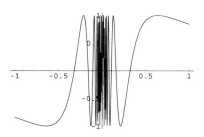

Fig. 5.

The graph near $x = 0$ is too confusing to identify. We try to 'zoom in' the interval near $x = 0$. Namely, we only draw the graph in interval $[-0.1, 0.1]$ or in $[-0.01, 0.01]$. The graph is in Fig. 6.

We see in Fig. 6 that the graph is more and more confusing with the magnifying of the interval. This means that when x approaches 0, the graph vibrates between -1 and 1 more and more quickly and madly. Even though the function $y = \sin \frac{1}{x}$ takes value in a finite interval $[-1, 1]$, it has no limit when x closes to 0.

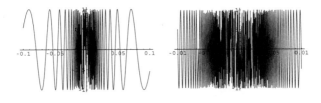

Fig. 6.

The graph of $y = \sin\frac{1}{x}$ near $x = 0$ is confusing and ugly. Now let x take a series of values $1, \frac{1}{2}, \frac{1}{3}, \ldots, \frac{1}{5000}$ closing to 0, and take the corresponding points $(\frac{1}{k}, \sin k)$ $(1 \leq k \leq 5000)$ from the graph of $y = \sin\frac{1}{x}$. Let us observe what the set of these points looks like. Since they are taken from a confusing and ugly figure. You may guess it must be more confusing and ugly.

```
T=Table[{1/k,Sin[k]},{k,1,5000}];
P=ListPlot[T]
```

Here the first sentence `T=Table[1/k,Sin[k],k,1,5000]` defines a set T consisting of 5000 points $(\frac{1}{k}, \sin k)$ $(1 \leq k \leq 5000)$, while the second sentence `P=List[T]` draws all these points.

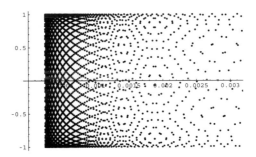

Fig. 7.

You may be surprised to see that the figure of these points looks neither confusing nor ugly. Conversely, it looks orderly and beautiful. It seems that the figure consists of graceful curves. Naturally we hope to know what are these curves? Can we find the expressions of functions whose graphs are these curves? If we cannot, it is good enough to choose certain set points among these 5000 points to form one of these curves.

We try to settle the problem in this way: for any point $P_1 = (\frac{1}{n}, \sin n) \in$ T we look for a point $P_2 = (\frac{1}{m}, \sin m)$ in T close to P_1. Certainly $(\frac{1}{n\pm1}, \sin(n \pm 1))$ is not close to P_1, since $\sin(n \pm 1)$ is usually far from $\sin n$. For large n, m, the x-coordinates $\frac{1}{n}$ and $\frac{1}{m}$ are close to each other. If we can choose n, m with the difference $m - n \approx 2k\pi$ for an integer k, then $\sin n$ and $\sin m$ are close to each other. We know $\pi \approx \frac{22}{7}$ and thus $2\pi \approx \frac{44}{7}$, hence $44 \approx 7 \times 2\pi$. We take points $(\frac{1}{k}, \sin k)$ in T with $k + 44t$ ($t = 0, 1, 2, \ldots$) ranging over an arithmetic progression of step 44. And connect these points one by one to form a smooth curve. This can be done by the following command, with the result in Fig. 8. We see in Fig. 8 that the two curves we obtain coincide well with two of the curves hidden in Fig. 7.

```
d=44;
T1=Table[{1/k,Sin[k]},{k,3,5000,d}];
T2=Table[{1/k,Sin[k]},{k,6,5000,d}];
P1=ListPlot[T1,PlotJoined->True];
P2=ListPlot[T2,PlotJoined->True];
Show[P,P1,P2]
```

Notes to the above commands.

(i) In the definition of the set T1, $\{k,3,5000,d\}$ means that k ranges over a sequence $3, 3 + d, 3 + 2d, \ldots, 3 + md, \ldots$ with each term obtained by adding the same constant d to the last term, and all the terms not exceeding 5000. Similarly, in the definition of T2 the expression $\{k,6,5000,d\}$ means k ranges over $6, 6 + d, 6 + 2d, \ldots \leq 5000$.

(ii) The function of the option "PlotJoined-->True" in the definition of the graphs P1,P2 is to connect the successive points into a smooth curve.

(iii) The command "Show[P,P1,P2]" is used to display the graphs P,P1,P2 (which was defined before) again in the same coordinate system.

We see in Fig. 8 that the two curves we obtain coincide well with two of the curves hidden in Fig. 7.

2. How to Calculate π?

As is well known, the circumference ratio π is the ratio of the circumference of a circle to its diameter on a plane. It is equal to $3.1415926\ldots$.

Are you interested in trying to calculate the value of π by making use of your knowledge? And you can do it with the help of a computer.

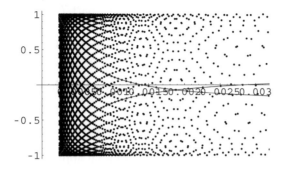

Fig. 8.

2.1. Method of Numerical Integral

We know that the area of a unit circle is π, where a unit circle is a circle with radius 1. So we can obtain the value of π by calculating the area of a unit circle.

Example 2.1. Construct a rectangular coordinate system with its origin at the center of the given unit circle, and calculate the area $\frac{\pi}{4}$ of the part of this circle in the first quadrant. Namely, we calculate the area of the graph bounded by the curve $y = \sqrt{1 - x^2}$ with $0 \le x \le 1$ and the coordinate axis. One way to do this is to use a set of lines $x = \frac{1}{n}, x = \frac{2}{n}, \ldots, x = \frac{n-1}{n}$ parallel to y axis to partition the area into many narrow parts $T_1, T_2, \ldots, T_n$ as showed in Fig. 9.

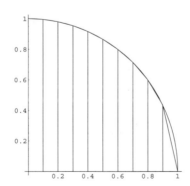

Fig. 9.   Calculate the area by Trapezoid formula

When n is very large, the wide $\frac{1}{n}$ of each part T_k is very small, we can view it as a trapezoid with two bases on lines $x = \frac{k-1}{n}, x = \frac{k}{n}$ parallel to y axis and height on x axis. The two bases of the k-th part T_k have lengths $y_{k-1} = \sqrt{1 - (\frac{k-1}{n})^2}, y_k = \sqrt{1 - (\frac{k}{n})^2}$ respectively, and its height is $\frac{1}{n}$. Viewing T_k as a trapezoid (and as a triangle when $k = n$ and $y_n = 0$) we obtain an approximation

$$S_k = \frac{1}{2} \frac{1}{n} (y_{k-1} + y_k)$$

of its area. Summing all these S_k we obtain an approximation

$$S = S_1 + S_2 + \cdots + S_n = \frac{1}{n} \left[\frac{y_0 + y_n}{2} + (y_1 + y_2 + \cdots + y_{n-1}) \right]$$

of the total area $\frac{\pi}{4}$. Taking a large enough n one can obtain a good approximation of π.

The area $\frac{\pi}{4}$ we calculate in example 2.1 is precisely the integral $\int_0^1 \sqrt{1 - x^2}\, dx$. The method we used there can be generalized to calculate the integral $\int_a^b f(x)\, dx$ for any continuous function $f(x)$ over any interval $[a, b]$, obtaining the following formula, called *Trapezoid formula*.

$$\int_a^b f(x)\, dx \approx \frac{b - a}{n} \left[\frac{f(a) + f(b)}{2} + (f(x_1) + f(x_2) + \cdots + f(x_{n-1})) \right],$$

where $x_k = a + \frac{k(b-a)}{n}$ for $k = 1, 2, \ldots, n - 1$.

In fact, we can obtain an approximation π by calculating the integral $\int_0^1 \frac{1}{x^2+1}\, dx$ instead of $\int_0^1 \sqrt{1 - x^2}\, dx$.

The Trapezoid formula is obtained by viewing the region T_k bounded by lines $x = x_{k-1}, x = x_k, y = 0$ and curve $y = f(x)$ as a trapezoid, namely, by viewing the curve segment $y = f(x)$ $(x \in [x_{k-1}, x_k])$ as a line segment. For more accurate calculation we can view such curve segment as the parabola segment passing through the 3 points $(x_{k-1}, y_k), (x_{k-0.5}, y_{k-0.5}), (x_k, y_k)$, where $x_i = a + \frac{i(b-a)}{n}$ and $y_i = f(x_i)$ for $i = k - 1, k - 0.5, k$. By calculating integral we obtain the area S_k of such a T_k under the parabola segment to be

$$S_k = \frac{1}{6} \frac{b - a}{n} (y_{k-1} + 4y_{k-0.5} + y_k)$$

Summing all the S_k $(k = 1, 2, \ldots, n)$ we obtain an approximation of $\int_a^b f(x)\, dx$ as follows:

$$\int_a^b f(x)\, dx \approx \frac{b - a}{6n} [(y_0 + y_n) + 4(y_{0.5} + y_{1.5} + \cdots + y_{n-0.5}) + 2(y_1 + \cdots + y_{n-1})]$$

This is known as *Simpson formula* for numerical integral.

As an exercise, one can use Simpson Formula to calculate approximations of $\int_0^1 \sqrt{1-x^2}\,dx$ or $\int_0^1 \frac{1}{x^2+1}\,dx$, thus obtain approximations of π.

2.2. Method of Using Taylor's Series

Example 2.2. Use Taylor's series

$$\arctan x = x - \frac{x^3}{3} + \frac{x^5}{5} - \cdots + (-1)^k \frac{x^{2k+1}}{2k+1} + \cdots$$

to calculate π.

Solution. (1) Putting $x = 1$ we obtain $\frac{\pi}{4} = 1 - \frac{1}{3} + \frac{1}{5} - \cdots + (-1)^k \frac{1}{2k+1} + \cdots$.

Using the following Mathematics command we can obtain an approximation of the sum $1 - \frac{1}{3} + \frac{1}{5} - \cdots$.

```
T[x_,n_] := Sum[(-1)^k*x^(2k + 1)/(2k + 1), {k, 0, n}];
N[4*T[1, 30000]]
```

The first sentence in the command defines a function $T(x,n) = \sum_{k=0}^{n}(-1)^k\frac{x^{2k+1}}{2k+1}$. The second sentence N[4*T[1,30000]] calculate the value of $4T(1,30000)$ to obtain an approximation of $4\arctan 1 = \pi$. Run this command in Mathematica. After a long time (1 minute) it gives the result $\pi \approx 3.14163$, which is not good. You may try larger n (i.e. $n = 50000$), and see what happens.

The defect of this calculation is that we take a too large value $x = 1$ and thus the Taylor's series $\arctan x$ converges too slowly. If we take a value of x much smaller than 1, then the term $\frac{x^{2k+1}}{2k+1}$ would decrease very fast with the increasing of k, and thus the Taylor's series converges fast.

(2) We try to decompose the angle $\arctan 1 = \frac{\pi}{4}$ into the sum $\frac{\pi}{4} = \alpha + \beta$ of two small angles $\alpha = \arctan x$ and $\beta = \arctan y$. For example, put $x = \frac{1}{2}$, then

$$y = \tan(\frac{\pi}{4} - \alpha) = \frac{\tan \frac{\pi}{4} - \tan \alpha}{1 + \tan \frac{\pi}{4} \tan \alpha} = \frac{1 - \frac{1}{2}}{1 + \frac{1}{2}} = \frac{1}{3}$$

So we obtain a formula

$$\frac{\pi}{4} = \arctan \frac{1}{2} + \arctan \frac{1}{3}$$

Now we can use the function $T(x,n)$ defined above to calculate approximations of $\arctan \frac{1}{2}$ and $\arctan \frac{1}{3}$ to obtain a good approximation of $\pi = 4(\arctan \frac{1}{2} + \arctan \frac{1}{3})$. This can be done by the command

```
T[x_,n_] := Sum[(-1)^k*x^(2k + 1)/(2k + 1), {k, 0, n}];
N[4*(T[1/2, 250] + T[1/3, 200]), 150]
```

where the sentence `N[4*(T[1/2,250]+T[1/3,200]), 150]` calculates the approximation of $4(T(\frac{1}{2}, 250) + T(\frac{1}{3}, 150))$ to 150 digits. Running the command in Mathematica. It gives the result

$$\pi \approx 3.141592653589793238462643383279502884197169399375105$$
$$8209749445923078164062862089986280348253421170679$$
$$82148086513282306647093844609550582231725359408113$$

in a very short time (0.03 second). Compare this result with the first 150 digits of π obtained by Mathematica command `N[Pi,150]`). We find that all the 150 digits we obtain are correct.

There is a better decomposition

$$\frac{\pi}{4} = 4\arctan\frac{1}{5} - \frac{1}{239},$$

known as *Maqin formula*. Using this formula we can calculate π faster.

3. Geometric Transformations

We consider the transformations on a plane Π. Construct a rectangular coordinates system on Π, represent each point $P \in \Pi$ by a unique coordinates (x, y). Given 4 real constants a_1, b_1, a_2, b_2 determine a transformation φ on Π sending each point $P \in \Pi$ with coordinates (x, y) to a point $P' = \varphi(P)$ with coordinates $(x', y') = (a_1 x + b_1 y, a_2 x + b_2 y)$. And it sends each vector $\overrightarrow{OP}$ on Π to $\overrightarrow{OP'}$ with $P' = \varphi(P)$. Such a transformation is called a linear transformation on Π. Moreover, φ sends each graph C in Π to a graph consisting of the images $\varphi(P)$ of all the points P in C.

3.1. Invariant Properties Under a Linear Transformation

Example 3.1. Draw a figure C consisting of curve segments.

Choose 4 constants a_1, b_1, a_2, b_2, say $a_1 = 1.1, b_1 = 0.3, a_2 = 0.2, b_2 = 0.9$, to determine a linear transformation $\varphi : (x, y) \mapsto (x', y')$ with $x' = a_1 x + b_1 y$, $y' = a_2 x + b_2 y$. Draw the image $\varphi(C)$ of C under φ. Compare the shapes of C and $\varphi(C)$. What do you find out?

As an example, we draw some curves to form a graph like a 'bird'. And we draw lines parallel to x-axis and y-axis respectively to form a grid

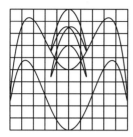 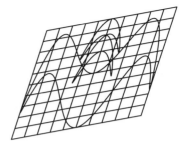

Fig. 10. Graphs before and after a linear transformation

consisting of squares as a background of the 'bird'. Observing the change of the grid will help you in imaging how the 'bird' changes.

We find out that, when C changes to $\varphi(C)$, its shape changes, the distances between points and the angles change, squares change into parallelograms ; but the images of lines are still lines, images of parallel lines are still parallel lines, and the images of parallelograms are still parallelograms.

In the above we choose constants a_1, b_1, a_2, b_2 satisfying the condition $a_1b_2 - a_2b_1 \neq 0$. Choose constants with $a_1b_2 - a_2b_1 = 0$ and observe what happens.

3.2. *Eigenvectors*

Example 3.2. Take the same linear transformation φ determined by same constants a_1, b_1, a_2, b_2 as in example 3.1. Investigate how the directions of vectors change under the action of φ.

Choose a positive integer n. Take the n points $P_k \left(\cos \frac{2k\pi}{n}, \sin \frac{2k\pi}{n}\right)$ $(0 \leq k \leq n-1)$ which divide the unit circle into n equal parts. Let $P'_i = \varphi(P_i)$ be the image of P_i under the transformation φ defined by the matrix A. Draw lines from the origin O to all the n points P_k $(0 \leq k \leq n-1)$. And draw line segments from each P_k to its image P'_k. The graph is in Fig. 11.

Observe the difference between the directions of each vector $\overrightarrow{OP_k}$ and $\overrightarrow{P_kP'_k}$, and thus find how the direction of $\overrightarrow{OP_k}$ changes to that of $\overrightarrow{OP'_k}$. We find that some $\overrightarrow{OP_k}$ turns anti-clockwise to the direction of $\overrightarrow{OP'_k}$, some turns clockwise. And there are four $\overrightarrow{OP_k}$ which do not turn their direction, these $\overrightarrow{OP_k}$ change to their images $\overrightarrow{OP'_k}$ just by lengthening or shortening in their origin direction. Namely, each of these $\overrightarrow{OP_k}$ is sent by φ to a multiple $\overrightarrow{OP'_k} = \lambda_k \overrightarrow{OP_k}$ of itself.

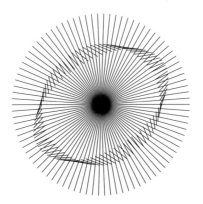

Fig. 11.   Changes of the directions of vectors under linear transformation

In general, if a nonzero vector u is sent by a linear transformation to a multiple λu of itself, then u is called an eigenvector of φ, while the scalar λ is called an eigenvalue. Those $\overrightarrow{OP_k}$ in Fig. 11 keep their direction invariant under φ satisfying the condition $\varphi(\overrightarrow{OP_k}) = \lambda_k \overrightarrow{OP_k}$ with $\lambda_k > 0$, hence they are eigenvectors with eigenvalue being positive real numbers. Notice that these 4 eigenvectors $\overrightarrow{OP_k}$ lie in two different lines through the origin $(0,0)$. And all the nonzero vectors along these two lines are eigenvectors.

Example 3.3. Take the same linear transformation φ and draw the same 'bird' as in example 3.1. But we draw a grid different from that in example 3.1. Instead of lines parallel to coordinates axes we choose lines parallel to eigenvectors to form a grid consisting of parallelograms. The graph is in Fig. 12. Observe the change of the 'bird' and the grid under the action of φ.

Each of the edges of the grid is parallel to an eigenvector, hence it does not turn the directions under the action of φ but just lengthens or shortens its along its own direction. If we construct a new coordinates system with two non-collinear eigenvectors as a basis, thus with its two coordinates axes along two edges of our grid, then φ sends a point of coordinates (x, y) to $(\lambda_1 x, \lambda_2 y)$. Namely, the action of φ just multiplies two real numbers λ_1, λ_2 on two coordinate x, y respectively. With respect to such a coordinates the action of φ becomes easier to understand.

Usually we write the linear transformation $\varphi : (x, y) \mapsto (a_1 x + b_1 y, a_2 x + b_2 y)$ in matrix form $\begin{pmatrix} x \\ y \end{pmatrix} \mapsto \begin{pmatrix} a_1 & b_1 \\ a_2 & b_2 \end{pmatrix} \begin{pmatrix} x \\ y \end{pmatrix}$, and call $\begin{pmatrix} a_1 & b_1 \\ a_2 & b_2 \end{pmatrix}$ the

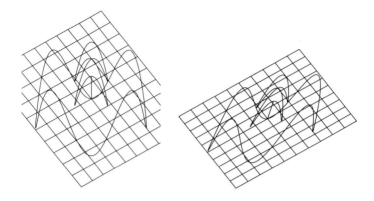

Fig. 12.   Diagonalization of a linear transformation

matrix of φ. In the new coordinates system in example 3.3, φ becomes $\begin{pmatrix} x \\ y \end{pmatrix} \mapsto \begin{pmatrix} \lambda_1 & 0 \\ 0 & \lambda_2 \end{pmatrix} \begin{pmatrix} x \\ y \end{pmatrix}$, with its matrix $\begin{pmatrix} \lambda_1 & 0 \\ 0 & \lambda_2 \end{pmatrix}$ having simplest form: all the non-diagonal entries are zero. Such a matrix is called a diagonal matrix. In general, for a linear transformation φ on a vector space V, if there exists a set of eigenvectors of φ which forms a basis of V, then the matrix of φ with respect to this basis is a diagonal matrix. Such a linear transformation is said to be diagonalizable.

3.3. *Projective Transformations*

A linear transformation $\varphi : (x,y) \mapsto (a_1 x + b_1 y, a_2 x + b_2 y)$ is determined by two linear functions $f_1(x,y) = a_1 x + b_1 y$, $f_2(x,y) = a_2 x + b_2 y$. Naturally we can consider two functions $f_1(x,y)$, $f_2(x,y)$ of other type, to determine a transformation $\varphi : (x,y) \mapsto (f_1(x,y), f_2(x,y))$.

Example 3.4. Define a transformation $\varphi : (x,y) \mapsto (x',y')$ with $x' = \frac{x}{1-x}$, $y' = \frac{y}{1-x}$.

Draw the following graphs and their images under φ.

(1) Several lines through a same point $(1,b)$ on the line $x = 1$. For example, we choose lines $y = k(x-1) + b$ with $b = 0.5$ and $k = 0.1, 0.5, -0.5, 1.5$ respectively.

(2) Several circles having the same center at the origin $(0,0)$, and having different radii $r < 1, = 1, > 1$ respectively. Say $r = 0.8, 1.0, 1.2$.

The graphs of (1) and (2) are in Figs. 13 and 14 respectively.

Observe the graphs. We see some strange and interesting phenomena:

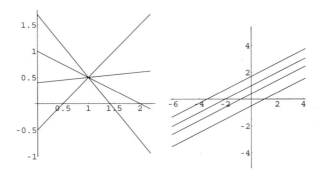

Fig. 13.

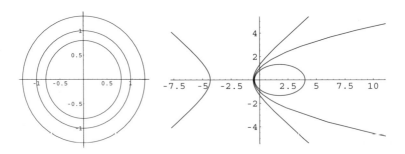

Fig. 14.

(1) Observe Fig. 13. We find out that the images of lines are still lines. But a set of lines intersecting at a same point $(1, b)$ transform to a set of parallel lines. Why this strange thing happens? If you try to calculate the image of the point $(1, b)$, you see that $(1, b)$ has no image.

The functions $f_1(x, y) = \frac{x}{1-x}$, $f_2(x, y) = \frac{y}{1-x}$ have denominator $1 - x$, which takes value 0 for $x = 1$. So the points on the line $x = 1$ have no images under φ. Strictly say, φ is not a transformation on the whole plane, but is only a mapping from the remaining part of the plane after deleting the line $x = 1$. Notice that when a point (x, y) closes to the line $x = 1$ the coordinates $(\frac{x}{1-x}, \frac{y}{1-x})$ of its image go to infinity. So we can say that the images of points on $x = 1$ are infinitely far from the origin, and called them infinite points. Appending 'infinite points' to the plane Π we obtain a set Π^* called *projective plane*, φ can be regarded as a transformation on Π^*, called a *projective transformation*.

In particular, the common point $(1, b)$ of our lines has no image under φ, so the images of these lines have no common points and thus have to be mutually parallel. In other words, when we regard that the image of $(1, b)$ is a finite point, then the images of these lines through $(1, b)$ are lines intersecting at an infinite point and thus are parallel.

Keep k invariant, but try different values of b. Observe what happens.

(2) Observe Fig. 14. We find that the images of the concentric circles are ellipse, parabola and hyperbola respectively. This sounds reasonable: A circle with radius < 1 has no common points with the line $x = 1$, its image should still be a curve surrounding a finite region. An ellipse satisfies this condition. The circle with radius 1 has exactly one common point $(1, 0)$ with the line $x = 1$. This point goes to infinitely far under φ, the circle is 'pulled apart' from this point and becoming a parabola. A circle with radius > 1 is divided by the line $x = 1$ into two separate parts. These two parts transform to the two branches of a hyperbola.

In general, given any 3×3 invertible matrix

$$\begin{pmatrix} a_1 & b_1 & c_1 \\ a_2 & b_2 & c_2 \\ a_3 & b_3 & c_3 \end{pmatrix}$$

(having determinant nonzero), we can define a transformation $\varphi : (x, y) \mapsto (x', y')$ defined by rational functions

$$x' = \frac{a_1 x + b_1 y + c_1}{a_3 x + b_3 y + c_3}, \quad y' = \frac{a_2 x + b_2 y + c_2}{a_3 x + b_3 y + c_3},$$

which is called a projective transformation. When $a_3 = b_3 = c_1 = c_2 = 0 \neq c_3$, it is a linear transformation.

A projective transformations can be understood as follows. Imagine the planar figures are drawn on a piece of glass Π. Use a point light source to irradiate on the glass plane such that the shadows of the figures project into the wall Π' (not necessarily parallel to Π). Then the transformation of the figures from Π to Π' is a projective transformation. Notice that lines on the glass plane Π intersecting at a common point can project to a set of parallel lines. A circle on glass plane Π maps to a conical section on the wall, which may be an ellipse, a parabola or a hyperbola.

Reference

1. Shangzhi Li, Falai Chen, Yaohua Wu and Yunhua Zhang, *Mathematics Experiments* (World Scientific, Singapore, 2003).

CREACOMP:
EXPERIMENTAL FORMAL MATHEMATICS FOR THE CLASSROOM*

GÜNTHER MAYRHOFER[1], SUSANNE SAMINGER[2]
and WOLFGANG WINDSTEIGER[3]

[1] *Institut für Algebra, guenther.mayrhofer@students.jku.at*
[2] *Institut für Wissensbasierte Mathematische Systeme, susanne.saminger@jku.at*
[3] *Institut für Symbolisches Rechnen, wolfgang.windsteiger@risc.uni-linz.ac.at*
JKU Linz, Altenbergerstraße 69, A-4040 Linz, Austria

CREACOMP provides an electronic environment for learning and teaching mathematics that aims at inspiring the creative potential of students. During their learning process, students are encouraged to engage themselves in various kinds of interactive experiments, both of visual and purely formal mathematical nature. The computer-algebra system *Mathematica* powers the visualization of mathematical concepts and the tools provided by the theorem proving system *Theorema* are used for the formal counterparts. We present a case study on the concept of equivalence relations and set partitions, in which we demonstrate the entire bandwidth of computer-support that we envision for modern learning environments for mathematics.

Keywords: Automated theorem proving, computer-algebra system, mathematical education.

1. Introduction

Both in classroom and in scenarios of distance learning of mathematics, the use of computer-algebra systems has become more and more popular. Until now, computer-support focuses on *(symbolic) computations*, e.g. calculating limits, derivatives, integrals, polynomial and matrix computations, and *visualization*, e.g. plotting real-valued sequences or functions or other mathematical objects in 2D or 3D: the availability of powerful algorithms allows to solve certain problems even in situations when the method would

---

*This work is done within the project "CreaComp: E-Schulung von Kreativität und Problemlösekompetenz" at the Johannes Kepler University of Linz sponsored by the Upper Austrian government.

require a tremendous computational effort when executed by hand or when no solution method is known to the students at a certain level of education. Additionally, different visual representations of the computational objects contribute to qualitative data analysis and exploration of non-obvious mathematical relationships. It is clear that modern symbolic computation systems are powerful enough to carry out all computations done in high-school mathematics and most of the computations taught at undergraduate university level. Hence, the questions of which methods should be taught to students in the first place, and for which tasks we rely on the help of the computer, are of utmost importance. There is no absolute answer to this and the "White-Box Black-Box principle", see [3], usually serves as the didactic guideline, by which, depending on the didactical goals, certain methods are taught in detail in one phase of education, the white-box phase, whereas they can be applied as black-boxes in later phases.

On the other hand, most of the available electronic learning material for mathematics only rarely focus on computer-support for acquiring such crucial mathematical skills as "exact formulation of mathematical properties" and "rigorously proving mathematical properties correct", for exceptions see e.g. [1,12]. In any case, computers can support students and teachers, but they can also introduce new obstacles compared to traditional learning/teaching, see e.g. [8].

In this paper we present the CREACOMP project, whose main goal is to develop electronic course material for self-study and also for use in classroom. In its current state, CREACOMP comprises approximately 15 (only loosely connected) learning units on an undergraduate level, such as e.g. equivalence relations, polynomial interpolation, or Markov processes. The computer-aid provided in CREACOMP units follows the didactical guidelines set up in the MEETMATH project, see Section 2, and it promotes an approach of self-paced learning that has been centered around "gaining insight into mathematical concepts through computational and graphical interaction". In addition to this, the CREACOMP approach now adds *formal reasoning* as a third important component by integrating the *Theorema* system, see [5–7]. *Theorema* is designed to become a uniform environment in which a mathematician gets support during all periods of his/her mathematical occupation. For the CREACOMP project, however, *Theorema* mainly provides the mathematical language and the possibility of fully automated or interactive generation of mathematical proofs. Both MEETMATH and *Theorema* are based on the well-known computer algebra system *Mathematica*, see [14].

There is often the distinction between *experimental mathematics* and *formal mathematics* and computer-supported teaching/learning is primarily associated with experimental mathematics whereas all proving-related mathematics is predominantly considered to be done "by hand". The discussion is then "experimental mathematics vs. formal mathematics" and the question is to what extent can formal mathematics be supplemented/accompanied/enriched/replaced by experimental mathematics and vice versa, see [2]. The CREACOMP approach should be seen much more as "experimental formal mathematics", we aim to combine the experimental approach of discovering mathematics through interactive visualizations and computations with the rigorous approach of proving every claim that is made. By using the *Theorema* system for automatically generating human-readable proofs, an experimental flavor can also be given to the formal part, i.e. students can observe with little effort how the *available knowledge influences success or non-success of a proof*, how *tacit assumptions* are often used in human arguments, or how *mathematical theories evolve* from sometimes simple definitions. Although CREACOMP is not intended as an environment for learning how to prove, the white-box nature of *Theorema* proofs may even assist the student in acquiring some proving skills.

In the sequel, we will briefly introduce the constituent components MEETMATH and *Theorema* and their combination in Section 2, the main part will be an exemplary case study presenting parts of a CREACOMP unit on equivalence relations and set partitions in Section 3. Mathematically, the learning unit on equivalence relations and set partitions starts from

- the *definition of binary relations* and elementary properties such as *reflexivity, symmetry*, and *transitivity*,
- then introduces *classes* and *factor sets*,
- proceeds with *set partitions* and *induced relations*,
- develops the theorems that *the factor set of an equivalence forms a set partition* and that *the induced relation of a set partition is an equivalence relation*, and
- finally concludes with the theorems that *building the factor set (of an equivalence relation)* and *building the induced relation (of a set partition)* are *inverse* to each other.

At all stages, interactive visualization tools are provided to illustrate the new concepts and their properties in small and easily comprehensible examples. For all theorems as well as for all auxiliary lemmata required in the proofs, we allow for automated proofs in natural language to be generated interactively by the students, i.e. we provide an interface to *Theorema*-provers that allows the student to generate fully automated proofs.

2. The CreaComp Project: An Overview

2.1. *The Components MeetMath and Theorema*

MEETMATH denotes a family of interactive mathematics course-ware based on *Mathematica* equipped with a Java^{TM}-based navigation. The basic course MEETMATH@Business&Economy and the didactic concepts for MEETMATH course-ware have been initially developed in the framework of the project IMMENSE (for *I*nteractive *M*ultimedia *M*athematics *E*ducation in *N*etworked universities for *S*ocial and *E*conomic sciences) initiated by the Johannes Kepler University Linz already in 1999. For more detailed information about the project and partners see [11].

The development of any course material including electronic supplement demands to focus not only on, possibly new, technology but on the corresponding didactic framework as well. MEETMATH course units are structured as "didactical rooms", where different rooms reflect different phases of the learning process. Basically, four different types of didactical rooms have been distinguished:

(i) "Motivation/linking": motivation/linking addresses the students' knowledge about and their attitude to deal with certain content.
(ii) "Acquisition/confrontation": the central new concepts are presented in a complete and carefully paced argumentation. Relevant information, thoughts, and illustrations should be offered in a way that students are able to build up their own ideas and concepts and/or to modify existing, incorrect concepts.
(iii) "Strengthening": these rooms allow to verify and inspect newly developed concepts and ideas. Experiments and interactive elements enable students to stabilize the concepts and allow to identify incorrectly developed concepts by trial and error. Both success and failure are possible and allowed during strengthening.
(iv) "Assessment": assessment is a necessary tool for supervising the learning process. Since students are responsible for the development of their knowledge, they need some tools for measuring the progress and/or for finding out the status quo.

Theorema is a system that intends to bring computer-support during all phases of mathematical activity, such as proving, solving, and computing. The *Theorema* system provides a uniform language and logic, in which many of the above activities can be carried out, see [4]. The overall design principle of the *Theorema* system is to communicate with the user in mathematical textbook style. The syntax of the language in *both input and output* is close to common mathematical notation, including special mathematical characters and two-dimensional syntax as typically used in mathematics. The *Theorema* language is a version of higher-order predicate logic with pre-defined basic mathematical objects such as numbers, sets, and tuples. The main focus in the development of the *Theorema* system over the past years has been put on the development of various general and special-purpose fully automated theorem provers.

Since *Theorema* is built on top of the well-known *Mathematica* system, we use the *Mathematica* notebook front-end as the user-interface for *Theorema*. When generating mathematical proofs, *Theorema* displays the full proof in a separate notebook document with each proof step explained in natural language. The structure of the proof is reflected in the cell structure of the proof notebook, so that the standard *Mathematica* technology of opening/closing nested cells by mouse-click can be used to collapse entire proof branches. This allows the reader to get an overview over the structure of the proof and then to zoom into parts of the proof by subsequently opening just the relevant cells. As an alternative to fully automated proof generation the *Theorema* system also allows for interactive proving, see e.g. [10]. For details on the *Theorema* system, the language, available provers, and applications of the *Theorema* system, we refer to the introductory papers [5–7]. Notably, an overview on CREACOMP as an application of *Theorema* in education has been given in [13].

2.2. *The Combination of MeetMath and Theorema*

The most dangerous scenario of computer-supported mathematics is that the extensive use of computation and visualization leads to a tradition of "proof by inspecting particular examples" instead of "proof by mathematical proving". In our view, examples can and should accompany the development of mathematical content, they can contribute to shaping the students' intuition about mathematics, and the content presented in examples is typically well memorized. However, examples — even if many and well-chosen — can (almost) never substitute a proof of a proposition. It is one of the main goals of this project to highlight the importance of rigorous formal mathematical arguments in all facets of mathematical work, including for instance also software development.

The combination of MEETMATH and *Theorema*, which is investigated in the frame of the CREACOMP project, therefore aims at providing computer aid for visualization, computation, but most importantly also for proving. Whereas computation and visualization ought to fertilize the *intuition* about mathematical objects, the proving phase should establish and enhance the *understanding* of mathematical argumentation, in particular that "validity in some examples" does not necessarily always mean "validity in *all cases*". An additional benefit of a theorem proving system as the student's assistant is that the students must think carefully about tacit assumptions they use in their argumentation, because the automated prover forces them to state all usable knowledge explicitly, see also e.g. [9]. Moreover, we think that by having a machine to give formal proofs of all statements and therefore being forced to fill all gaps in the proofs, the students can understand the evolution of mathematical theories much better. We consider this experience, even if maybe not necessary for a pure user of mathematics, as very enlightening for students of mathematics.

The interplay of MEETMATH and *Theorema* is facilitated by the common underlying *Mathematica* technology, since both are based on the capabilities of the *Mathematica* notebook-frontend. CREACOMP educational units are distributed in the form of *Mathematica* notebooks containing normal text intermixed with formal mathematical texts (definitions, theorems, lemmata, etc.) written in the *Theorema* language. Furthermore, we provide visualizations of the mathematical objects studied in the units. In addition to static plots we involve the students in actively exploring mathematical properties by providing *interactive visualizations* based on *Mathematica*'s GUIKit, a toolbox supporting the implementation of Java applications fed with *Mathematica* data. Finally, we encourage students to also prove their conjectures after their experiments. In this stage, they may use the *Theorema* provers both in interactive or in fully automated mode.

Although the *Mathematica* notebook-frontend is often called a graphical user interface (GUI), *Mathematica* propagates a command-centered interaction pattern. In order to trigger a *Mathematica* computation, a command has to be typed into the notebook and then needs to be evaluated by pressing certain keys. For the CREACOMP interface we make heavy use of interactive notebook elements like buttons and hyperlinks in order to prevent students from struggling with unfamiliar input syntax. Students' experiments are mainly based on common modern user interface actions such as selecting items by clicking radio-buttons or checkboxes, opening dialogs by button-click, etc.

In the spirit of MEETMATH's didactical framework, the interactive visualizations serve mainly for motivation and acquisition. After introducing a new mathematical concept, we provide tools aiming at graphical visualizations of important properties that are to be investigated in the current unit. The user can interactively "play" with the tool, the on-line help gives instructions which phenomena can and should be observed. These interactive tools are always designed in such a fashion that in addition to pre-defined examples they allow to run user-defined examples as well as randomly generated examples. A symbolic computation system is indispensable as the engine behind these tools, because an instructive visualization often needs the computation of the problem's solution in the background. Symbolic computation methods can be applied for generating pre-computed symbolic solutions depending on example parameters, such that for visualization of a random example only the example parameters need to be instantiated in the symbolic solution.

During this phase, the students get an intuition about the new concept and in the best case they observe some of the intended properties during their experiments. Still staying in an "acquisition room" (see Section 2.1) we then formulate some conjectures in the *Theorema* language, which looks very much like standard mathematical formula language. Changing into a "strengthening room", we then ask the user to prove the conjecture using *Theorema*. Again, we provide a button interface for the prover call in order not to confuse the students with syntax details thereby distracting them from their main focus, the proof. The learning goal and, thus, the user interaction in this phase consists of choosing the appropriate knowledge base and observing its influence on the generated proof. Furthermore, students can investigate possible modifications in the formulation of the conjecture and/or parts of the knowledge in order to obtain a successful proof.

CREACOMP consists of several thematic units that are intended for use in standard undergraduate courses for studies in mathematics and computer science as well as in mathematics courses for non-mathematical studies, e.g. business, marketing, social sciences, etc. Units are available for basic set theory, relations, functions, real-valued sequences and limits, continuous functions, fast computations using modular arithmetic, polynomial interpolation, Markov chains, cryptology, Gröbner bases, and other topics to be developed. We do not discuss content selection, i.e. the CREACOMP environment does not define rules, *what* should be taught and what not and, in particular, what should be presented as white-box and what should be considered black-box. Rather, the above topics have been selected by the authors to be taught as white-boxes, and CREACOMP provides a common frame *how* to present these in the particular computer environment.

In the remainder of this paper, we want to illustrate the structures described above in a case study showing parts of the CREACOMP unit on equivalence relations and set partitions.

3. The Case Study: Equivalence Relations and Set Partitions

Following the didactic principles taken from MEETMATH, the typical flow of a CREACOMP unit is to

- motivate the students by some real-world example,
- present new concepts by defining new objects or properties,
- let the students experiment with the new entities on concrete data,
- guide the students in their experiments such that possibly they are able to conjecture new properties,
- guide the students in rigorous proofs of their conjectures.

We try to illustrate the flavor of computer-support given in a CREACOMP unit in the example chapter on "equivalence relations and set partitions".

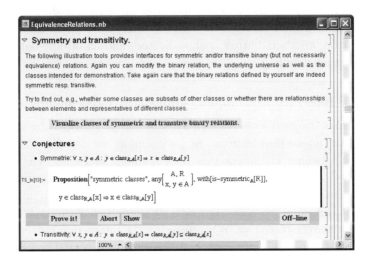

Fig. 1.   A typical CREACOMP educational unit.

Figure 1 shows a screen-shot of a part of the notebook on equivalence relations containing the most important interactive interface elements. We see structured text containing inline mathematical formulae hierarchically grouped in nested cells intermixed with formal parts (e.g. definitions, theorems, etc.) written in the *Theorema* language. *Theorema* blocks are written in *Mathematica* input cells and they differ in layout from the surrounding text blocks so that they can easily be recognized as active content. These cells must be evaluated in order for their content to be accessible in the *Mathematica*-kernel later. *Theorema* input can use most of the common mathematical notation[a], notably all sorts of quantifiers written in appealing two-dimensional form and, thus, *Theorema* input hardly differs from inlined mathematical formulae in the text.

Although *Mathematica* and *Theorema* provide palettes and keyboard shortcuts for inputting two-dimensional expressions, *Theorema* input is always prepared in advance and the users are usually not required to type *Theorema* formulae. Only occasionally, we leave parts of a formula blank and indicate with a "□"-placeholder that formula parts need to be inserted for the placeholder. CREACOMP *interaction buttons* indicate the availability of an interactive experiment and they appear as gray boxes, the text above and on the button roughly explains the associated experiment. The unit shown in Fig. 1 contains an interaction button for visualizing classes of symmetric and transitive relations, which will be described in more detail in Section 3.1. Mathematical conjectures are formulated in *Theorema* language immediately followed by a CREACOMP *prove panel* containing a prove-button, an abort-button, a show-button, and an off-line-button, see Section 3.2 for details.

3.1. *The Interface to Computer-Supported Experiments*

The interface to interactive experiments is always provided by so-called CREACOMP interaction buttons. As an example, we describe the visualization tool behind the interaction button shown in Fig. 1. The notions "symmetry" and "transitivity" of a binary relation R on a universe A and the notion of a "class of an element x w.r.t. R and A" have been introduced earlier. At this point we want to investigate properties of classes when R is symmetric and/or transitive. When pressing the interaction button, a new window as shown in Fig. 2 appears on the screen. The window essentially

---

[a]Some notation is supported already by standard *Mathematica*, like subscripts, fractions, summation/integration, and a bunch of special characters. Input syntax is configurable and *Theorema* uses this feature to support most of the common mathematical language. *Theorema* uses the braces $\{,\}$ for sets and anglebrackets $\langle,\rangle$ for tuples, which contrasts *Mathematica*, which uses braces for lists, i.e. tuples, and which does not have sets as distinguished objects.

contains 4 components:

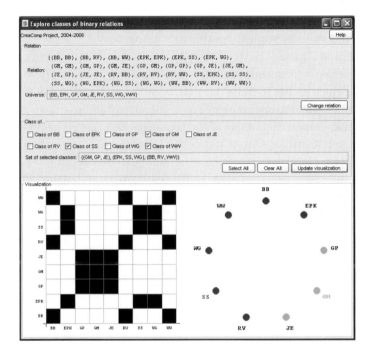

Fig. 2.   Interactive visualization of classes.

(i) The top box displays the relation R as a set of pairs in *Theorema* no-
    tation and the universe set A. The relation R can be changed by either
    explicitly giving a new set of pairs or by having a random symmetric
    and/or transitive relation automatically generated by the system.

(ii) The middle box allows to select the classes to be visualized and it
    displays the respective classes as a set of sets in *Theorema* notation.

(iii) The bottom box shows graphical visualizations of the relation and the
    selected classes. The raster on the left corresponds to R's adjacency
    matrix and the arrangement of disks on the right indicates A's ele-
    ments and each of the selected elements' class by color: each element
    is assigned a unique color shown by the color of its label and all ele-
    ments in its class have their disk in the same color. Since intersecting
    classes are a key-feature to be discovered by this experiment, we dis-
    play elements belonging to more than one class by a grey disk. The
    absence of grey disks in the visualization in Fig. 2 indicates disjoint

classes in this example.

(iv) The help button in the top-right corner displays individual help for this experiment by explaining which interactions can be made and which phenomena the student is expected to investigate.

Interactive visualizations are implemented using *Mathematica*'s GUIKit, which allows to build Java GUIs containing *Mathematica* data. In the example, the bottom graphics are re-calculated and re-drawn whenever there is user-interaction in one of the top boxes and this is the prototypical interaction pattern for CREACOMP experiments: mathematical objects are visualized by *Mathematica* graphics that adapt to user-input given through intuitive interface elements such as check-boxes, radio-buttons, roll-down menus, etc., and special dialog windows that allow *Theorema* input that will be correctly parsed and processed before the respective graphics are re-generated. The on-line help explains the possible interactions and, as a side-effect, it is meant to lead the students' experiments into a "reasonable direction" so that they might conjecture "relevant knowledge". Students have the freedom in exploiting the interactive tools in arbitrary manner, but it is important to provide them some guidelines in what to try and what to observe, otherwise there is the danger that they get lost if they deviate from the intended track through the unit.

For all interactive tools, their design is learner centered, i.e. the developer of a unit needs to decide which visualizations are instructive at which place in a unit. For each case it needs to be decided whether available visualizations in *Mathematica* (including the numerous extension packages) can be re-used or whether specialized graphics need to be programmed. Finally, the interaction patterns need to be developed and implemented in the Java interface in such a fashion that the desired learning process is supported best. We observe that the *Mathematica* programming part is almost neglectable (regardless of availability of visualizations in packages) compared to the interface design and programming, having in mind unexperienced users that should intuitively follow intended paths as inspired by the interface layout and its behavior, respectively.

3.2. *The Interface to Automated Proving*

We discuss the CREACOMP interface to *Theorema* provers using the example shown in Fig. 1. In plain *Theorema*, the command to generate the proof would be

Prove[Proposition["symmetric classes"], by → SetTheoryPCSProver,
using → {Definition["symmetry"], Definition["class"]}, ProverOptions →
{GRWTarget → {"goal","kb"}, UseCyclicRules → True},SearchDepth→50]
In practice we have often realized, that the call of the appropriate prover
with the appropriate options turns out to be a real hurdle, not only for
students. The problem is not syntax but a successful call requires detailed
knowledge about available provers, their exact names, their options, and
the influence of these options on the generation of the proof. Since the
primary goal of the course is to learn about equivalence relations rather than
learning how to use *Theorema* (or *Mathematica*), we decided to hide the
concrete prover calls and instead provide a uniform interface to *Theorema*'s
automated provers by a so-called CREACOMP prove panel, see Fig. 1.

The prove panel is a highlighted part in the notebook directly following
a proposition to be proven, and it consists of buttons controlling a *Theorema* prover. The prove-button on the left has a call to a *Theorema* prove
method with appropriate parameters and options as shown above associated
to its "button-pressed"-event. Every *Theorema* prover needs the knowledge
base to be used in the proof as a parameter, thus, before actually starting
the proof the user can compose the knowledge base in an interactive dialog[b]. Figure 3 shows such a dialog window: it displays the formula to be
proven and it lists all definitions, propositions, theorems, etc. available at
this stage. The user simply selects by mouse-click and sends the knowledge
base to the prover by pressing the "Prove"-button in the dialog's bottom-
right corner. Pressing the "Hint"-button in the bottom-left corner selects
just the appropriate portion of knowledge for a successful proof. The appropriate knowledge for a certain proof cannot be detected automatically,
the developer of the unit needs to code this information within the prove
panel so that the knowledge base composition tool can access it from there.

The abort-button in the prove panel aborts a running proof, the show-
button shows the proof attempt, typically after having aborted the prover.
The off-line-button on the right-margin of the prove panel allows to view
a pre-generated successful proof. Both pre-generated and live-generated
proofs appear in a separate window as shown in Fig. 4. The proof comes in
human-readable format and explains each proof step in natural language.

---

[b]This feature will not be used in every proof. Sometimes the appropriate knowledge base
will be hardcoded in the prove-button.

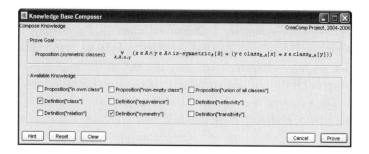

Fig. 3.   Interactive knowledge base composition.

3.3. *The Entire Unit*

After having explained the interaction possibilities that are spread all over the material whenever appropriate we can now browse through the unit "Equivalence Relations and Set Partitions", which introduces the students

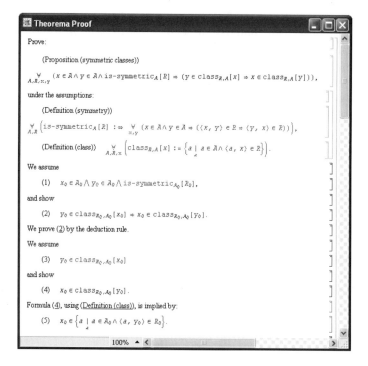

Fig. 4.   *Theorema* proof.

to the correspondence between equivalence relations and set partitions. First of all we introduce the mathematical objects to work with in this theory. The definitions are given in *Theorema* language and start with the definition of relations as a subset of some cartesian product. Since we want to study classes and factor sets of equivalence relations, we restrict our theory to binary relations on some universe set. For other kinds of relations there are links to other CREACOMP units, which focus on e.g. general relations or order relations. Furthermore, the first section of this unit defines the main properties interesting for equivalence relations, namely reflexivity, symmetry, and transitivity.

In order to develop some intuition on these properties of relations, we provide a visualization tool to illustrate these properties. The students can experiment with different relations, some are pre-defined, some are randomly generated or user-defined. This tool is similar to the one shown in Fig. 2 only that there is no mentioning of the concept of classes yet.

The next step is to introduce the concept of classes for binary relations. Traditionally, (equivalence) classes are defined for equivalence relations only. This is due to the nice properties of classes that can be proven in this setting. However, in the spirit of theory exploration, see e.g. [5], we find it interesting and natural to define *classes for arbitrary relations* and then study the dependence of properties of classes from properties of the underlying relation. In the *Theorema* language the definition of a class looks similar to common mathematical language, so the students can read and understand this definition easily without learning additional syntax:

Definition["class", any$[x, A, R]$,

$\quad$ class$_{R,A}[x] := \{a \in A | \langle a, x \rangle \in R\}$]

Even for relations with only few properties, e.g. only reflexive, they can prove certain (weak) properties of classes; the stronger the properties of the relation the nicer the properties of the classes, until finally, towards the end of the unit, we find the classical results for equivalence classes. We think this evolution of the theory is an interesting aspect for students to experience.

Of course, conjectures proposed by the students or suggested in our material need not really be true. Some are false in general, but they may be valid in special cases. For example, after inspecting relations in the visualization tool some students might conjecture the following:

Proposition["in own class", any$[A, R]$,

$\quad \underset{x \in A}{\forall} \; x \in$ class$_{R,A}[x]$]

After trying the proof they would realize that the prover fails to prove this proposition. In general, failure of a *Theorema* proof can have various reasons: the provided knowledge is insufficient or the proposition as stated is not provable, maybe not even true. This is just what we want to emphasize in teaching mathematics, and conventional learning material does not provide room for this experience. Finally, failure can also be due to an inappropriate proving method or inappropriate parameters for the method, but we eliminate these sources by packing the call to the prover into the prove-button.

Theorema's possibility to inspect failing proof attempts comes very handy at this point, so students can investigate, which part of the proof led to failure. In the example above, they detect that the prover closes all branches successfully, only $\langle x_0, x_0 \rangle \in R_0$ needs to be proven for arbitrary x_0 and R_0. Thorough inspection of the available knowledge at that stage shows that only $x_0 \in A_0$ is known and the student might learn that the proposition as stated *cannot be proven* unless more is known about R_0. In general, there are various possibilities how to modify the setup for the next proof attempt: the proof goal can be modified, assumptions can be changed, new assumptions can be added, or even a different proving method could be applied. We assist the student by writing a skeleton of a new formula into the notebook at this point, thereby fixing which kind of modification is sensible. In the above example, a side-condition to the proof goal is the way to go. In *Theorema* this can be done using the with[...] expression and we provide

Proposition["in own class", any[A, R], with[□],

$$\underset{x \in A}{\forall} \ x \in \text{class}_{R,A}[x] \ ]$$

where the student is asked to substitute some condition for the "□"-placeholder. Of course, in order to succeed with the above proof, R_0 must have the property that $\langle x, x \rangle \in R_0$ is true for all $x \in A_0$, i.e. R_0 must be reflexive on A_0. Hence, they must put the side-condition "is-reflexive$_A[R]$" and can then successfully prove the adapted proposition. This proof is not particularly difficult, still the formal rigor in which it is carried out is instructive for students.

The remaining content of this unit explains some properties of sets of sets. In particular, the students can learn about the factor set of a relation and set partitions and they can investigate properties that turn a set of sets into a partition. Moreover, the concept of an *induced relation* is introduced, namely

Definition["induced relation", any[A, S],

induced-relation$_A[S] := \{\langle x, y \rangle \underset{x,y \in A}{\mid} \underset{M \in S}{\exists} x \in M \wedge y \in M\}$]

In each step the procedure is similar:

- *introduce* new objects or properties,
- *visualize* the properties in order to gain insights,
- *guess and propose* conjectures,
- *formalize* the conjectures precisely, and
- *prove* them automatically with *Theorema*.

The key observations are then:

- if R is an equivalence relation on A then factor-set$_A[R]$ is a partition of A and induced-relation$_A$[factor-set$_A[R]$] = R.
- if P is a partition of A then induced-relation$_A[P]$ is an equivalence relation and factor-set$_A$[induced-relation$_A[P]$] = P.

All these theorems including also all auxiliary lemmata necessary for compact proofs of the main statements are proved fully automatically within this learning unit. In order to demonstrate the readability of *Theorema* proofs, we show one proof in all details *as it is generated in the* Theorema *system*, compare its appearance also to Fig. 4.

Lemma["induced relation is transitive", any[A, P], with[is-partition$_A[P]$],

is-transitive$_A$[induced-relation$_A[P]$]]

In the knowledge base for this proof, we have the definitions of transitivity and induced relation and an auxiliary proposition proved earlier, namely

Proposition["intersecting classes are equal", any[A, P], with[is-partition$_A[P]$],

$\underset{X,Y \in P}{\forall} X \cap Y \neq \emptyset \Rightarrow X = Y$]

Proof. We assume

(1)   is-partition$_{A_0}[P_0]$

and show

(2)   is-transitive$_{A_0}$[induced-relation$_{A_0}[P_0]$].

Formula (2), using (Definition (transitivity)), is implied by:

(3) $\underset{x,y,z \in A_0}{\forall} \langle x, y \rangle \in$ induced-relation$_{A_0}[P_0] \wedge \langle y, z \rangle \in$ induced-relation$_{A_0}[P_0]$

$\Rightarrow \langle x, z \rangle \in$ induced-relation$_{A_0}[P_0]$.

We assume

(4) $x_0 \in A_0 \land y_0 \in A_0 \land z_0 \in A_0 \land$
$\langle x_0, y_0 \rangle \in \text{induced-relation}_{A_0}[P_0] \land \langle y_0, z_0 \rangle \in \text{induced-relation}_{A_0}[P_0]$

and show

(5) $\langle x_0, z_0 \rangle \in \text{induced-relation}_{A_0}[P_0]$.

Formula (5), using (Definition (induced relation)), is implied by:

(8) $\langle x_0, z_0 \rangle \in \{ \langle x, y \rangle \underset{x,y \in A_0}{|} \underset{M \in P_0}{\exists} x \in M \land y \in M \}$.

In order to prove (8) we have to show

(9) $\underset{x,y \in A_0}{\exists} (\underset{M}{\exists} M \in P_0 \land x \in M \land y \in M) \land \langle x_0, z_0 \rangle = \langle x, y \rangle$.

Since $x := x_0$ and $y := z_0$ solves the equational part of (9) it suffices to show

(10) $x_0 \in A_0 \land z_0 \in A_0 \land \underset{M}{\exists} M \in P_0 \land x_0 \in M \land z_0 \in M$.

Formula (10.1) is true because it is identical to (4.1)
Formula (10.2) is true because it is identical to (4.3)
Formula (4.4), by (Definition (induced relation)), implies:

(12) $\langle x_0, y_0 \rangle \in \{ \langle x, y \rangle \underset{x,y \in A_0}{|} \underset{M \in P_0}{\exists} x \in M \land y \in M \}$.

From (12) we know by definition of $\{ T_x \underset{x}{|} P \}$ that we can choose an appropriate value such that

(13) $\underset{M}{\exists} M \in P_0 \land x1_0 \in M \land x2_0 \in M$,

(14) $\langle x_0, y_0 \rangle = \langle x1_0, x2_0 \rangle$.

Formula (14) simplifies to

(16) $x_0 = x1_0 \land y_0 = x2_0$.

By (13) we can take appropriate values such that:

(17) $M_0 \in P_0 \land x1_0 \in M_0 \land x2_0 \in M_0$.

Now, let $M := M_0$. Thus, for proving (10.3) it is sufficient to prove:

(21) $M_0 \in P_0 \land x_0 \in M_0 \land z_0 \in M_0$.

Formula (21.1) is true because it is identical to (17.1).

Formula (21.2), using (16.1), is implied by:

(22) $x1_0 \in M_0$.

Formula (22) is true because it is identical to (17.2).
Proof of (21.3) $z_0 \in M_0$: Formula (4.5), by (16.2), implies:

   $\langle x2_0, z_0 \rangle \in$ induced-relation$_{A_0}[P_0]$

which, by (Definition (induced relation)), implies:

(23) $\langle x2_0, z_0 \rangle \in \{\langle x, y \rangle \underset{x,y \in A_0}{|} \underset{M \in P_0}{\exists} x \in M \wedge y \in M\}$.

From (23) we know by definition of $\{T_x \mid P\}$ that we can choose an appropriate value such that

(24) $\underset{M}{\exists} M \in P_0 \wedge x3_0 \in M \wedge x4_0 \in M$,

(25) $\langle x2_0, z_0 \rangle = \langle x3_0, x4_0 \rangle$.

Formula (25) simplifies to

(27) $x2_0 = x3_0 \wedge z_0 = x4_0$.

By (24) we can take appropriate values such that:

(28) $M_1 \in P_0 \wedge x3_0 \in M_1 \wedge x4_0 \in M_1$.

Formula (21.3), using (27.2), is implied by:

(32) $x4_0 \in M_0$.

Formula (17.3), by (27.1), implies:

(33) $x3_0 \in M_0$.

From (28.2) together with (33) we know

(35) $x3_0 \in M_1 \cap M_0$.

From (35) we can infer

(36) $M_1 \cap M_0 \neq \emptyset$.

Formula (36), by (Proposition (intersecting classes are equal)), implies:

(37) $\underset{A,P}{\forall}$ is-partition$_A[P] \wedge M_0 \in P \wedge M_1 \in P \Rightarrow M_1 = M_0$.

Formula (1), by (37), implies:

(71) $\quad M_0 \in P_0 \Rightarrow (M_1 \in P_0 \Rightarrow M_1 = M_0)$.

From (17.1) and (71) we obtain by modus ponens

(72) $\quad M_1 \in P_0 \Rightarrow M_1 = M_0$.

From (28.1) and (72) we obtain by modus ponens

(73) $\quad M_1 = M_0$.

Formula (32) is true because of (28.3) and (73). $\qquad\qquad\qquad\qquad$ □

The proof as shown above will appear in a separate window and features interactive elements that cannot be rendered in the above "static reproduction": All formula references are active button elements, which will display the referenced formula in a separate window, proof goals and assumptions can easily be distinguished by color, see also Fig. 4, and the structure of the proof tree is reflected by the nested cell structure of the proof notebook, so that entire proof branches can be collapsed by a single mouse-click. In the configuration used for the above proof, *Theorema* does not display every single proof step it applies. In this example, for instance, it tacitly splits conjunctions in the goal and the knowledge base into its parts. This explains formula labels referring to formulae not actually present in the proof, e.g. formula (4.1) refers to the first conjunct in formula (4).

4. Conclusion and Future Work

CREACOMP is work in progress. Therefore we do not have results on evaluation of the units in classroom yet. Further work will go into computer-supported assessment, which has already been implemented in the frame of MEETMATH, see [11]. Assessment is heavily based on randomly generated test exercises based on example patterns, where the power of a symbolic computation system in the background is essential for both generating the exercises as well as checking correctness of user solutions. Although proving forms an essential part of our approach to teaching, we plan to assess neither the students' performance in proving nor their use of an automated theorem proving system. Rather, we test facts about mathematical concepts and we hope that proving enhances students' understanding of the mathematics involved. As a different branch, the use of *Theorema* provers for checking user answers can be investigated.

References

1. R. B. Andrews, C. E. Brown, F. Pfenning, M. Bishop, S. Issar, and H. Xi. ETPS: A System to Help Students Write Formal Proofs. *Journal of Automated Reasoning*, 32:75–92, 2004.
2. J. M. Borwein. The Experimental Mathematician: The Pleasure of Discovery and the Role of Proof. *International Journal of Computers for Mathematical Learning*, 10(2):75–108, May 2005.
3. B. Buchberger. Should Students Learn Integration Rules? *ACM SIGSAM Bulletin*, 24(1):10–17, January 1990.
4. B. Buchberger. Symbolic Computation: Computer Algebra and Logic. In F. Bader and K.U. Schulz, editors, *Frontiers of Combining Systems, Proceedings of FROCOS 1996 (1st International Workshop on Frontiers of Combining Systems, Munich, March 26–28, 1996)*, volume 3 of *Applied Logic Series*, pages 193–220. Kluwer Academic Publisher, Dordrecht - Boston - London, The Netherlands, 1996.
5. B. Buchberger, A. Craciun, T. Jebelean, L. Kovacs, T. Kutsia, K. Nakagawa, F. Piroi, N. Popov, J. Robu, M. Rosenkranz, and W. Windsteiger. Theorema: Towards Computer-Aided Mathematical Theory Exploration. *Journal of Applied Logic*, 4(4):470–504, 2006. ISSN 1570-8683.
6. B. Buchberger, C. Dupre, T. Jebelean, F. Kriftner, K. Nakagawa, D. Vasaru, and W. Windsteiger. The Theorema Project: A Progress Report. In M. Kerber and M. Kohlhase, editors, *Symbolic Computation and Automated Reasoning (Proceedings of CALCULEMUS 2000, Symposium on the Integration of Symbolic Computation and Mechanized Reasoning, St. Andrews, Scotland, August 6–7, 2000)*, pages 98–113. Copyright: A. K. Peters, Natick, Massachusetts.
7. B. Buchberger, T. Jebelean, F. Kriftner, M. Marin, E. Tomuta, and D. Vasaru. A Survey of the Theorema Project. In W. Kuechlin, editor, *Proceedings of ISSAC'97 (International Symposium on Symbolic and Algebraic Computation, Maui, Hawaii, July 21–23, 1997)*, pages 384–391, ACM Press, 1997. ISBN 0-89791-875-4.
8. P. Drijvers. Learning Mathematics in a Computer Algebra Environment: Obstacles are Opportunities. *Zentralblatt für Didaktik der Mathematik*, 34(5):221–228, 2002.
9. G. Hanna. Proof, Explanation and Exploration: An Overview. *Educational Studies in Mathematics*, 44:5–23, 2000.
10. F. Piroi and T. Kutsia. The Theorema Environment for Interactive Proof Development. In G. Sutcliffe and A. Voronkov, editors, *Logic for Programming, Artificial Intelligence, and Reasoning. Proceedings of the 12th International Conference, LPAR'05*, volume 3835 of *Lecture Notes in Artificial Intelligence*, pages 261–275. Springer Verlag, 2005.
11. S. Saminger. MeetMATH — Visualizations and Animations in a Didactic Framework. In M. Borovcnik and H. Kautschitsch, editors, *Technology in Mathematics Teaching (Special groups and working groups). Proceedings of ICTMT 5, Klagenfurt (Austria)*, volume 26 of *Schriftenreihe Didaktik der Mathematik*, pages 217–222, Wien, 2002. öbv & hpt Verlagsgesellschaft.

12. R. Sommer and G. Nuckols. A Proof Environment for Teaching Mathematics. *Journal of Automated Reasoning*, 32:227–258, 2004.
13. R. Vajda. E-training of Formal Mathematics: Report on the CreaComp Project at the University of Linz, June 26, 2006. Contributed talk at ACA 2006.
14. S. Wolfram. *The Mathematica Book*, 5th edition. Wolfram Media, Inc., 2003.

FREE SOFTWARE SSP FOR TEACHING MATHEMATICS*

JING-ZHONG ZHANG

Engineering Center for Educational Information Technology
Huazhong Normal University, Wuhan, 430079, China
Chengdu Institute for Computer Applications, Chinese Academy of Sciences
Chengdu, 610041, China
Institute for Educational Software, Guangzhou University
Guangzhou, 510006, China
E-mail: zjz101@yahoo.com.cn

HUI-MIN XIONG

Department of Mathematics & Statistics, Huazhong Normal University
Wuhan, 430079, China
E-mail: xiong_hm@tom.com

XI-CHENG PENG

Engineering Center for Educational Information Technology
Huazhong Normal University, Wuhan, 430079, China
E-mail: pxc417@126.com

SSP (Super Sketchpad) is educational software in Chinese. Teachers and students can do almost everything for teaching and learning mathematics by using SSP. Even the free version of SSP still has a lot of surprising functions. This paper provides an introduction to the design, implementation, and capabilities of the free version of SSP.

Keywords: SSP, dynamic geometry, mathematical teaching, symbolic computation.

1. Introduction: What Is SSP?

SSP (Super Sketchpad) is dynamic geometry software developed for mathematical teaching, which integrates multiple features. There is only a Chinese version till now.

---

*This work is supported in part by NKBRSF-G2004CB318003 from National Key Basic Research Program of China (973 Program).

Using the dynamic geometry software, we could plot a dynamic geometry graph on computer screen. By 'dynamic' we mean a graph for which geometric attribute imposed initially remains consistent after some point or line is dragged, such as middle point is still middle point, perpendicular lines are still perpendicular lines, etc. By the dynamic evolution of geometry graph, the geometric law that could not be observed on paper could be shown, and thus students have chance to understand fundamentals of geometry more directly and deeply. In the mean time, according to geometry knowledge mastered previously, students could plot unlimitedly changeable graph using various drawing method provided by dynamic geometry software, which makes themselves feel really the beauty of geometry and thus promotes their interest in study and improves teaching effect.

The mechanism of dynamic geometry has been described in detail in [1]. The first dynamic geometry software GSP[2] (The Geometer's Sketchpad) appeared in 1987. Up till now, there are dozens of dynamic geometry software all over the world, among which GSP, Cabri-Geometry[3] and Cinderella[4] are the most well-known ones.

The international education community has reached a consensus about the positive impact of dynamic geometry on education. But school mathematics includes not only geometry, but arithmetic, algebra and analysis as well. And geometry is not only about plotting and reading graphs, but also reasoning and calculus. In order to satisfy the demand of mathematical education, it is suggested that dynamic geometry software should integrate more features and be used much easier and faster.

For example, in [5] and [6], the issue about how to combine geometry drawing and reasoning was raised. The software GeoGebra, which addresses combination of algebra, calculus and dynamic geometry, has been introduced in [7]. It was mentioned in [8] that mathematical software should be much easier to use and more intelligent in the future. The dynamic geometry software SSP, which has been designed mainly for use in school mathematics, takes all the above-mentioned demands into account. Apart from the functions of dynamic geometry, the SSP can also do the following things.

(1) Automated proving for geometry theorems based on users' drawing and question.

(2) Elementary symbolic computation: calculation about large integers and fractions; addition among polynomials or fraction expressions; multiplication and power; factorization of polynomial in several ele-

ments with integral coefficients; derivation and computation about the most elementary indefinite integral.

(3) Dynamic measurement for geometric quantity and expression; Measurement for coordinate of point as well as equation of line or conic curve; Dynamic numerical calculation.

(4) Construction of dynamic curve or table of values for functional, parametric and polar coordinates equation(s), whose expression might contain some new parameters and is input directly by keyboard or copy-paste way.

(5) Drawing, symbolic computation and numerical calculation by programming.

(6) Simulation for chance phenomenon by random function and compilation of statistical chart or table.

(7) Dynamic modification for parameter or formula that is related to computation and drawing.

(8) Transformation from dynamic pages to interactive web pages.

(9) Protection for the intellectual property rights of user by fixing an lock on their works.

(10) Production of courseware analogous to ppt file for demonstration in a lecture.

There is a free version of SSP, which has all functions except for (1), (8) and (9) (Fig. 1). But some operations in it could be performed only by text instructions and not by menu as in a registered version.

SSP has not only satisfied almost all the demands of mathematical teaching and studying for computer system, but its operation method is also easy and simple for its design oriented to humanization, intelligence, visualization, dynamism and stylization.

In the remainder of this paper we mainly discuss the elementary features of the free version of SSP, its special in operation and application in teaching. We first introduce and illustrate the dynamic drawing (Section 2), the symbol computation and dynamic measurement (Section 3) and the programming environment (Section 4). Then we present more examples (Section 5). Finally, we outline future directions for research in this area (Section 6).

The free version of SSP can be downloaded from the following website: http://www.zplusz.org, www.qiusir.com and www.maths-edu.net.

It has been described in detail in [9] about how to use the free version of

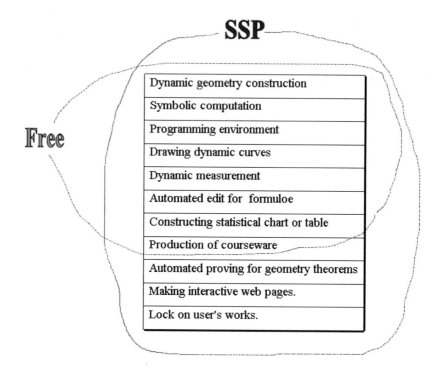

Fig. 1.

SSP to assist mathematical teaching and studying. The DVD in this book includes the free version of SSP and 200 examples written by one of the authors.

2. What Is the Special of SSP in Dynamic Drawing?

Similar to SSP, some good dynamic geometry software attributes drawing of graph to that of geometric elements such as point, line (line segment, half line and straight line included), circle, and so on, which follows the mathematical tradition of axiomatization. But they all use different tools for drawing point, line, and circle. It is ridiculous just thinking whether we change frequently our drawer or not in order to draw them in common situation. Why to use three pens if one pen is enough? On the contrary, SSP[a] only uses an intelligent drawer to do these. After entering intelligent

---

[a]In the rest of this paper, 'SSP' indicates the free version of SSP if no special explanation is attached.

drawing state by clicking the icon 'drawer', the mouse becomes an intelligent drawer as a chalk by which we can without any shift between menus and tools draw almost all elementary geometric graph, such as free point, line segment (or straight line, half line), circle, point on straight line or conic section, point of intersection between straight lines or between straight line and conic section, and so on.

For example, when you want to get the mid-point of a line segment, it is enough to move the cursor to approach the mid-point until the word 'mid-point' appears nearby and then click the mouse. If you want to draw a straight line (or line segment, half line) parallel with the other known one, what is needed to do is clicking the left button without releasing, dragging the mouse to draw line in the course of which the orientation of line should be adjusted to be close to parallel with the known one, and then loosening the left button when the known line has changed color and the word 'parallel' appears nearby. If you also want to draw the tangent line of a circle, what is needed to do is clicking the left button without releasing, dragging the mouse to draw line in the course of which the orientation of line should be adjusted to be close to tangent with the known circle, and then loosening the left button when the known circle has changed color and the word 'tangent' appears nearby. It is worth mentioning that the tangent point could not be obtained at the same time when drawing the tangent line, but if needed, it could be drawn as stated above. Of course the foregoing are all dynamic geometry graphs.

Example 1 A dynamic geometry graph for producing ellipse locus

(1) Select intelligent drawer, double-click the left button to origin O, hold down, move the mouse to some point A on axis x, and release the left button. Thus, a circle is constructed with point O as its center and with point A on its circumference.

(2) Create point B and C as being a point on segments OA and on the circumference respectively, and then draw line segments BC and OC.

(3) Move the mouse to near the midpoint of BC, click the left button when the word 'midpoint' appears, hold down, drag the mouse along OC, and release the left button the moment that the words 'perpendicular and intersecting' appears. Thus midpoint D and perpendicular bisector DE of BC are constructed.

(4) Click the right button to point E, and select 'trace' in the emerging menu.

(5) Click the right button to point C, and select 'animation' in the emerging menu and 'once' as moving type in the following dialog box.

(6) Click the animation button, and thus ellipse would be produced (Fig. 2).

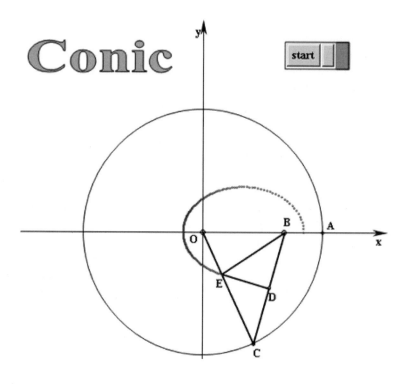

Fig. 2.

All dynamic geometry software can produce ellipse as above. The difference between SSP and other software lies on intelligence of its drawer. With the help of system's hint, graph could been drawn directly by clicking and dragging mouse, which needs no shift between menus or tools as well as no shortcut key.

SSP also supplies abundant text instruction to plot some graphs not obtained directly by intelligent drawer, as shown in the following example.

Example 2 A theorem about 5 circles

As shown in Fig. 3, plot a cross pentagon $ABCDE$ and all 5 intersection points F, G, H, I and J between its sides. The following steps are taken to

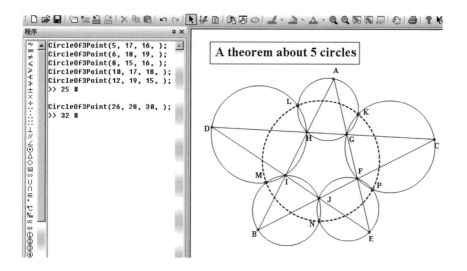

Fig. 3.

draw 5 circumcircles of triangles, where text instruction is used to substitute for intelligent drawer ahead.

(1) Input text instruction

```
Circleof3point(5,17,16);
```

in programming area, where 5, 17 and 16 are ordinal numbers of object A, H and G respectively in which they are introduced. These numbers could be retrieved in object area or be captured under drawing window after clicking these points.

(2) Input similar 4 instructions by copy-paste way in the programming area, and then modify their parameters.

(3) Move the cursor to the last instruction, and then press Ctrl+Enter.

The resultant circles produce 5 intersection points K, L, M, N and P again, which locate on the same circle as an interesting theorem says.

There is no need to bear these text instructions in mind, as well as to input them word for word by keyboard. SSP provides dialog box for them, which is open after clicking the item 'draw by text' being under the menu 'drawing'. After selecting the instruction being needed from instruction list in dialog box and double-clicking it, it would be copied to edit column. It is all right if filling parameters and clicking the button 'Run' (Fig. 4).

122

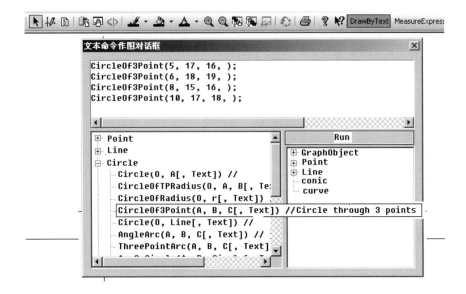

Fig. 4.

Besides these previous ways, the complete version of SSP provides drawing by menu or icon. In addition, the complete version also supports automated reasoning, by which the theorem's readable proof written in traditional style could been obtained after several seconds.

It is also convenient for SSP to plot functional or parametric curve, which could be constructed simply by inputting expression with parameter. The variable ruler of the parameter also could be constructed for suiting us to adjust its value continuously. If dragging the slide of variable ruler, we could observe corresponding change of curve.

Example 3 Dynamic graph of the function $y = a\sin(bx + c)$

We could plot the graph of the function $y = a\sin(bx + c)$ for the values $x \in [-10, 10]$ by running the following instruction in the programming area or by dialog box

```
Function(y=a*sin(b*x+c), -10,10,n,);
```

where n denotes the number of sample points for drawing.

All above-mentioned parameters could be exchanged with number or character. For the latter, SSP would plot the graph according to some appropriate defaulted values before they are assigned by user.

To make the adjustment convenient for the value of parameter a, a variable ruler could be constructed by the following instruction

```
Variable(a,);
```

Similarly, the variable ruler of b, c and n could be obtained. The result after running is shown in Fig. 5.

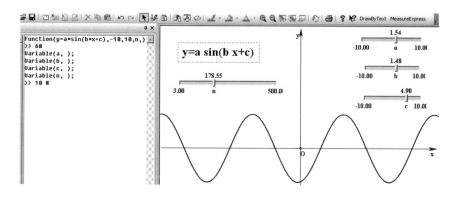

Fig. 5.

As far as we know, other dynamic geometry software or drawing software oriented to functional curve could not plot curve by directly inputting analytic expression with parameter, as SSP can do. Some software such as GSP even does not support copying the expression written before in the dialog box.

With regard to functional curve, there is more which SSP could accomplish, such as taking dynamic point, drawing tangent line, making a table of values for sample points, making integral cut and measuring corresponding integral sum, modifying analytic expression, performing geometric transformation, tracing image variation, and so on.

3. Symbolic Computation and Dynamic Measurement for Expression

SSP supports symbolic computation and with which writing of formula is linked. The feature could assist students in constructing some basic concepts about algebraic operation such as power, as well as in carrying on mathematical calculus and checking up on computation result. Thus, Teachers also can feel more convenient and relaxed in lecture.

124

Symbolic computation is performed in programming area. All instructions must be input in English state and end with ';'. If there is '//' in some instruction line, the words follow it is only note and not as instruction. The result of computation begins with '>>', which appears in screen after running by pressing 'CtrL+Enter'.

Example 4 Construction for the concept of power using symbolic computation

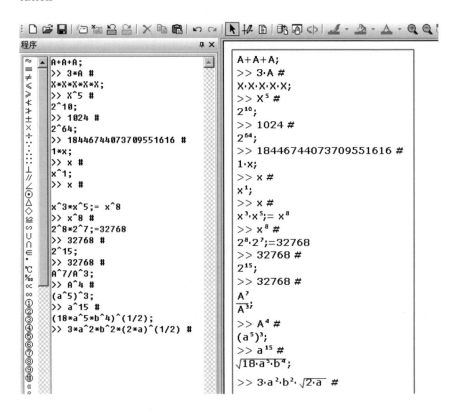

Fig. 6.

As is shown in Fig. 6, after performing a series of symbolic computation in programming area under teacher's direction, students could make a summary about the meaning and operational rule of power.

Figure 7 gives more examples about symbolic computation. These expressions and their computation results all have been typeset automatically in the right of programming area and thus an editable document comes into

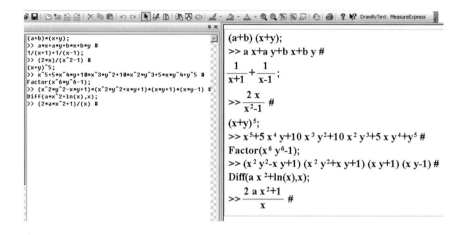

Fig. 7.

being.

SSP also provides dynamic numerical calculation, as shown in the following example.

Example 5 Exploration for a maximizing problem by dynamic numerical calculation

The following question is very common in school textbook: given that the perimeter of a rectangle is 20, find the maximum among all its possible areas.

Let x be the length of the Rectangle, so its width is $10 - x$ and its area $x(10 - x)$. Measure its length and area using the following instructions

```
MeasureExpress(x);
MeasureExpress(x*(10-x));
```

and construct the variable rule of x. When adjusting the value of x, it is easy to find that when x reach 5, the relevant area goes up to the maximum. If the point $(x, x(10-x))$ is also drawn and then traced, the conclusion will be easier to be perceived through the senses (Fig. 8).

4. Programming Environment in SSP

SSP provides a programming environment, namely programming area, which supports programming using basic programming statement includes assignment statement, conditional statement, for loop statement and while

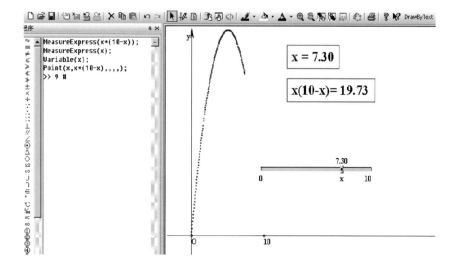

Fig. 8.

loop statement, as well as permits users to define function themselves. For example

Assignment statement:

```
a=3; b=7; h=4;
V=pi*(a^2+b^2+a*b)*h/3;
>> (316*pi)/(3) #
```

Conditional statement and definable function to user[b]:

```
g(a,b) {if (a<b) {a;} else {b;}}
m(a,b,c){g(a,g(b,c));}
>>g(a,b)
  m(a, b, c) #
m(3,-1,8);
>> -1 #
```

Relying on the support of SSP's programming environment, students themselves could define a function and then calculate some function values, which could make them understand function concept better. For example,

---

[b]An example for picking up the minimum among three real number a, b and c.

after students complete those operations which are shown in Fig. 9, it is easy for them to grasp the meaning of function calculus.

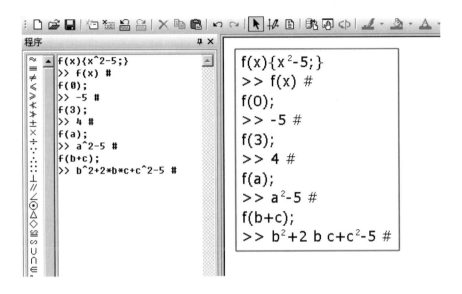

Fig. 9.

It is also very convenient to produce dynamic graph by programming, the following example is not common.

Example 6 Taylor polynomial for sin function

An animation could be designed to show how Taylor polynomial of sin function approximates itself when lengthening the number of terms of polynomial. The following program with 10 lines is a simple approach to obtain it.

```
TS(x,n,k){i=0; f=x;
          while (i<k)
          {i=i+1;
          f=f+sign(n,i)*(-1)^i*x^(2*i+1)/Factorial(2*i+1);}}
S=Function(x,TS(x,n,50),x,-10,10,100,0);
Function(x,sin(x),x,-10,10,100,0);
Trace(S);
MeasureExpress(floor(n));
Variable(n, );
```

```
AnimationVar(n, );
```

Line 1 to line 4 constitute a loop, by which function TS is defined. Though $TS(x, n, k)$ contains $k + 1$ terms of Taylor polynomial in form, it actually only have n terms because function $sign(n, i)$ causes the ith term become 0 when $i \geq n$ ($sign(x, y)$ is defined as follows: if $x > y$, $sign(x, y) = 1$, else $sign(x, y) = 0$). And as n is a variable parameter, it is a dynamic expression. After understanding these 4 lines, readers can try to plot more dynamic graphs similar to it.

Line 5 plots dynamic graph of Taylor polynomial by text instruction, in which x ranges -10 to 10, sample points is 100, and function TS defined above is used.

Line 6 plots the graph of sin function by text instruction.

Line 7 traces the dynamic graph of Taylor polynomial.

Line 8 measures $floor(n)$ to show the number of terms.

Lines 9 and 10 produce variable ruler and animation button of parameter n respectively.

After running animation, the result is shown in Fig. 10.

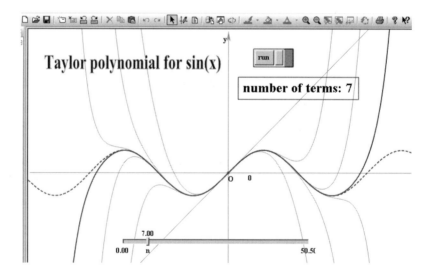

Fig. 10.

Some of other dynamic geometry software also could plot dynamic graph of Taylor polynomial for some functions. But they rely mainly on such geometric function as iteration and tracing rather than a suitable working bench similar to programming environment, and so great skill is needed for performing some transformation. The operations are so complicated that an ordinary user feels it difficult to grasp them. On the contrary with the help of programming environment, SSP could use common instruction to obtain ingenious design instead. If only users who understand Taylor expansion know some basic programming syntax and algorithm such as recursion here, they could plot dynamic graphs for functions with ease. What they need to do is only retelling the same mathematical meaning with programming language.

In summary, the dynamic geometry software mainly used in school could develop students' potential and strengthen their capability of operation. Specially, the programming environment of SSP also could provide for users chance of the second time development and thus there is more space to reveal their talent. In addition, SSP could make students master some elementary programming and algorithm knowledge, which is beneficial for them to study mathematics and computer in college in the future.

5. More Examples

Example 7 Explanation for Pythagoras theorem by piecing areas together
  SSP can produce an animation for piecing areas together to prove

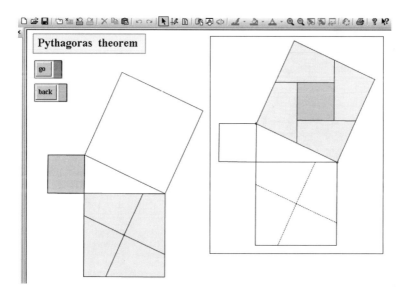

Fig. 11.

Pythagoras theorem, as shown in Fig. 11. Click the button 'go', and then the figure on the left will transform continuously into the one on the right.

There are more than 400 kinds of method used to prove Pythagoras theorem, of which the most elementary one is based on the following principle: sum of areas keeps fixed before and after piecing areas together. The above figure is a classic example using it. The dynamic proof is both visual and rigorous, by which students could experience the process of exploring and verifying Pythagoras theorem. Thus, their desire of exploration will be stimulated and ability of plausible reasoning be developed. It is beneficial for them to understand the thought of combining algebra and geometry, as well as to engage actively in experiment, guess, verification, inference and communication.

Example 8 Buffon Needle experiment

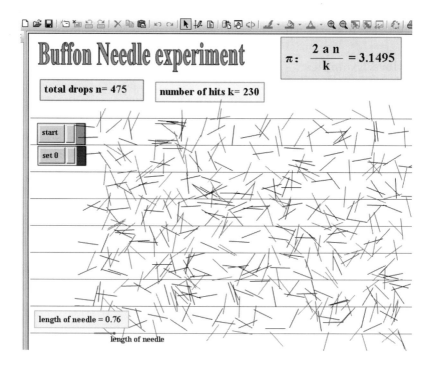

Fig. 12.

Buffon Needle is one of the oldest problems in the field of geometric probability, which was first stated in 'Essai d'arithmétique morale' pub-

lished in 1777. It involves dropping a needle of length a on a lined sheet of
paper with distance d apart and determining the probability of the needle
crossing one of the lines. The remarkable result is that the probability is
$P = 2a/\pi d$, which directly related to the value of π, and thus the approximate value of π could be obtained by means of probability experiment. As
shown in Fig. 12, SSP could simulate the animation of the experiment in
which random function is used.

By SSP, performing the experiment becomes more quickly and easily,
but which takes much labor and great effort originally. The simulation
experiment based on SSP is very effective for developing students' capability
in the fields of independence, cooperation, exploration and creation.

Example 9 Locus based on 3 circles

Fig. 13.

The graphs shown in Fig. 13 are geometric locus from the same equation
with different parameters. Actually the steps in need are very simple, as
follows.

(1) Draw 3 circles with point A, C and E as their centers and B, D and F
as a point on circumferences respectively.

132

(2) Create point G (No. 14) on the circumference of circle A and point H (No. 15) on circle C.

(3) Draw a line that join point G and H, and select point I on it.

(4) Create point J (No. 18) on the circumference of circle E and K (No. 20) on line IJ.

(5) Run the text instruction

```
Locus(14,15,18,20);
```

to construct locus of point K.

(6) Run the text instruction

```
Variable(m);
Variable(n);
```

to get variable rules of parameter m and n.

(7) Modify locus attributes in order that any 2 of 3 maximum values in it become `floor(2*m)*pi` and `floor(2*n)*pi`.

By adjusting parametric values, dragging point I and K or changing size and position of 3 circles, we will get far more unexpected graphs than those in Fig. 13, as shown in Fig. 14.

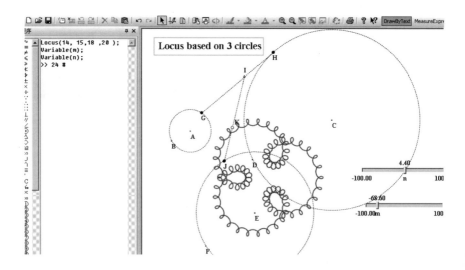

Fig. 14.

Example 10 Iteration image

The full version of SSP supports iteration for drawing. The free version also could fulfill it by programming. It is interesting that iteration for function could be accomplished conveniently by using measurement for expression.

The fundamentals of iteration by measurement lie in that measurement could embed in itself in SSP. The result of measurement will be named automatically after its sequence such as $m000, m001, m002, \ldots$, and so on. So if the expression of the first measurement $m000$ contains itself, then when data is renewed every time, $m000$ in the expression would be substituted by its current value, and thus iteration would appear. For example, supposing the expression of the first measurement is $m000 + 1$, the result of measurement would add 1 once data is renewed. Generally, suppose the expression of some measurement such as the third one is $f(m002)$, then the function f will be used once when data is renewed every time. If animation is also executed, then data will be renewed continually and thus iteration for function f also will occur continually.

Select any two functions $f(x, y)$ and $g(x, y)$. A series of points begin with point (x, y) would be obtained by the following calculus:

$$x_1 = f(x, y), \quad y_1 = g(x, y);$$
$$x_2 = f(x_1, y_1), \, y_2 = g(x_1, y_1);$$
$$x_3 = f(x_2, y_2), \, y_3 = g(x_2, y_2);$$
$$\ldots$$

After the parameters in the expressions of f and g are adjusted, these points maybe construct some unexpected and interesting images.

Let

$$f(x, y) = x^2 - y^2 + a - trunc(x^2 - y^2 + a)$$
$$g(x, y) = 2xy + b - trunc(xy + b)$$

For some appropriate values of parameter a and b, if iteration point is traced, the resultant image could be highly fascinated, as shown in Fig. 15.

6. Prospect

Based on the demand of mathematical teaching and studying, further study about SSP would be necessary. Besides improving its running efficiency and stability, the following issues should also be considered:

- Providing support for dynamic drawing of 3D figure

134

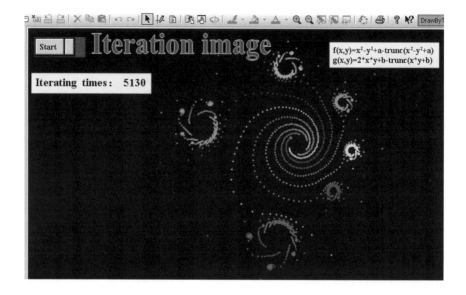

Fig. 15.

- Augmenting programming function, such as supporting for array, and so on
- Developing English version
- Strengthening animation feather suitable to teaching in primary school
- Enhancing the internet service.

Welcome for more suggestion, as well as more cooperation and communication with us.

References

1. Ulrich H. Kortenkamp, Foundations of Dynamic Geometry, Ph.D. thesis, Swiss Federal Institute of Technology Zurich (1999).
2. Nicholas Jackiw, The Geometer's Sketchpad (software) (Key Curriculum Press, Berkeley, 1991–1995).
3. Jean-Marie Laborde and Franck Bellemain, Cabri-Geometry II (software) (Dallas, Texas Instruments, 1993–1998).
4. Jürgen Richter-Gebert and Ulrich H. Kortenkamp, The Interactive Geometry Software Cinderella (Springer-Verlag, Heidelberg, 1999).
5. Ulrich H. Kortenkamp and Jürgen Richter-Gebert, Using Automatic Theorem Proving to Improve the Usability of Geometry Software, in Proceedings of Mathematical User-Interfaces Workshop (MathUI), Bialowezia, 2004.
6. Sean Wilson and Jacques D. Fleuriot, Combining Dynamic Geometry, Au-

tomated Geometry Theorem Proving and Diagrammatic Proofs, in Proceedings of the European Joint Conferences on Theory and Practice of Software (ETAPS) Satellite Workshop on User Interfaces for Theorem Provers (UITP), Edinburgh, 2005 (Elsevier, Amsterdam, 2006).

7. Markus Hohenwarter and Karl Fuchs, Combination of Dynamic Geometry, Algebra and Calculus in the Software System GeoGebra, in Proceedings of Computer Algebra Systems and Dynamic Geometry Systems in Mathematics Teaching Conference, Pecs, 2004, pp. 128–133.

8. Ulrich Kortenkamp, The Future of Mathematical Software, in Proceedings of Multimedia Tools for Communicating Mathematics (MTCM), Lisbon, 2000 (Springer-Verlag, Heidelberg, 2001), pp. 191–202.

9. Jingzhong Zhang, Free Trip with Super Sketchpad (Science Press, Beijing, 2006) [in Chinese].

BRINGING MORE INTELLIGENCE TO DYNAMIC GEOMETRY BY USING SYMBOLIC COMPUTATION

FRANCISCO BOTANA

Department of Applied Mathematics I, University of Vigo
36005 Pontevedra, Spain
E-mail: fbotana@uvigo.es
webs.uvigo.es/fbotana

This article describes through some selected case studies how symbolic computing can be used to improve dynamic geometry software. Focusing on some of
the key problems around the dynamic geometry paradigm, such as general discovery and loci derivation, we review some of our algorithms and tools relating
computer algebra based methods and dynamic geometry environments.

Keywords: Dynamic geometry, symbolic computation, computer algebra software, intercommunication.

1. Introduction

Dynamic geometry software refers to computer programs where construction of geometric configurations can be done. The key characteristic of this
software is that unconstrained objects of the construction can be updated
and, as they do, all other elements automatically self-adjust, preserving
all dependent relationships and constraints. Two such pieces of software
were launched ending the eighties: Cabri Geometry[8,15] and The Geometer's
Sketchpad[12,13] (the references point out to more recent versions). Their ease
of use, simplicity, multi-platform distributions, and the interest of a substantial number of teachers, mainly at non university levels, led up to a
generalized presence of these environments at schools, currently configur-
ing a duopoly in this educational market. In fact, both tools have evolved
from their academic origins to their current corporative status: The Geometer's Sketchpad was originally designed at the Swarthmore College by
Nick Jackiw as an academic product and it currently is the star product of
Key Curriculum Press, a corporation specialized in educational materials

for schools. On its side, Cabri, developed at the IMAG institute of the University of Grenoble, is currently commercialized by Cabrilog, a company founded and led by the main Cabri developer, Jean Marie Laborde.

Since the launching of these products two points attracted attention from users: the capability of drawing the locus of an object (usually a point) constrained by user-specified conditions, and the anomalous behavior of some constructions under extreme conditions. Furthermore, one of the environments (Cabri) provides a "property checker", a tool able to answer simple questions about geometric properties of a construction. These abilities are based on numerical computations: checking, for instance, the collinearity of three points in Cabri internally reduces to test if the coordinates of a point satisfy the equation of the line defined by the others, so relying on the numerical accuracy of computer representation of real numbers.

Reacting against the numerical approach taken by The Geometer's Sketchpad and Cabri, various alternatives to the dynamic geometry paradigm have been proposed since the beginning of the nineties. The common basis of such approaches lies on symbolic computation and mathematical background. For instance, as early as 1991, first results on a system for automated proving of geometric theorems, GEOTHER,[18] were reported. This software, currently updated and exhibiting more dynamic features[19] makes an extensive use of the Ritt–Wu theory of characteristics sets. GDI,[4,5] on its side, uses Groebner bases to perform automated discovery on a dynamic geometry environment. While these tools use external computer algebra systems (Maple in GEOTHER, and Mathematica and CoCoA[9] in GDI) for some tasks, other systems embed their symbolic algorithms into the program code. In this way, Geometry Expert[11] offers an extensive collection of methods for automatic theorem proving, besides their standard dynamic geometry procedures. Cinderella[10,14] shows a very efficient handling of continuity, inscribed in a nice dynamic geometry environment and based on complex analysis.

In this paper, we review our contributions to the subject of enriching the dynamic geometry paradigm by means of computer algebra systems and tools. We describe the main problems around the dynamic geometry paradigm (continuity, loci computation, proof and discovery), how they can be solved from a symbolic viewpoint, and some work in progress relating communication within dynamic geometry programs and with computer algebra systems.

2. Continuity and Discontinuity

The problem of continuity occurs in situations when a small movement of an element in a construction involves unexpected or counterintuitive changes in some part of the construction. The canonic example is shown in Fig. 1: Studying one point of the intersection of two circles, one of them fixed (thick line) and the other moving along the horizontal line (thin line, multiple instances drawn), most dynamic geometry systems show a jump of the intersection point from one pole to the other when both circles coincide.

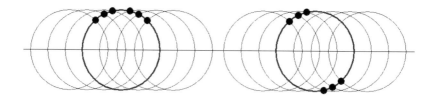

Fig. 1.   The canonic example for non continuity

The continuity issue has been efficiently solved by Cinderella, using methods of complex analysis. No other dynamic geometry system exhibits a comparable behavior regarding continuity. As stated in Ref. 7, "the continuity problem is not simply an issue about finding the right implementation strategies for visualization: it is mathematically involved and it is related to the so called *conservative* or *deterministic* behavior (namely, that for any concrete position of the base points in a construction, the position of all the constructed elements should be uniquely determined) of the dynamic geometry software". Developers must choose between continuity and determinism, since these properties cannot be present simultaneously.[14]

Another source of discontinuity stems from the computation of loci. Following the above notion of continuity, it is easy to produce constructions where the loci obtained by standard systems suffer sudden changes for small movements of its defining elements, as shown in Fig. 2. A conchoid is the locus of points X such that O, X, and P are collinear, the distance between X and P is constant, O is any fixed point and P is another point moving along a line. Note that the loci in the bottom of the figure are anomalous, and small movements of point O will cause dramatic changes in the shape of the locus.

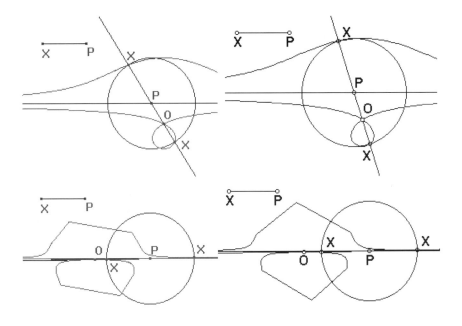

Fig. 2. Two conchoids in Cabri (left) and The Geometer's Sketchpad (right)

3. Loci Computations

A symbolic approach will be more fruitful for determining loci. Most dynamic geometry systems share the strategy for tracing loci: selecting an object, the *driver object*, with a predefined path, the locus of another object depending on the former is drawn by sampling the path and plotting the locus object for each sample. Usually, the system will obtain the locus as a continuous line by joining contiguous points, leading this heuristic frequently to extraneous loci, as illustrated for the conchoid. Cinderella, although exploiting its treatment of continuity, also suffers this problem. Furthermore, its strategy of returning loci as the positions only accessible by real continuous moves (see Ref. 14, p. 137) sometimes avoids their correct generation. Geometry Expert does not link the locus points, trying to eliminate the above problem, so getting some loci as mere suggestions (Fig. 3).

In Ref. 2, where a thoroughful discussion of loci generation strategies in dynamic geometry environments is developed, we postulate that the traditional way for generating loci is outperformed by a new class of methods

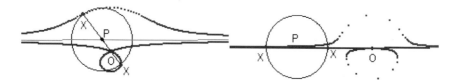

Fig. 3.   The conchoid in Geometry Expert

coming from algebraic geometry. Elimination techniques have been successfully used for deriving loci equations. Inspired by the elimination theory of
Seidenberg and the Ritt–Wu's characteristic set method, Wang[20] has proposed efficient elimination algorithms with applications in loci derivation.
Applying the Groebner bases method, Botana and Valcarce[4] have embedded a simple elimination algorithm in GDI, a dynamic geometry environment able to compute the equations for a wide class of algebraic loci. For the
sake of illustration we will consider the obtaining of the conchoid in GDI.
Once constructed the basic elements of the construction, the locus point X
must be defined as a free one (at first sight, this is a unconventional way
with respect to standard environments, but this approach allows to extend
the class of computable loci, as described below), and it must be constrained
by the collinearity condition of O, X, P, and the distance condition between
X and P (Fig. 4).

The algebraic description of the construction is given by the coordinates
of the points $O(2, -0.5)$, $A_1(0,0)$, $A_2(1,0)$(which define the support line of
$P(x_1, x_2)$), $X(u_7, u_8)$, and the following relations:

$$x_2 = 0$$
$$(x_2 + 0.5) * (u_7 - x_1) - (u_8 - x_2) * (x_1 - 2) = 0$$
$$(u_7 - x_1)^2 + (u_8 - x_2)^2 = 1.$$

A simple elimination of the x variables in the above equations gives the
locus equation. This equation and its plot is then returned by GDI, with
the locus drawn by an internal algorithm (as is the case shown in Fig. 5)
or by the graphics abilities of Mathematica.

Note that the equation simultaneously describes both branches of the
conchoid. Most of tools force to define both intersections of the line OP
with the circle OX in order to get the whole graphical locus. Furthermore,
the locus equation remains unknown. As stated in Ref. 20, "in general, one
cannot tell only from the geometric description what a locus looks like.
When its equations are found, the geometric figure can be much clearly

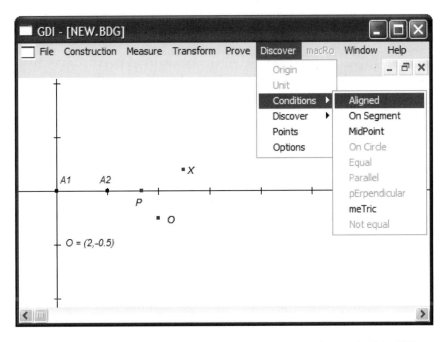

Fig. 4. Imposing the alignment of O, P, X for discovering the conchoid in GDI

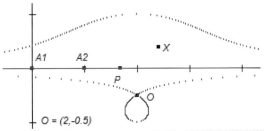

If there is a construction with properties:
Aligned(P,A1,A2)
then the locus of point X(u[7],u[8]) such that: Aligned(X,P,O)
distance(X,P)=1 is (or is contained in):

1.- the curve: 4u[7]^2u[8]^2 + 4u[8]^4 - 16u[7]u[8]^2 + 4u[8]^3 + 13u[8]^2 - 4u[8] - 1 = 0

Fig. 5. The equation and plot of the conchoid

analyzed and explained according to its algebraic structure". According to the significance of knowing the loci equations, the last version of Cabri has been extended to give them. Nevertheless, given the numerical character of the used algorithm, equations are inexact by definition: for instance, placing the point O at $(1.90, -0.02)$ the user obtains as equations of the loci

$$0.96x^2y + 10xy^2 - 0.63y^3 - 4.76xy - 8.69y^2 + 0.02x + 3.69y - 0.08 = 0$$
$$0.04x^2y + 1.09xy^2 + 10y^3 - 0.10xy + 0.34y^2 + 0.12y = 0,$$

that is, two cubic equations (one for each branch of the conchoid), instead of just a quartic! Furthermore, even the degree of these equations changes when dragging some basic element in the construction, while a symbolic approach such as the one in GDI is able to give the exact equation in real time.

We recently report in Ref. 1 an external add-on for Cabri and The Geometer's Sketchpad which complements these programs when searching for loci equations.

The tool (located at `http://nash.sip.ucm.es/GLI/GLI.html`) accepts uploading loci-defining files from Cabri or The Geometer's Sketchpad, and returns the equation and plot of such loci. Nevertheless, care should be taken when using this resource, given the differences between standard interactive approaches and our symbolic proposal to loci. Fig. 6 shows a capture of the web page for the following Cabri construction: a point moving along a line is the center of a circle of fixed radius that contains a point which locus is searched for. While Cabri returns as locus a line parallel to the first one, our symbolic approach concludes that the locus is contained in the whole plane, since the true locus is the set of all possible points of the circle when it sweeps the line.

As said above, an adequate combination of the interactive environment and our symbolic approach for loci computation extends the class of computable loci. Consider, for instance, computing the locus of C in the plane triangle ABC, where the bisector $\angle CAB$ intersects the side BC at point A_1, and the bisector of $\angle CBA$ intersects the side AC at point B_1 such that $|AA_1| = |BB_1|$. This locus (also studied in Ref. 22) cannot be investigated in standard environments since the point C with the given constraints cannot be constructed in general using common dynamic geometry tools: it is implicitly defined by simultaneous conditions rather than depending on a single parameter. Defining C as a free point and imposing that A_1 and B_1 lie on the bisectors and the equality of segments AA_1 and BB_1, GDI easily obtains the locus equations, shown in Fig. 7 by means of webDiscovery,[3] a Java application that remotely offers the symbolic abilities of GDI for computers only running the interactive version of the tool.

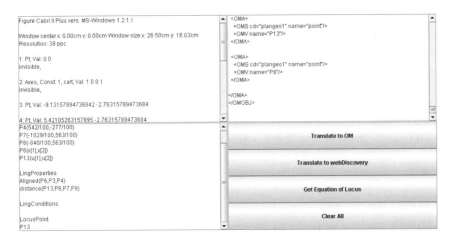

Fig. 6. An applet for performing symbolic loci discovery from standard environments

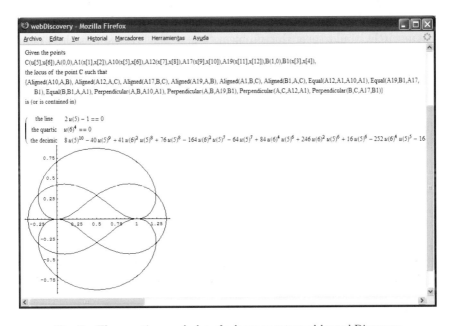

Fig. 7.   The equations and plot of a locus as returned by webDiscovery

4. Automatic Discovery

Automatically proving theorems in elementary geometry has been extensively studied during the last decades by means of symbolic algebraic tech-

niques. Efficient automatic provers integrate, jointly with the traditional computer algebra engines, a dynamic environment where the user can sketch geometric configurations and ask about the truth of stated properties. Even a standard environment such as Cabri offers, as said earlier, an option to test some elementary geometric properties. Nevertheless, its numerical character again prevents an in-depth use of this ability. Imagine, for instance, that a student has conjectured that the projections from a point to the sides of a triangle are collinear if the point lies on the circumcircle. Drawing such a point on the circumcircle things go right. Nevertheless, if the user does not know the Simson line, a reasonable procedure would be experimenting with a free point on the plane. Dragging it to different positions, the conjecture becomes more convincing and the user draws the circumcircle and carefully places the point on it, asking the system about the collinearity of projections. The answer is that the conjecture is wrong! The property checker tests if the coordinates of the point satisfy the circle equation, but the system does not recognize the point as placed on the circle, given the high numerical accuracy used. Although redefining the point to be on the circumcircle would solve this problem, a new algebraic approach is more promising. Using the method proposed by Recio and Vélez,[16] GDI offers a graphical environment where some kind of discovery can be performed in an automatic way. As a real class example and for illustration purposes we recall from Ref. 7 the following exercise proposed by Richard:[17] Given a circle of diameter AB, its bisector d, and a point C in the intersection of d and the circle, decide which statements are true:

- The construction is impossible
- The triangle is isosceles
- The triangle is equilateral
- It is a right triangle
- None of the above

Constructing C as a free point in the plane, O as the center of the circle, and imposing that C is in the intersection, the textual output of GDI is:

```
If there is a construction with these properties
Midpoint(O,B,A)
then the necessary condition(s) for
Equal(A,C,B,C)
Equal(B,O,O,C)
is(are)
"The point A is on a circle with center C passing through B"
```

"The triangle CBA is isosceles on C"
"CB is perpendicular to CA"

Besides obtaining elementary conclusions, GDI can also be used for performing discovery of unknown relations. We will illustrate this point with a formula due to Euler which relates the radii of the incircle and the excircle of a triangle with the distance between their centers. This problem, also studied in Ref. 7, has been previously discussed by Wang and Zhi in Ref. 21 using an automated proving approach. The basic construction is shown in Fig. 8.

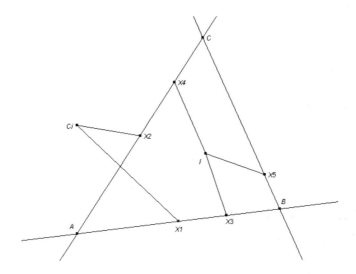

Fig. 8.   The construction for discovering Euler's formula

Note that since GDI is able to discover relations only about free points, both the incenter I and the circumcenter Ci are constructed without any *a priori* constraint, imposing the required conditions via an *ad hoc* menu. So, we have a triangle $A(0,0), B(1,0)$ and $C(u_5, u_6)$, the midpoints of AB and AC, X_1, X_2, three points on the triangle sides X_3, X_4 and X_5, the incenter $I(u_7, u_8)$, and the circumcenter $Ci(u_9, u_{10})$, being defined these centers through the conditions $AB \perp IX_3, AC \perp IX_4, BC \perp IX_5, |IX_3| = |IX_4|, |IX_3| = |IX_5|$ and $AB \perp CiX_1, AC \perp CiX_2$, respectively. Once done the construction, GDI tries to eliminate, by using CoCoA, all the variables of points X_i in order to get a relation just involving the coordinates of points A, B, C, I and Ci. Using webDiscovery, the returned answer is given in Fig. 9. Apart from the degenerated condition $(Aligned(A, B, C))$, GDI, in its current version, ends by giving the conjunction of eight polynomials. Some post-process must be done by the user: calling $r = u_8$ the radius of the incenter, $c^2 = u_9^2 + u_{10}^2$, the square of the radius of the circumcenter, and $d^2 = (u_9 - u_7)^2 + (u_{10} - u_8)^2$, the squared distance between centers, and eliminating again all variables u_i we get the formula $d^4 - 2d^2c^2 - 4r^2c^2 + c^4 = 0$, extending Euler's formula since it is valid for all different incenters.

Given a construction with points

A (0,0),B(1,0),C(u[5],u[6]),X1(x[1],x[2]),X2(x[3],x[4]),X3(x[5],x[6]),X4(x[7],x[8]) ,X5(x[9],x[10]),I(u[7],u[8]),Ci(u[9],u[10]) ,

described by

{Midpoint(X1,A,B) , Midpoint(X2,A,C), Aligned(X3,A,B), Aligned(X4,A,C), Aligned(X5,B,C) },

the necessary condition(s) for

(Perpendicular(A,B,X1,Ci), Perpendicular(A,C,X2,Ci) , Perpendicular(A,B,I,X3),

    Perpendicular(A,C,I,X4), Perpendicular(B,C,I,X5), distance(I,X3)=distance(I,X4), distance(I,X3)=distance(I,X5))

is(are)

$2u(9) - 1 == 0 \wedge u(5)^2 - u(5) + u(6)^2 - 2u(6)u(10) == 0 \wedge (\{Aligned(A, B, C)\} \vee -u(7)^2 + 2u(5)u(7) + u(8)^2 - u(5) + 2u(6)u(8) - 4u(8)u(10) == 0) \wedge$

$(\{Aligned(A, B, C)\} \vee 2u(7)u(6) - u(6) - 2u(5)u(8) - 2u(7)u(8) + 2u(8) == 0) \wedge$

$(\{Aligned(A, B, C)\} \vee 2u(8)^3 - 8u(10)u(8)^2 + 2u(7)^2u(8) - 2u(7)u(8) - 2u(8) + u(6) == 0) \wedge$

$(\{Aligned(A, B, C)\} \vee 2u(7)^3 - 3u(7)^2 + 2u(8)^2u(7) - 8u(8)u(10)u(7) - u(8)^2 + u(5) + 4u(8)u(10) == 0) \wedge$

$(\{Aligned(A, B, C)\} \vee -4u(8)^4 + 16u(10)u(8)^3 - 8u(6)u(10)u(8)^2 + 4u(8)^2 - 4u(6)u(8) + u(6)^2 == 0) \wedge$

$(\{Aligned(A, B, C)\} \vee -8u(7)u(8)^3 + 4u(8)^3 - 16u(5)u(10)u(8)^2 + 16u(7)u(10)u(8)^2 - 6u(5)u(8) + 2u(7)u(8) + 2u(8) + 2u(5)u(6) - u(6) == 0)$

Fig. 9. A partial discovery for Euler's formula

5. Finding Elementary Extrema

As a final illustration of the potentialities of cooperation between dynamic geometry environments and computer algebra systems, we describe a new way for computing, in an automatic manner, critical points in elementary extrema problems described through interactive diagrams. Although preliminary results have been obtained for the 3D case, here we restrict to optimization problems in one variable. Furthermore, only problems admitting a plane modelization in a dynamic geometry setting are considered. Let us describe our approach with a simple exercise: *Two vertical poles OA and PB are secured by a rope AXB going from the top A of the first pole to a point X on the ground between the poles and then to the top B of the second pole. If the length of poles are 1 and 2, find the position of X that requires the least rope.*

The construction involves three fixed points $A(0, 1), P(2, 0), B(2, 2)$ and a dependent point $X(x_1, x_2)$, which lies on the horizontal axis (Fig. 10). Once done the construction, the user specifies the magnitude to optimize and the point on which it depends $(X, distance(A, X) + distance(B, X))$

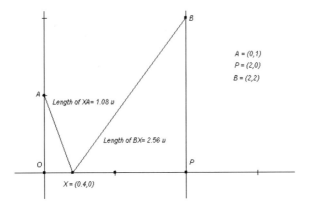

Fig. 10.   A diagram for an optimization problem

and the system launches a computer algebra system for performing the following tasks:

- read the construction points and constraints and the optimization items,
- solve the polynomial constraints $(x_2 \to 0)$,
- solve the optimization constraints
  $(x_3 \to \pm\sqrt{x_1^2 + (1 - x_2)^2}, x_4 \to \pm\sqrt{(2 - x_1)^2 + (2 - x_2)^2})$,
- for each combination of the preceding solutions

  - solve the derivative of the optimization condition with respect to the unbound variable of the optimization point (x_1),
  - compute the coordinates of the construction dependent points,
  - add this set of points to a list of possible solutions,

- return this list.

These ideas have been implemented as an add-on to GDI (see Ref. 6 for an extended description). In the case we describe, two solutions are found: the expected one, $x_1 = 2/3$, and a spurious answer, $x_1 = -2$, which appears since we work in a strict algebraic setting.

6. Conclusion

We described part of our past and current work relating the use of symbolic techniques and computer algebra software for enhancing the dynamic geometry paradigm. Features like automatic discovery of geometric properties, derivation of unknown properties, and generation of equations of loci are made really possible by mixing symbolic computation with interactive environments.

Acknowledgments

This work has been partly supported by grant MTM2004-03175 from the Spanish MEC.

References

1. Abánades, M., Escribano, J., Botana; F.: Computing loci equations for standard dynamic geometry environments. *Proc. 7th International Conference on Computational Science* (ICCS 2007), LNCS, 4488, 227–234 (2007)
2. Botana, F.: Interactive versus symbolic approaches to plane loci generation in dynamic geometry environments. *Proc. I International Workshop on Computer Graphics and Geometric Modeling* (ICCS 2002), LNCS, 2330, 211–218 (2002)
3. Botana, F.: A Web-based intelligent system for geometric discovery. *Proc. 2nd International Conference on Computational Science* (ICCS 2003), LNCS, 2657, 801–810 (2003)
4. Botana, F., Valcarce, J. L.: A software tool for the investigation of plane loci. *Mathematics and Computers in Simulation*, 61(2), 141–154 (2003)
5. Botana, F., Valcarce, J. L.: Automatic determination of envelopes and other derived curves within a graphic environment. *Mathematics and Computers in Simulation*, 67(1–2), 3–13 (2004)
6. Botana, F., Valcarce, J. L.: Automated discovery in elementary extrema problems. *Proc. International Conference on Computational Science* (ICCS 2006), LNCS, 3992, 470–477 (2006)
7. Botana, F., Recio, T.: Towards solving the dynamic geometry bottleneck via a symbolic approach. *Proc. V International Workshop on Automated Deduction in Geometry* (ADG 2004), LNCS, 3763, 92–110 (2006)
8. http://www.cabrilog.com
9. Capani, A., Niesi, G., Robbiano, L.: CoCoA, a system for doing Computations in Commutative Algebra. Available via anonymous ftp from: cocoa.dima.unige.it
10. http://cinderella.de
11. Gao, X. S., Zang, J. Z., Chou, S. C: *Geometry Expert*. Nine Chapters Publ., Taiwan (1998)
12. Jackiw, N.: *The Geometer's Sketchpad*. Key Curriculum Press, Berkeley (1997)
13. http://www.keypress.com/x5521.xml
14. Kortenkamp, U.: Foundations of dynamic geometry, Ph.D. Thesis, ETH, Zurich (1999)
15. Laborde, J. M., Bellemain, F.: *Cabri Geometry II*. Texas Instruments, Dallas (1998)

16. Recio, T., Vélez, M. P.: Automatic discovery of theorems in elementary geometry. *Journal of Automated Reasoning*, 23, 63–82 (1999)
17. Richard, P.: *Raisonnement et stratégies de preuve dans l'enseignement des mathématiques*. Peter Lang, Berne (2004)
18. Wang, D.: GEOTHER: A geometry theorem prover. *Proc. 13th International Conference on Automated Deduction* (CADE 1996), LNCS, 1104, 166–170 (1996)
19. Wang, D.: GEOTHER 1.1: Handling and proving geometric theorems automatically. *Proc. IV International Workshop on Automated Deduction in Geometry* (ADG 2002), LNCS, 2930, 194–215 (2004)
20. Wang, D.: Reasoning about geometric problems using an elimination method. *Automated Practical Reasoning*, eds. J. Pfalzgraf and D. Wang, Texts and Monographs in Symbolic Computation, 147–185 (Springer, 1995)
21. Wang, D., Zhi, L.: Algebraic factorization applied to geometric problems. *Proc. Third Asian Symposium on Computer Mathematics* (ASCM '98), Lanzhou University Press, Lanzhou (China), 23–36 (1998)
22. Wang, D.: *Elimination Practice: Software Tools and Applications*. Imperial College Press, London (2004)

COMBINING CAS AND DGS — TOWARDS ALGORITHMIC THINKING

ULRICH H. KORTENKAMP

Institute for Mathematics and Computer Science
University of Education Schwäbisch Gmünd
73525 Schwäbisch Gmünd, Germany
E-mail: Ulrich.Kortenkamp@ph-gmuend.de
http://www.ph-gmuend.de

This article discusses some ways to combine software for interactive geometry and computer algebra, with an emphasis on using this software in teaching. Some arising mathematical problems and necessary software specific paradigms that have to be adjusted are considered, and solutions to these problems are presented. The article also highlights some of the aspects that drove the development of the mathematics software *Cinderella.2*, which integrates an interactive geometry software package, a physics simulation engine, and an all-purpose functional programming language.

Keywords: Interactive geometry, computer algebra, HCI, Cinderella, CAS, DGS, OpenMath, mathematics education.

1. Introduction

In mathematics teaching today the use of software seems to be an accepted practice. In almost all national curricula, the use of a computer is obligatory, or at least strongly recommended. In this article, we will not discuss whether the use of software in mathematics is indeed helpful *per se* when compared to more traditional approaches, but we will rely on the hypothesis that it is at least a different approach to teaching that might add to the portfolio methods and as such it is at least worth to be tried.

If we accept this, then we should make sure that

(a) the theoretical foundation for such a software reflects the necessities of the subject (here: mathematics),

(b) the software adheres to usability standards and does not introduce additional things to learn that do not contribute to the original teaching goals, and

(c) new educational approaches can be explored through the software.

We will try to serve an answer to all three requests. Before we start, we briefly review the three main types of software that are currently in use in schools and universities for math teaching.

1.1. *Spreadsheets*

Spreadsheets (usually *EXCEL*, or its open source alternative *OpenOffice.org Calc*) are highly useful in mathematics teaching.[1-3] They provide an easy way to organize calculations and to gather data. Paired with the immediate visualization through, say, pie charts or other graphs they are particularly useful in applied mathematics teaching. Also, they play an important part in teaching basic computing skills (as required, for example, by the NCTM standards).

Probably, spreadsheets do such a good and important job because they (almost) replace the concept of a variable, which is usually very hard to understand and to teach, by the concept of a *cell*. A cell explicitly corresponds to an area of the work sheet, and it inherits its name automatically.[a]

1.2. *Computer Algebra Software*

Computer algebra software (Maple, Mathematica, Derive, and many more, commonly referred to as *CAS*) makes symbolic manipulation, as opposed to pure calculation, available. It takes away many of the burdens of doing mathematics. The extended abilities to *solve* equations (or other formula-based things) deserve special attention: At the very least, the availability of such methods must make us re-think the way of teaching, the contents we teach, and the goals of a mathematics education that contributes to *allgemeinbildung* (general knowledge).

While spreadsheets organize the user interaction in matrix form[b], the user interface of Computer Algebra software is linearly ordered. It is a kind

---

[a]Naming a variable, say a, in a mathematical formula, for example Pythagoras' theorem, $a^2 + b^2 = c^2$, is confusing, because this name may be re-used in other formulas with a different meaning, or one might re-name it to, say, x, without changing the mathematical semantics. This is different if cells are being used: re-using is only possible if a new sheet is used, and then the students easily know that this is not related to the old one, and re-naming is only possible if the cells' content is moved to another location, which connects the re-naming to an action carried out by the student.
[b]This is still the main item of distinction for spreadsheet software, and it was a feasible approach to use the whole computer screen even in times when one had to rely to the keyboard as only input device!

of dialogue between the user and the software, the latter answering the requests of the former. For prepared teaching or demonstration material this makes it necessary to have a special command like *shift-enter* to evaluate the expressions step-by-step. We will come back to this mode of operation in Sect. 4.2.

1.3. *Dynamic Geometry Software*

A software type that brought much excitement into the computer-based teaching community is dynamic (or *interactive*) geometry software, also known as *DGS*. Pioneered by the packages *Geometers' Sketchpad* and *Cabri Géomètre*, the direct, visual, mouse-driven interaction with geometric constructions, have now become an important part of mathematics education in many curricula.

The basic principle of DGS is to have two kinds of (geometric) objects, free ones and dependent ones. The free objects can be manipulated with the mouse (for example, a free point can be moved in the plane), the dependent objects are re-calculated according to the changes of the free or other dependent objects (the perpendicular bisector of a segment is automatically adjusted when the start and end vertices of the segment move). There must be no circular dependencies between elements (i.e., the recalculation graph is acyclic) for this approach to work. For a description of all the mathematical subtleties of dynamic geometry we refer to the thesis [4].

Historically, the invention of DGS was connected to the widespread introduction of a – at that time innovative – hardware device, the *mouse*. The mouse-driven interaction enables users to use the whole screen without limitation, as opposed to the coarse cell raster sported by spreadsheets. Again, we refer to Sect. 4.2 where we distinguish these modes.

2. Using DGS in Teaching

Before we are going to combine DGS with computer algebra software, we want to briefly review some aspects of using DGS in teaching mathematics (and other sciences).

2.1. *Reasons to Use DGS at All*

Most people agree on the fact that DGS can help to teach mathematics. In this section we want to quickly categorize some of the aspects in order to have them available for review later. Our final goal is to enable more interaction between CAS and DGS, and we want to take care that the benefits listed below are not sacrificed for the sake of software interaction. The separation into pedagogical and mathematical issues is not as strict as it might look like – in fact, both are connected in a dialectic way.

2.1.1. *Pedagogical Aspects*

It is immediate that an interactive way of learning concepts as it is available with DGS is preferable to a *consuming* way.[c] Just watching a demonstration or listening to it is inferior to learning with all senses, through multiple channels, or, to quote Confucius:

> I listen and I forget, / I see and I remember, / I do and I understand.

This has been repeated by education experts over and over again for centuries, and is today backed by empirical studies as well.[5] We want to stress the importance of *immediate* feedback – if the actions of the learner are not directly coupled then we cannot hope for a positive effect.

Many topics in mathematics are very abstract and hard to understand for those students who cannot build a mental model of the abstract setting. The process of building such a mental model has been studied extensively, and during the last years the first empirical data has been collected and analyzed that supports the hypothesis that the immediate experience of mathematical facts through computer software can help.[6–8] In particular, the method of supplantation,[9] where an external representation of a mental representation that the learner should build up internally is presented in addition to the abstract setting, seems to promising.[6]

2.1.2. *Mathematical Aspects*

Many publications are available that discuss the various opportunities by DGS.[10–12] Unfortunately, most are restricted to describing possibilities, and still some research must be done to validate the assumptions made there. Nevertheless, we want to highlight a few aspects that are relevant to our further argumentation.

From a mathematical point of view, DGS contributes to the possibilities of teaching by extending the toolbox of the learner, and by this also the range of theories that are accessible in the class. DGS makes it possible to work with mathematical problems that otherwise would be infeasible

---

[c]Unfortunately, despite this common knowledge, many teachers still disregard this fact.

in lessons just because of their sheer complexity. Hand-drawn constructions need much more time and drawing skills than computer sketches; if the primary goal of the teaching is the mathematical content and not the development of such skills then one can take a short-cut here.

By providing a microworld[13-15] for exploration, DGS also serves as a virtual laboratory for experimentation. Great care has to be taken that the software is really a valid environment, i.e. mathematically correct and able to support unforeseen situations that the learner might encounter.[16]

While images and figures are static entities, a construction adds time as another dimension.[d] This additional dimension can be used to strengthen the understanding of functional relationships.[17] Furthermore, it is possible to directly experience functional relationships that come without any other visual hints – a way to avoid fatal misconceptions based on misunderstood visualizations.[18]

A last advantage of DGS over traditional methods is the automatic or semi-automatic processing of constructions by the software, which can create hints or visual clues that would not be available on paper. The software can, for example, show whenever two lines are parallel by construction, or point out interesting identities like equal angles in a construction.[19] These relations are based on mathematical knowledge that is 'built into' the software; we will come back to this important point in Sect. 6.2.

2.2. E-Learning/E-Teaching Scenarios

With the observations from above we can derive several E-Learning or E-Teaching scenarios with DGS. A DGS can be used to . . .

- to *present and demonstrate* mathematical situations to students, either in front of the class using a beamer or another projection device connected to a single computer, or more individually using prepared animations on the web
- to let students *explore* mathematical situations by working with pre-made examples directly,
- to let students *create* their own work (which in turn can be presented to others and explored by others again)

We cannot guarantee that students really *learn* things by being exposed to the software. A major part in instruction should be the ability to *exercise* – how can DGS help there?

---

[d]Like a movie, which is the narrative counterpart to an interactive construction

2.2.1. *Assessment and Guidance*

If we assume that a teacher is always present, then all traditional ways of creating exercises are available. If we do not want to loose the independence from a physically available teacher that is one major plus of computer based teaching, then we have to find a way to automatically *assess* exercises. If we identify a method to do this assessment, it is not restricted to the final judgment, but we can also use the information generated by it to draw conclusions on the progress of the learner and show relevant hints that might help him.[20]

So, the computer has to "know" what the student is doing. At the same time we do not want to sacrifice creativity and we want to allow for individual ways of working!! This means that the Computer has to decide whether two (or more) constructions are equivalent – otherwise, we are back to a multiple-choice like test method. These considerations lead to a strong relation between DGS and CAS from an educational point of view, which is explicated in the next section.

3. Automatic Theorem Proving

In the field of Automatic Theorem Proving (ATP) the attempt is made to find algorithms to solve mathematical problems, and to set up the corresponding structures that make the mathematical problems accessible to these algorithms. Geometry has been a primary field of application for ATP, due to several reasons. First, (Euclidean) Geometry has a long tradition of proof, much longer than any other field of mathematics. The formalization of Geometry has been carried out early, much earlier than, say, in number theory. Also, Geometry is a very nice field for applying ATP, because most proofs (or at least conjectures) can be illustrated by a figure.

As such, much research has been done, and several methods have been invented. A good overview can be found in Wang's paper,[21] and we just want to highlight Wu's method,[22] Groebner bases,[23] and Cylindrical Algebraic Decomposition. They all share the fact that they work on algebraic representations of geometric figures, and the proofs generated by the methods using computer algebra software (!) are more or less unreadable. Also, in most situations the time to generate a proof is in the range of several seconds or more.

The latter will probably change in the future, and more and more theorems might become accessible to "immediate" solutions that are found automatically. Still, conceptually, there will always be constructions that are intractable by computer algebra methods, if there is a time limit.

DGS has been used as an *input tool* to ATP algorithms for many years now. In fact, the software Cinderella[24] described below started its career as an input tool for the method of binomial proving.[25] The binomial prover was also included in the pre-commercial Java-version Cinderella's Café (Fig. 1): When the user conjectured an incidence (like, three lines concur for any position of the free points), he could select these and then start the binomial prover. After a short calculation time[e], the prover eventually found a symbolic proof for that fact. Unfortunately, the method is not suitable for disproving, nor is it universal in the sense that all geometric incidence theorems can be proved.

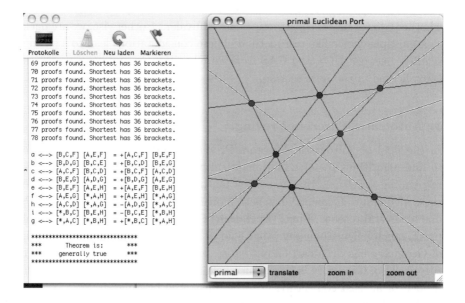

Fig. 1. A proof produced automatically with the first Java-based version of Cinderella using the binomial method.

4. Combining DGS and CAS

Today, there are much more advanced geometry tools that include symbolic provers, for example Geometry Expert[26] or MMP/Geometer[27] that evolved

---

[e]at that time in the range of several seconds, with modern computers this reduces to a fraction of a second

over a long time. You can choose from a large set of different provers, and you will get very elaborate proofs, in symbolic or graphic form, and even in natural language.

Still, the way of integration has not changed much. The user may create a figure using interactive tools, and then use the geometric data as input for a symbolic prover – it is a two-step process, which means you are not using a DGS and a CAS at the same time, but one after the other. In this section we will present reasons for that lack of integration, but also, after an analysis of the user interaction paradigms for mathematical software, solutions that can lead to better integration.

4.1. *Continuity vs. Discreteness*

As pointed out in Ref. 4, the notion of *theorem* is not as clear as it might seem at first. Sure, if you have an algebraic description of the hypotheses and the conjecture, there is a well-defined semantic of that. But if you approach proving from the DGS point of view, the translation into the algebraic description is not at all straight-forward.

Let us give an example for this fact: Given two circles of equal radius around A and B, and the line connecting the two intersections of the circles, i.e. the radical axis. The radical axis will pass through the midpoint of A and B. This theorem is generally true, at least in the complex setting. In the real setting, we have to add the constraint that the distance between A and B is less than the radius of the circles – otherwise there are no (real) intersections of the circles. Depending on the prover, we might have to add this information or not.

So, what is the correct notion of *theorem* for DGS? It should be connected to the user experience: If a condition (like incidence or equality) holds not only for a special placement of the free points, but for all configurations that are reachable from the current configuration by moving points, then this constitutes a theorem. This can be formulated exactly in terms of geometric straight-line programs and continuous evaluations.[28,29]

4.1.1. *Principle of Continuity*

What we described in the paragraph above can be traced back historically to Poncelet,[30] who claimed[f]

---

[f]Cited from Ref. 31, translation by the author.

A relation that has been determined with sufficient generality for
a figure is also valid for all other figures that can be deduced from
it by a continuous change of position.

Much later this has been formalized, and Felix Klein notes[31] that it is obvious (at least for him) that this is the prosaic description of the fundamental theorem of complex analysis in the setup of analytic continuations.

Indeed, the obvious postulation of a smooth (and continuous) user experience implies that the software has to use analytic continuations on Riemann surfaces internally.[32] This makes it difficult to have continuity and user-defined functions at the same time, because even simple things like the absolute value function are incompatible with this. There seems to be no way to link a DGS properly to a CAS, i.e. use the CAS calculations within the geometry part of the software. We have to examine the situation in more detail in order to come up with solutions that go beyond the "use the DGS as input tool for a CAS" strategy.

4.2. Usage Paradigms for Math Software

How do we use math software – what are the usage paradigms for the DGS and CAS? We contrast the two approaches in Table 4. 1.

Table 4. 1.   Aspects of Mathematics Software

Dynamic Geometry	computer algebra
interactive	Input/Output based
continuous/analytic	algorithmic
immediate	asynchronous
realtime	long calculations allowed
visual	symbolic

This table drastically shows that we cannot expect that DGS and CAS can be used at the same time from within the same user interface. A user who moves a point in a DGS figure expects a correct visual feedback within fractions of a second, and it is not at all possible to start a lengthy calculation and show the result later. Or, from the other perspective, we cannot expect that typing symbolic instructions will move the elements of the figure as easily as we can do by using the mouse.

On the other hand, it is highly desirable to close this gap. And indeed, we can find a successful mode of interaction between the two, as is described in the next paragraph.

4.3. *Successful Interaction Between CAS and DGS*

The solution for the problem described above is surprisingly easy, although the devil is in the details. We describe the ingredients needed.

4.3.1. *CAS as a User*

The first step is to *make the CAS a user of the DGS*. Users who move free points do not do it in an analytic way, they just move them as they like to. This observation lead to the first working interaction of the CAS Mathematica and the DGS Cinderella, as demonstrated in 2000 in Lisbon.[33]

Let us quickly review what was done there: From within the Mathematica user interface (a Mathematica *notebook*) the Cinderella software is started using the J/Link toolkit.[g] Once running, geometric elements that are present in the Cinderella kernel can be moved using Mathematica code. The code actually simulates a users' action dragging a point from one position to the other, only bypassing the conversion from screen coordinates to the homogeneous coordinates used internally.

Information about the elements, in particular their coordinates, can be retrieved from the geometry kernel calling special Java APIs that Cinderella provides. This makes it easy to create a point C that uses the x-coordinate of a point A and the y-coordinate of another point B. This very basic example can be taken as a proof of concept for the interaction. Another, more elaborated example is to simulate how a ball bounces off a wall; the calculations, including gravity, can be done easily in the CAS.[h]

Still, there is a serious drawback: All control logic is located in the Mathematica kernel, and for a true interactive update of the display the Mathematica kernel has to *poll* the data from the Cinderella kernel, usually from an infinite control loop. While this is a working approach (see Fig. 2 for a pong-style game that was written in Mathematica, using Cinderella as I/O device), it is not a sustainable approach for serious work. Apart from using system resources excessively, the design of such a control loop is overly complicated and contradicts the intuitive approach of a (geometry) tool to be used in teaching and research.

---

[g]http://www.wolfram.com/solutions/mathlink/jlink/
[h]These first examples gave rise to the integration of *CindyLab* into Cinderella.2, a basic physics simulation engine.

160

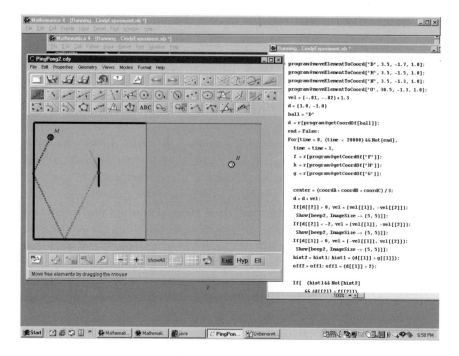

Fig. 2. A simple pong game, implemented in Mathematica, using Cinderella as I/O device. Created by Jürgen Richter-Gebert.

4.3.2. *Make CAS Results Available to Geometry*

The next step is to make the computational power of the CAS available to the DGS at places where no interactive update is necessary, i.e. when it is safe to spend a longer time for the calculation.

Again, we present an example: If you want to set the coordinates of a point to a certain position based on the coordinates of other points, say, the barycenter, then this can be achieved by typing in the appropriate formula in the DGS, which is then passed to the computer algebra system, which does the calculation and simulates a user action, and then returns. During the calculation time the DGS will not accept other input, but is waiting for the other action to finish. From a users' perspective, this user-initiated process is fully acceptable.[i]

There are similar scenarios: An ATP engine that tries to prove a con-

---

[i]Of course, calculating the barycenter is not a very time-consuming task, but you may replace this with your favorite calculation.

jecture and sends back a counter-example if it finds one, or a construction macro that creates a barycentric subdivision of a triangulation, or a routine that optimizes the area of a figure under some constraints, etc.

Note that this interaction already goes beyond the one-way communication that takes place when using DGS as an input tool only. The output of the CAS is used immediately and without further user interaction to manipulate the (former) input. The I/O-based communication that has been identified in Sect. 4.2 has been changed.

4.3.3. *Discretization: Event-based Calculation*

In a last step, we replace the last obstacle for true interactive use of both software types from within one package, the user input that initiates the communication.

The example above, where a point "inherits" the coordinates of two other points, is worth to be analyzed in more detail. The calculation does not need much time, and it is clearly possible to have it done constantly, i.e. for every new position of A and B. Whenever a point is moved, then point C should be adjusted according to the new situation.

In fact, this is the whole idea of *events* or *triggers*. A DGS that supports a mechanism where user-defined calculations in a CAS are started automatically at given moments of time – something moves, the screen is redrawn, the mouse is moved/dragged/clicked, a time interval has passed, etc. – can serve as a common user interface for both packages.

4.4. *CindyScript and Other Scripting Languages*

After the first experiments with computer algebra integration in Cinderella, we decided not to rely on an external CAS, but to integrate a functional programming language called *CindyScript* into Cinderella.2. This language allows for very easy, but still powerful, calculations using a syntax that is very similar to standard mathematical notation. There is no symbolic manipulation of formulae, instead all features of a complete programming language, like loops, conditional branching, recursion, list handling, are included. It is also possible to connect to arbitrary Java objects, thus it is possible to interface to any software that offers a Java-based API.

More details about CindyScript are in the documentation, which is available online at http://doc.cinderella.de. Here we want to concentrate on the way CindyScript is integrated into Cinderella: As identified in Sect. 4.3.3, the execution of CindyScript can be triggered automatically.

The user can attach as many scripts to any event. Mainly for debugging purposes and on-the-fly calculations there is also a *shell mode*, which is similar to the line-by-line mode of interaction with CAS (Fig. 3).

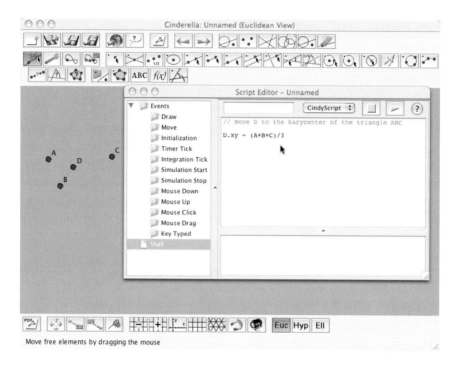

Fig. 3. The Script Editor in shell mode. The coordinates of D are set to the barycenter of A, B and C. While it is possible to retrieve the coordinates of a point using just its name, it is nevertheless required to explicitly refer to .xy to set the (affine) coordinates of D. Writing D = (A+B+C)/3 overwrites the value of the variable D (which is defaults to the point D) with the vector that contains the barycenter's coordinate.

As an easy way to add results of calculation directly to the displayed figure, one can type in a line of code that is evaluated on every recalculation of the geometric figure. The result will be shown in text form or as a function graph, both embedded into the geometric view. In addition, it is possible to write output to the screen and draw (inactive) figures using special statements in CindyScript.

The *calculate-once-and-be-happy* approach as described in Sect. 4.3.2 is also employed in Cinderella, not only in the shell mode, but also in inspection panels (Fig. 4). For example, it is possible to set the coordinates of a point to a calculated value.

Fig. 4. Setting the coordinates of point A using the built-in scripting language. The expression is evaluated once, and the coordinates of A are set. Subsequent mouse actions on A are still possible, and the expression itself is no longer used.

The language CindyScript, though recommended for beginners and built-in, is only one possibility for adding computer algebra features to the DGS kernel. As an alternative, we provide the scripting language Python,[j] and a plug-in architecture is in the works. This would allow for having a true computer algebra system like Maple or Mathematica to be used.

5. Consequences for Educational Setups

Besides the technical and mathematical challenge, the unification of DGS and CAS was started with the consequences for educational setups in mind. It is obvious that students who can stay inside one system for their mathematical work face a gentler learning curve for their tools than those who have to handle two systems. They can concentrate on content and mathematical competencies instead.

Also, in the light of holistic approaches to learning, they have easier access to simultaneous representations of mathematics. Switching the frame of reference is made easy; there is a direct connection between figures and symbolic entities. With the approach presented in the last section the usage paradigm of DGS, which is intuitive, immediate, interactive, and probably more easily to understand for beginners, is transferred to the symbolic, I/O-oriented, linearly ordered way of computer algebra, which is more suitable to advanced students and teachers.

---

[j]Based on Jython, see http://www.jython.org

But in addition to bridging the two worlds, we also open new application areas for and aspects of using mathematics software in teaching. Below, we elaborate on three of them.

5.1. *Algorithmic Thinking*

Algorithms[k] are able to enrich the mathematics curriculum. In particular, the aspect of modeling real world examples using the appropriate mathematical models has gained a lot of attention. Because a good, abstract model can be treated algorithmically on a computer, the continuous refinement circle of modeling is supplemented by a faster way of comparing the results within the abstract model and the real world.

This parallels the development in Applied Mathematics: Optimization of real-world processes has become a more and more important part of mathematics, partially due to the massive computational power available today.

The importance of the subject is reflected in more and more school curricula, and also in the standards that are adopted by teachers' associations and governmental bodies responsible for education.[34] Students' shall learn to do modeling and be able to *think mathematically*.

5.1.1. *Example: Discrete Mathematics*

A highly relevant topic that may serve as an example for the kind of mathematics described above is Discrete Mathematics, in particular Combinatorial Optimization.[35]

Cinderella.2 sports an extension package *Visage* – short for *Vis*ualizing *A*lgorithms in *Ge*ometry Software – that offers basic graph algorithms (depth-first and breadth-first search, bipartite matchings, minimum spanning trees, shortest paths, etc.) that can be used interactively.[36] Due to the tight integration with the DGS, students do not have to learn another software, but they can use and refine their media skills directly with the new content and new problems.

Also, all the features of the DGS are available for the creation of advanced online material (Fig. 5). For example, one can export exercises or pre-made animations, and use CindyScript for direct or subliminal hints.[37]

---

[k]Not *routines*, which are just recipes to guide students through standard exercises. Those are important to develop a certain *routine*, but they do not encourage mathematical thinking.

In Sect. 5.3 we discuss this as one important preliminary for bringing teachers back into charge.

Fig. 5. Example from a computer enhanced lesson about Euler Tours. Students work on a digital map that depicts the vicinity of their school, and they can directly draw the graph representation of the streets onto the map. Then, they can run a Euler Tour algorithm in order to explore the properties of their model. The map used in this lesson is © ViaMichelin.com.

In this example we can see the success of the usage paradigm integration: Algorithms, in particular for optimization, are usually unsuited for direct manipulation in an interactive environment. Using the separation process described in Sect. 4.3 we arrive at a solution that offers both ways of thinking in one interface.

5.2. *Creating Things to Think About*

Continuity in interactions seems to be problematic for teaching. A student who interacts with a construction or, worse, just watches a continuous animation, lacks 'points of interest' which can be used to agglomerate knowledge.

One easy example that illustrates this problem is the following. Using a DGS, the area of a triangle can be measured immediately. Now, when changing the triangle with the mouse, the student can watch (and learn) that the area *changes* when the vertices of the triangle move. This (trivial) fact does not help him: In theory, the student could find out the proper way to calculate the area of a triangle using the DGS, provided that he moves the vertices into the right positions, followed by formulating a hypothesis and doing more experiments. However, he has to have a clear idea about this kind of *strategy*.

We can help the student by using a code snippet that changes the continuous display of measurement to a discrete one:

```
if( area(A,B,C) > 10 ,
   "The area is larger than 10 cm²",
   if( area(A,B,C) = 10,
      "The area is exactly 10 cm²",
      "The area is smaller than 10 cm²"
   )
)
```

Using this or similar code we reduce the changes that are not directly caused by the user to the minimum necessary. Moving a single vertex of the triangle will literally create a *line of events*, parallel to the baseline of the triangle at the distance that is 5 divided by the length of the baseline.

Moving the vertex will not create any unexpected behavior besides the flip between *larger* and *smaller*, thus focussing attention to this line, suggesting further inspection. In the unmodified example, students will experience *only* expected behavior: The area changes when the triangle changes.

5.3. *Bringing Teachers Back into Charge*

In the preceding sections we have seen that the combination of DGS and CAS is possible and can be fruitful for new media-based educational scenarios. At the same time, we are aware of the fact that many of these new scenarios can also be created using standard authoring tools (say, *Macromedia Director*) or general purpose programming languages with graphical interfaces like Java.[1]

There are important advantages of the demonstrated approach:

---

[1] http://www.java.com

(a) The available features of – and extension packages for – DGS and CAS make it easy to arrive at sophisticated electronic teaching material.

(b) By using mathematical tools, it is much easier to arrive at a mathematically correct endproduct. The built-in support of projective geometry in a DGS takes care of many pitfalls that are present when creating a custom geometry tool, just to name one example.

(c) Students do not have to learn new user interfaces.[m]

The final consequence of these advantages is that teachers are enabled to create or modify electronic activities *themselves*. Thus, they may continue teaching in their own, personal style for teaching. Like they create traditional activities or combine paper-based exercises into new ones, they can adapt available electronic assets, re-combine it, and complement it with their own works.

Instead of replacing teachers we enable them to teach better by offering them more options to their methods. They are not forced to adhere to common guidelines in order to make use of electronic material, but they can pursue their individual style, without sacrificing access to modern teaching material. This respects their role as human beings who can serve as good mentors to their students.

6. Further Integration and Other Approaches

In this last section we just want to mention some other approaches at the intersection of computer algebra and interactive geometry. Some of them are extensions of what we described above, some are alternatives or just supplements.

6.1. *OpenMath*

OpenMath[38] is an XML-based description language for mathematical content. In contrast to MathML it is specifically designed to capture the semantics of mathematics, not only the presentation.[n]

D. A. Roozemond[39,40] used a translation of a geometric statement into OpenMath code, followed by several transformations from one OpenMath

---

[m]Much educational software is written using Director, and each of them tries to invent new user interfaces for entering data, selecting options, etc. While these new metaphors are sometimes inspired by educational reasons, this always bears the danger of adding new interaction barriers.

[n]Recent developments for MathML make this distinction less acute, but the basic historic roots of each still support the statement.

encoding to another, to feed a geometric conjecture into GAP.[41] Then, a variant of the binomial prover written in GAP was used to prove the conjecture, if possible. The result was translated back into a readable proof, and the user could highlight the hypotheses used by the proof back in the geometric figure. Similar approaches were shown at the ADG conference 2006.[42]

A similar implementation was used by the author to translate figures described using the `plangeo` content dictionaries of OpenMath[43] into actual drawings using server-side-Java. This project has not been continued; instead, there is a European consortium of software providers and education specialists that started the Intergeo project°. Among other things, a common OpenMath-based geometry exchange language shall be developed within the project.

Finally, we want to mention GOOL, a new language for the description of geometry that is currently in development.[44] It is another proof for the rising importance of data exchange for mathematical software.

6.2. *Extended Use of Symbolic Computation for the Geometry Kernel*

Once a working link is established between a computer algebra kernel and a geometry software, more advanced calculations become available to the geometry kernel. These can be used for internal proving and also for advanced user interfaces.[19]

It is immediate to apply symbolic computation to the automatic recognition loci as algebraic curves – by translating the generated traces of a point into a symbolic form we already perform the paradigm shift from DGS to CAS. Lebmeir and Richter[45] describe a way to do this systematically using Eigenvalues, the most recent version of Cabri Geometry includes a heuristic approach that can find symbolic forms of many loci.[46] Gawlick[47] discusses the implications of such systems to education.

Another application is the use of advanced algorithms like PSLQ, though we will not discuss this here.

6.3. *Geometry Expressions*

Saltire software introduced the DGS *Geometry Expressions*, which also integrates a symbolic kernel.[48] The system provides an extremely easy way

---

°http://inter2geo.eu

to find symbolic representations and relations between elements (resp. their coordinates). Its user interface is similar to the user interface of other DGS, but internally the software is much more similar to a parametric CAD system. There is no notion of free or dependent elements, but all elements are considered equal.

The relations between elements are added manually or automatically. That is, a midpoint M of points A and B can be defined as a point on the line A and B that is equidistant to A and B. Geometry expressions then automatically finds appropriate symbolic descriptions of elements in terms of others. These are used for the automatic update on the movement of elements.

This approach is very appealing, but in its current implementation there are several issues that show how intricate it is for the final user experience. For example, the user has almost no control over the equation systems that determine the behavior of the construction. Constructions behave neither symmetric (the internal handling is dependent on the order in which the relations are added) nor truly predictable. In case of theorems (which should be an area of excellence for the software, as it "knows" much more than other DGS about the geometric situations) it can happen that it incorrectly claims that an additional constraint cannot be added.

From an educational point of view, it is questionable whether one really wants to loose the distinction between free and dependent elements. The traditional approach with its clear semantics that are similar to the kind of functional thinking needed in other areas of mathematics is lost. Instead, students experience a black box behavior. That contributes to the mystical appearance of mathematics in public that mathematics education tries to demystify.

That said, Geometry Expressions definitely is a promising and new development in the area of DGS, in particular for DGS and CAS integration.

6.4. *Feli-X*

Many other geometry packages claim to have computer algebra integration. Usually, this is just a way of stating that simple calculations that use functions can be done. Some packages, for example GeoGebra,[49] include some easy symbolic features like formal derivation. While these are useful features that might suffice for most school activities, they can hardly be counted as *computer algebra* integration.[50]

The package Feli-X of Reinhard Oldenburg[51,52] sticks out by providing a true integration based on an alternative interpretation of the user interface.

It is based on the computer algebra system MuPAD with custom extensions, with prior versions using Maple or Mathematica as the base system. The constraints are entered explicitly in form of symbolic equations (there are tools that allow for the easy addition of standard relations). Using plug-in strategies for re-adjusting the elements after an element has been moved, it is possible to fine-tune the behavior of any construction. Over-constrained systems are handled as well – instead of disallowing over-constraints as does Geometry Expressions, the defect of each unsatisfied constraint is shown.

Unfortunately, the system is not easily portable or distributable, so there have not been widespread tests in the classroom. It is clear, however, that such an advanced and powerful system needs properly educated teachers in order to be used in a sensible manner. Like Geometry Expressions, this software shows that there are still new exciting developments in the area of DGS.

Acknowledgements

I would like to thank Jürgen Richter-Gebert, who is responsible for most of the described extensions, in particular for CindyLab and CindyScript. Many thanks to Phil Todd who provided a license for Geometry Expressions.

The Visage project has been supported by the DFG Research Center MATHEON "Mathematics for key technologies" in Berlin.

References

1. J. E. Baker and S. J. Sugden, Spreadsheets in education — The first 25 years, *Spreadsheets in Education* **1**, 18 (2003).
2. S. Abramovich, Spreadsheet-enhanced problem solving in context as modeling, *Spreadsheets in Education* **1**, 1 (2003).
3. E. Neuwirth and D. Arganbright, *The Active Modeler: Mathematical Modeling with Microsoft Excel* (Brooks/Cole, Belmont, 2004).
4. U. Kortenkamp, Foundations of Dynamic Geometry, Dissertation, ETH Zürich, Institut für Theoretische Informatik, 1999, `http://kortenkamps.net/papers/1999/diss.pdf`.
5. D. Lewkowicz and K. Kraebel, The value of multimodal redundancy in the development of intersensory perception, in *Handbook of Multisensory Processing*, eds. G. Calvert, C. Spence and B. Stein (MIT Press, Cambridge, 2004).
6. M. Vogel, Mathematisieren funktionaler Zusammenhänge mit multimediabasierter Supplantation, PhD thesis, Pädagogische Hochschule Ludwigsburg, 2006.
7. J. Roth, Bewegliches Denken im Mathematikunterricht, PhD thesis, Universität Würzburg, 2006.

8. A. Kittel, Dynamische Geometrie-Systeme in der Hauptschule — Eine interpretative Untersuchung an Fallbeispielen und ausgewählten Aufgaben der Sekundarstufe, PhD thesis, Pädagogische Hochschule Schwäbisch Gmünd, 2007.

9. G. Salomon, Can we affect cognitive skills through visual media? An hypothesis and initial findings, *AV Communication Review* **20**, 401 (1972).

10. H. Schumann, *Schulgeometrisches Konstruieren mit dem Computer* (Metzler/Teubner, Stuttgart, 1991).

11. U. Kortenkamp and J. Richter-Gebert, Geometry and education in the Internet age, in *Proc. ED-MEDIA 98*, 1998.

12. P. Bender, Dynamische-Geometrie-Software (DGS) in der Erstsemester-Vorlesung — Ein Werkstatt-Bericht über ein Entwicklungs- und ein Forschungs-Projekt, in *Neuen Medien und Bildungsstandarts. Bericht über die 22. Arbeitstagung des Arbeitskreises Mathematikunterricht und Informatik*, eds. P. Bender, W. Herget, H.-G. Weigand and T. Weth (Franzbecker, Hildesheim, Berlin, 2004).

13. B. Lawler, Designing computer-based microworlds, in *New Horizons in Educational Computing* (Ellis Horwood, Chinchester, 1984).

14. C. Hoyles, Microworlds/schoolworlds: The transformation of an innovation, in *Learning from Computers: Mathematics Education and Technology* (C. Keitel and K. Ruthven, Berlin, 1993).

15. R. Hölzl, Im Zugmodus der Cabri Geometrie, PhD thesis, Universität Augsburg, 1994.

16. U. Kortenkamp, Experimental mathematics and proofs — What is secure mathematical knowledge? *Zentralblatt für Didaktik der Mathematik* **36**, 61 (2004).

17. P. Bender, Basic imagery and understandings for mathematical concepts, in *8th International Congress on Mathematics Education: Selected Lectures*, eds. C. Alsina et al. (S.A.E.M Thales, Sevilla, 1996) pp. 57–74.

18. U. Kortenkamp, Punkt- und Achsenspiegelungen, online teaching material, http://www.lehrer-online.de/url/spiegelungen.

19. U. Kortenkamp and J. Richter-Gebert, Using automatic theorem proving to improve the usability of geometry software, in *Proc. MathUI 2004*, ed. P. Libbrecht (Bialowiecza, Poland, 2004).

20. W. Müller, C. Bescherer, U. Kortenkamp and C. Spannagel, Intelligent computed-aided assessment in the math classroom: State-of-the-art and perspectives, in *Proc. IFIP WG 3.1, 3.3, & 3.5 Joint Conference "Imagining the Future for ICT and Education"* (Ålesund, 2006).

21. D. Wang, Geometry machines: From AI to SMC, in *Proc. Artificial Intelligence and Symbolic Mathematical Computation 3*, eds. J. Calmet, J. A. Campbell and J. Pfalzgraf, Lecture Notes in Computer Science, Vol. 1138 (Springer-Verlag, Berlin Heidelberg, September 1996).

22. W.-T. Wu, *Mechanical Theorem Proving in Geometries: Basic Principles. Transl. from the Chinese by Xiaofan Jin and Dongming Wang.* Texts and Monographs in Symbolic Computation (Springer-Verlag, Wien New York, 1994).

23. D. Cox, J. Little and D. O'Shea, *Ideals, Varieties, and Algorithms: An Introduction to Computational Algebraic Geometry and Commutative Algebra*, second edn. Undergraduate Texts in Mathematics (Springer-Verlag, New York, 1997).

24. J. Richter-Gebert and U. Kortenkamp, *The Interactive Geometry Software Cinderella*, Book & CD-ROM (Springer-Verlag, Berlin Heidelberg New York, 1999).

25. J. Richter-Gebert, Mechanical theorem proving in projective geometry, *Annals of Mathematics and Artificial Intelligence* **13**, 139 (1995).

26. S.-C. Chou, X.-S. Gao and J.-Z. Zhang, An introduction to geometry expert, in *CADE-13: Proc. 13th International Conference on Automated Deduction* (Springer-Verlag, Berlin Heidelberg, 1996).

27. X.-S. Gao and Q. Lin, MMP/Geometer — A software package for automated geometry reasoning, in *Proc. ADG 2002*, ed. F. Winkler (Springer-Verlag, Berlin Heidelberg, 2004).

28. J. Richter-Gebert and U. Kortenkamp, Complexity issues in dynamic geometry, in *Foundations of Computational Mathematics (Proc. Smale Fest 2000)*, eds. F. Cucker and J. M. Rojas (World Scientific, 2002). Also available as technical report TRB-2000/22, Freie Universität Berlin.

29. B. Denner-Broser, On the decidability of tracing problems in dynamic geometry, in *Proc. ADG 2004*, LNAI 3763, eds. H. Hong and D. Wang (Springer-Verlag, Berlin Heidelberg, 2006).

30. J.-V. Poncelet, *Traité des propriétés projectives des figures* (Gauthier-Villars, 1822).

31. F. Klein, *Elementarmathematik vom höheren Standpunkt aus.*, Die Grundlehren der mathematischen Wissenschaften in Einzeldarstellungen, Vol. 2, reprint 1968 edn. (Springer-Verlag, 1925).

32. J. Richter-Gebert and U. Kortenkamp, Grundlagen Dynamischer Geometrie, in *Zeichnung – Figur – Zugfigur*, eds. H.-W. Henn, H.-J. Elschenbroich and T. Gawlick (Franzbecker, Hildesheim, Berlin, 2001) pp. 123–144.

33. U. Kortenkamp, The future of mathematical software, in *Proc. MTCM 2000* (Springer-Verlag, 2001).

34. National Council of Teachers of Mathematics, Principles and standards for school mathematics (Reston, VA, 2000).

35. B. Lutz-Westphal, Kombinatorische Optimierung — Inhalte und Methoden für einen authentischen Mathematikunterricht, PhD thesis, Technische Universität Berlin, 2006.

36. A. Geschke, U. Kortenkamp, B. Lutz-Westphal and D. Materlik, Visage – Visualization of Algorithms in Discrete Mathematics, *Zentralblatt für Didaktik der Mathematik* **37**, 395 (2005).

37. U. Kortenkamp, Guidelines for using computers creatively in mathematics education, in *Proc. 1st KAIST Symposium on Enhancing University Mathematics Teaching*, ed. D. Arganbright (KAIST, Daejon, 2005).

38. The OpenMath Consortium, OpenMath, http://www.openmath.org.

39. D. A. Roozemond, Automatic geometric theorem proving, Bachelor Project, http://www.win.tue.nl/~amc/ow/bachproj/BachelorProjectAGTP.pdf

(July 2003).

40. D. A. Roozemond, Automated proofs using bracket algebra with cinderella and openmath, in *Proc. 9th Rhine Workshop on Computer Algebra (RWCA 2004)*, 2004.

41. The GAP Group, *GAP – Groups, Algorithms, and Programming, Version 4.4* (2004).

42. J. Escribano, M. Á. Abánades, J. L. Valcarce and F. Botana, On using Open-Math for enhancing reasoning abilities in dynamic geometry systems, in *Proc. ADG 2006*, 2006.

43. A. M. Cohen, H. Sterk and H. Cuypers, Plangeo Dictionaries for OpenMath, `http://www.win.tue.nl/~amc/oz/om/cds/geometry.html`.

44. T. Liang and D. Wang, Towards a geometric-object-oriented-language, in *Proc. ADG 2004*, LNAI 3763, eds. H. Hong and D. Wang (Springer-Verlag, Berlin Heidelberg, 2006).

45. P. Lebmeir and J. Richter-Gebert, Recognition of computationally constructed loci, in *Proc. ADG 2006*, 2006.

46. *Cabri Geometry II Plus* (Cabrilog, 2002).

47. T. Gawlick, Exploration reel algebraischer Kurven mit DGS, in *Zeichnung – Figur – Zugfigur*, eds. H.-J. Elschenbroich, T. Gawlick and H.-W. Henn (Franzbecker, Hildesheim, 2001).

48. P. Todd, Geometry expressions: A constraint based interactive symbolic geometry system, *Computeralgebra-Rundbrief* **39** (2006).

49. M. Hohenwarter, GeoGebra – Didaktische Materialien und Anwendungen für den Mathematikunterricht, PhD thesis, Universität Salzburg, 2006.

50. R. Oldenburg, GeoGebra: Dynamische Geometrie mit etwas Algebra, *Computeralgebra-Rundbrief* **36** (2005).

51. R. Oldenburg, Feli-X – Ein computeralgebra-gestütztes dynamisches Geometrieprogramm, *Computeralgebra-Rundbrief* **34** (2004).

52. R. Oldenburg, Feli-X – Ein Prototyp zur Integration von CAS und DGS, in *WWW und Mathematik – Lehren und Lernen im Internet. Berichte von der 21. Arbeitstagung des Arbeitskreis Mathematikunterricht und Informatik*, eds. P. Bender, W. Herget, H.-G. Weigand and T. Weth (Franzbecker, Hildesheim, Berlin, 2004).

INTEGRATING RULE-BASED AND INPUT-BASED APPROACHES FOR BETTER ERROR DIAGNOSIS IN EXPRESSION MANIPULATION TASKS

REIN PRANK*, MARINA ISSAKOVA, DMITRI LEPP, ENO TONISSON
and VAHUR VAIKSAAR

Institute of Computer Science, University of Tartu
Liivi 2-306 Tartu, 50409, Estonia
* E-mail: rein.prank@ut.ee

T-algebra is a project for creating interactive problem solving environment for basic school expression manipulation exercises: calculation of the values of numerical expressions; operations with fractions; solving of linear equations, inequalities and linear equation systems; operations with monomials and polynomials. This article describes and motivates solution step interface and error diagnostics developed in T-algebra.

Keywords: Problem solving environment, error diagnostics, elementary algebra.

1. Introduction

Expression manipulation skills are important for solving tasks in practically all fields of mathematics. Therefore the students solve in the school hundreds of technical exercises with fractions, monomials, polynomials, equations and systems of equations. However, we are often not satisfied with the results of learning in this area. Even many university students at the faculties of mathematics or computer science mix up elementary conversion rules and are unable to avoid numerous mistakes. One of the reasons for this seems to be the fact that the students do not get necessary feedback about their work during the school mathematics classes. The solutions of expression manipulation exercises are long and contain many details. The teachers are unable to supervise the students' training in real time, discover all the mistakes and correct them. The need for quick analysis of large volumes of information indicates that the training and testing of expression manipulation skills could be improved by using computerized environments.

This paper describes the design ideas and error diagnosing possibilities of interactive learning environment T-algebra developed at the University of Tartu beginning from 2004. The goal of this project is to create an environment for solving expression manipulation tasks in four areas of basic school mathematics:

- calculation of the values of numerical expressions
- operations with fractions
- solving of linear equations, inequalities and linear equation systems
- operations with monomials and polynomials.

T-algebra implements more than 50 problem types. Some of them are integrated types that summarize the content of an entire chapter in textbook (*"Solve linear equation"*), some others are devoted to one single step in algorithm (*"Move terms with unknown to left and constants to right"*).

Our aim is not to design a comfortable conversion machine to help strong students to solve advanced problems. Some existing programs[1,2] do this well enough. We try to support the weaker part of the students who often do not know the algorithms for solving the standard tasks, have problems with understanding the syntax of expressions, and make many mistakes when they execute the algorithm steps. Designing the solution dialogue for T-algebra, we have been guided by the didactical principle that all the necessary decisions and calculations at each solution step should be made by the student, and the program should be able to give hints and to understand mistakes.

In Section 2 of this paper we discuss suitability of rule-based and input-based dialogue schemes for diagnostic purposes. Section 3 describes our three-component solution step and input modes in T-algebra. Section 4 describes how the information entered by the students is used for diagnosing mistakes made at different stages of a solution step and what difficulties we have with diagnostics. In Section 5 the results and problems for further research are summarized.

2. What Type of Learning Environment Do We Need?

The history of learning environments for expression manipulation is considerably shorter than the history of elementary counting drills or the success story of dynamic geometry. Good programming tools for writing WYSI-WYG expression editors did not exist for a long time and even the computer algebra systems (CAS) had linear command-line input. Today we have already some more or less commonly accepted expression editing standards and these standards are sufficiently well supported by programming environments. As a result, practically usable programs for students are available.

We can point out two types of existing interactive environments with essentially different expression manipulation dialogue:

(1) Rule-based manipulation environments;
(2) Input-based manipulation environments.

A typical rule-based environment is MathXpert.[1] Using this program, the student begins each conversion step by marking some subexpression to be changed. The program displays then a menu with a list of rules, which are applicable to the marked subexpression. Then the student selects a rule and the program applies the rule to the marked subexpression (or to suitable parts of the marked subexpression) and writes the result together with unchanged parts of the previous expression to next line. MathXpert has hundreds of rules of different capacity and enables to construct solutions of different granularity. A similar scheme for conversion steps is used in programs developed in the framework of the Stanford Educational Program for Gifted Youth,[2] but this program asks in addition the student to fill sometimes some input boxes with coefficients, exponents, *etc.* The current version of Cognitive Algebra Tutor by Carnegie Learning[3] is likewise built on applying rules. AlgeBrain[4] is a small Intelligent Tutor for solving equations in rule-based interface. The use of computer algebra systems belongs also to rule-based work. But computer algebra systems have a serious disadvantage in comparison with programs written for educational use. They have very powerful commands for solving most task types of school mathematics in one step but do not have sufficiently detailed commands for construction of stepwise solutions. Such choice of rules is characteristic even for systems like WIRIS[5] that are designed and advertised especially for using in schools.

Input-based systems use paper-and-pencil-like dialogue design where a transformation step consists mainly of entering the next line. For example, Aplusix[6] copies the content of previous line (expression, equation or system of equations) to the next line and the student should edit it into the result of the step. The program displays between two lines the indicator of equivalence, giving the student feedback about correctness of the step. MATH-TEACHER[7] is another example of input-based solution environment but in this program the expressions are entered in old-fashioned linear form. An early version of Cognitive Algebra Tutor[8] used also purely entering of the result and the program tried to figure out what step was performed.

Let us now compare the dialogues of both types with the range of decisions that the student should make at each conversion step. At each solution step the student should

(1) Choose a transformation rule corresponding to a certain operation in the algorithm for current task (or some simplification or calculation rule known earlier);
(2) Select the operands (certain parts of expressions or equations) for this rule;
(3) Replace them with the result of the operation.

Some more "creative" tasks (such as factorization or integration) are taught in less algorithmic style but the solutions are expected to consist of operations of the same structure.

When solving a task in the rule-based system, the student's role is to know or to invent the solution strategy. The program executes all operations as a black box. In such scheme the learning of details of operations is passive and many typical mistakes are simply impossible. In order to learn to execute new operations and to test the expression manipulation skills we need an environment where all the decisions and calculations would be made by the student. It is clear that for such aims the environment should include input of new expression (or of the changed part of the expression) by the student.

In case of input-based dialogue the whole solution step is performed by the student. The student has the possibility to undertake whatever steps and to make arbitrary mistakes. His input is restricted only by syntax of expressions. The computer is now in the same situation as the teacher who should check a solution script on the paper: there is no explicit information about the student's decisions at the first two stages of the steps. Without knowing what operation was applied to what part(s) of previous expression and without restrictions on the number of operations applied during one step, it is very hard to diagnose errors more precisely than "expressions are not equivalent".

Experimental systems for diagnostics of algebraic errors in such situation were created in Intelligent Tutoring community already in the seventies of the last century. The programs used libraries of correct and buggy conversion rules (extracted by teachers from students' written solutions). If the entered expression was incorrect, then the program tried to model its underlying derivation, combining different buggy rules with correct ones. A good presentation about the ideas of that period is given in Ref. 9. Some subsequent trials are described in Ref. 10 and Ref. 11. It is clear that in expression manipulation the students really use some mixture of correct and buggy rules and therefore this approach seems to be adequate. Nevertheless we have not yet seen completed programs producing sufficiently detailed analysis of mistakes. Beside difficulties in detection of the source of the error, the systems with unrestricted extent of the step have also problems with providing intelligible feedback. The authors of the input-based version of Cognitive Algebra Tutor complained that "... the student's error might well have occurred at some intermediate step that the students were no longer fixated upon. It was very difficult to communicate to the student what the problem was." (Ref. 8, p. 42). After a period of silence quite serious new attempts of application of classical AI methods in expression manipulation exercises were reported at ITS 2006. The team of APLUSIX has started building rule-based diagnostics.[12] C. Zinn[13] presented the main ideas of rule-based reasoning and diagnostics of another system, SLOPERT, developed in Saarbrücken for tutoring of differentiation.

The task of error localization/diagnostics can be simplified when the program sets constraints to student's input. Some programs prescribe the form of entered expression, using less or more detailed textual instructions and/or splitting the input area in more than one specialized input boxes (for instance, separate boxes for numerator and denominator of fractions). Such measures are sometimes used already in quite primitive commercial products that then compare the student's input piecewise as strings with 'correct answer'. But such interface can be combined with more intelligent analysis. Similar effect can be achieved when the program tells what rule should be applied or the student has to choose the rule from the menu. For example, interactive exercises on addition of fractions in WIMS server (Ref. 14, OEF fractions/Guided addition) use both ways. For each step the student has to choose first the rule from the menu that contains together with correct choice also some buggy and some unsuitable rules. After that he has to enter different parts of the fractions into different boxes. But it seems that at every step the menu proposes only one correct way to continue the solution.

Several successful attempts have been made to incorporate computer algebra systems in error diagnosis and automated creation of solutions in expression manipulation tasks. The abovementioned Stanford program[2] used Maple. Several recent quiz systems are built on CAS. For example, AIM[15] uses Maple and STACK[16] uses Maxima. The quiz systems ask the student to enter the final answer of the task and therefore in general they are not the environments for stepwise solution. But the methods developed for questions about conversions can be suitable for arbitrary conversion steps. It is clear that the CAS can provide for quiz system the tools for checking of equivalence (equality) of student's answer and correct (CAS-computed) answer. Computer algebra systems have also utilities for checking whether the answer belongs to required syntactic category of expressions. For example, the factorization questions in AIM and STACK are designed to include checks whether the entered expression has completely factorized form, and they denote it even when the answer is completely wrong. Using the programming environment of corresponding CAS, it is possible for the authors of questions to implement nontrivial diagnostics for more precise assessment and feedback. But the required detailed work on a large number of question (task) types is only in the beginning stages.

Some design ideas of T-algebra originate from our earlier work in Tartu. In 1988–91 we developed a program package for exercises in Mathematical Logic.[17] One of the programs was interactive environment for stepwise solution of formula manipulation exercises in Propositional Logic (expression of formulas through $\{\&, \neg\}$, $\{\vee, \neg\}$ or $\{\supset, \neg\}$ and finding normal forms). The first version of this program worked with a pure input interface. At every step the student typed on the next line a new formula (having some copy-paste possibilities). The program checked the syntax, equivalence with the previous line and whether the target form of the expression was reached. We saw that the errors of misunderstanding of the order of operations were most dangerous. We were generally unable to diagnose them without explicit information about the object of conversion. In the second version[18] the step dialog was built using an Object-Action scheme. The student had to mark some subformula and to convert it then to the result of the step. The strings before and after the marked subformula were copied automatically. For the second substep the program had two working modes: input and selection of a conversion rule from the menu. As a result, the program was able to verify separately the selection of operand and the performed conversion. This addition of a marking phase gave us a level of feedback that was sufficient for that group of users (second-year students) and we did not have any further need to make it more precise.

3. Solution Step Dialogue in T-algebra

Our main concern in designing the dialog for T-algebra[19] has been to create preconditions for being able to diagnose and to give understandable feedback about mistakes at all three stages of a solution step. We have done this rather straightforwardly: the student enters not only the result of the step but also his first two decisions. At each solution step the student performs three actions:

(1) Selects an operation from the menu;
(2) Marks the operand(s) in expression;
(3) Enters the result of operation.

Unlike many other programs, T-algebra requires precise marking of operands for diagnostic purposes. For example, for the operation "Combine like terms" the student should mark only those terms that will be actually combined. (The program allows the preceding pluses and minuses to be marked or not.) For reducing the fraction where numerator and/or denominator consist of several factors, only those factors that will be actually reduced should be marked. Accordingly, the editor of T-algebra enables to mark more than one piece of the expression. Precise marking requires from the student more work at the second substep. However, leaving the parts that will not be changed unmarked means also that these parts will be copied onto the next line automatically and this reduces the amount of work at input.

Figure 1 demonstrates the solution window where the student has selected the rule *Multiply/Divide monomials* and has already marked two terms for multiplying.

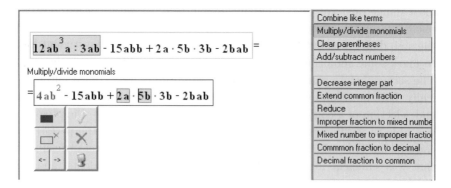

Fig. 1.   Solution window during execution of the first two stages of a step.

The first two substeps are not separated in T-algebra. At the beginning of our project we presumed that the three actions should be made in the abovementioned order and we named our interaction scheme "Action-Object-Input". When we started our first experiments with students, we wrote the order of substeps on blackboard. However, the program accidentally enabled to mark one subexpression already before selection of the rule (for copying). In the classroom we saw that the students often wanted to mark the operand(s) before selecting the rule from the menu. They suspected that the impossibility to mark the second operand before selection of the rule was a mistake in the program (we had told them that the program is not ready yet). Analyzing this experience, we decided to change the dialogue and to amalgamate the first two substeps. The student can mark the operands before, after, or even before and after selection of the rule. During the marking process the program checks only that each marked piece is a syntactically correct subexpression. Proper checking of Action and Object begins only when the student confirms both stages by clicking the green check button on the virtual keyboard. The student has to correct his first two decisions until they are accepted by the program.

When T-algebra accepts Action and Operands, the unmarked parts from the previous line will be copied onto the next line and the program asks the student to enter the result of applying the selected operation to the marked operands. T algebra has three input modes for entering the result of the step: *Free input*, *Structured input* and *Partial input*. In different input modes T-algebra offers different number and types of boxes for entering the result. The three different modes of an input stage following from the situation presented in Fig. 1 (after the third monomial is also selected for multiplying) are pictured in Fig. 2. The colored boxes are initially empty and the student enters their content during the stage.

Fig. 2.   Three input modes.

In the **free mode**, the entire resulting subexpression is entered into one single box. In case of operations where the result is not a single subexpression (some operations with fractions and equations) T-algebra offers two boxes. Free mode is implemented in principle in the same way for all the rules of T-algebra. In the free mode the student has almost the same degree of freedom as when writing solution steps on paper. All decisions about the structure of the result and about the values of component parts are made by the student. The student has the possibility to make almost arbitrary mistakes. Such mode is indispensable for testing the knowledge of students, even if the amount of input is high.

Besides free input we have also sought working modes where the program would support the student with some suggestions and/or would reduce the amount of keyboard work by displaying some obvious parts of the result automatically. In his Master thesis in 2003 D. Lepp tried to design natural dialogues for different operations with monomials and polynomials.[20] We saw that if we follow the essence of each operation too punctually we get a program where every rule has its own user interface. Therefore we decided to design two standardized additional input modes.

In the **structured mode**, the program prescribes the structure of the resulting subexpression(s), offering a set of boxes that enable to enter specific parts of the expression: signs, numbers, variables, monomials, powers, *etc.* For this T-algebra uses the received information about the intentions of the student, calculates the correct result and produces corresponding boxes for filling out. Nevertheless it is still possible not to write unary plus, coefficient or exponent 1, and even to leave all boxes empty if the member has coefficient zero. In some cases we do not want to prescribe the complete structure of the result. For example, in the case of multiplication of polynomials we do not want to predict the number of resulting monomials. The program creates only some monomial-structured groups of boxes and the virtual keyboard contains a button for adding the next group. Input in prescribed structure helps the student to some extent. On the other hand, it gives the possibility to formulate more precise error messages and to indicate the position of errors.

In the **partial mode**, T-algebra fills some parts of the structured result automatically the user has to enter only the critical parts of the result. For example, in the case of combining like terms, only the sign and coefficient of the resulting monomial should be entered; variables and their powers are filled automatically. Input modes of T-algebra are described more precisely in Ref. 21.

There are a few transformations where the way they are performed in the first school exercises necessitated some additions to our general input scheme. For instance, in the case of addition of fractions in two structured modes we decided to ask and check separately the common denominator and extenders before entering the complete result (Fig. 3). The rule for multiplication/division of both sides of equation asks about corresponding factor, *etc.* A more detailed description of the solution dialogue together with exceptions is given in Ref. 22.

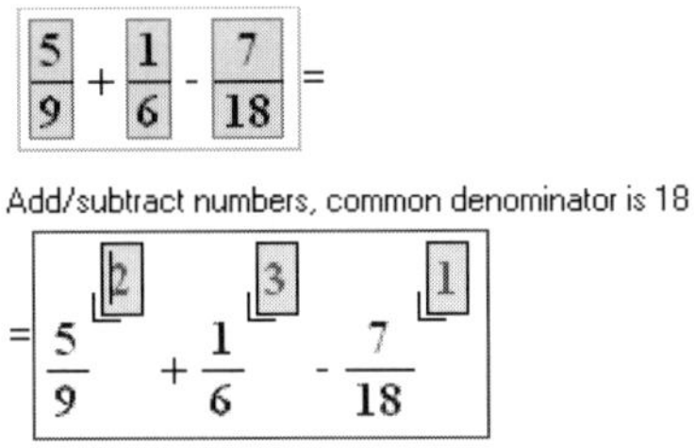

Fig. 3. Input of intermediate result when adding/subtracting fractions with different denominators.

In the current version of T-algebra, the input mode for each exercise is predefined by the teacher/author in a problem file and cannot be changed by the student. In the future it would be conceivable to change the mode dynamically: if the student does not cope with work in the free mode the program would deliver the tasks in more detailed modes for a certain period.

After description of the step dialogue we can appraise how much work our interface requires from the student. It is obvious that in the rule-based environments the student mostly does not enter the expressions and so the amount of input is considerably smaller and the input itself is simpler. Let us compare the work in T-algebra with pure-input interface.

In our interface the student should: select a rule, mark operand(s) in initial expression and enter the changed part of the expression. The first substep requires only one click of the mouse. The third substep is required in a pure-input interface too. Consider our second substep. In pure-input interface the student should form the next-line expression from empty input box or from previous-line expression. In the first case he should mark and copy the unchanged parts from the previous line one by one or enter them from keyboard. In the second case he should mark and delete all changed parts. So we see that marking of all bounds of operands is concealed in a pure-input interface as well (if not replaced by total input of the whole new line). Consequently our interface requires practically the same amount of input work as pure-input interface.

The first experiments with students already demonstrated that our concept of a three-component interface is understandable to students and teachers. Some difficulties arise with students who are not confident in terminology and have troubles with understanding the names of rules.

4. What Can We Diagnose in A-O-I-Interface?

4.1. *What Can Be Decided About the Selected Operation?*

It is quite easy to decide that the selected operation:

(1) cannot be applied to any subterm(s) of the current expression
(2) does not correspond to the algorithm to be learned (if such exists for actual problem type).

However we prefer not to check the selected rule separately. When the student confirms both the selection and marking then T-algebra checks the possibility to apply the selected rule to the marked subexpression(s).

In fact, checking of the possibility is implemented in T-algebra for other purposes. If the student selects an impossible rule and asks for help for marking the operands then T-algebra responds that the application of the selected rule is impossible. However after confirming an impossible rule together with some marked subexpression(s) the message explains what should be the form of the operand(s) for the selected rule.

Concerning the second issue we intend to add in the future warning messages if the selected operation does not correspond to the "official" algorithm and is not a simplification or calculation rule. After such message the student can continue or cancel the rule.

4.2. *Checking the Operation and Marking of Operands Together*

T-algebra diagnoses the following errors of selection of operands:

(1) Marked term is not a syntactically correct expression;
(2) Marked expression is not a proper subexpression (order of operations misunderstood);
(3) Operand does not have the form required for selected rule;
(4) Operands do not satisfy the compatibility requirements (are not like terms, *etc.*);
(5) Operands do not satisfy the location requirements (do not belong to the same sum, fraction, product, *etc.*);
(6) Number of marked operands does not correspond to selected operation (only one needed, at least two needed, *etc.*).

The first two issues are checked already when the student marks pieces of the expression as operands. The next four depend on the selected rule and are checked when the student confirms both rule and operands.

It is important to note here that our wish to diagnose errors 4–6 has lead us to certain restriction in making expression manipulation steps: T-algebra does not permit parallel use of rule in one step (collection of several groups of like terms, multiplication of more than one group of terms, *etc.*). This is in slight contradiction with mathematical practice on paper and gives rise to some error messages of types 4–6 in the beginning of use of T-algebra but these problems disappear quickly. Exclusion of parallel conversions makes the solution longer but does not cause additional typing work because the program copies unchanged parts of the expression automatically to the next line. It also improves the readability of the resulting solution script.

Errors of types 1 and 6 can be often simply oversight errors where the student has marked something else than he wanted (only one of two brackets included, no operands marked at all, *etc.*). In the pure-input interface where the student does not have to mark arguments he cannot make such errors and therefore produces a correct step. The same can sometimes be true for other error types as well but often the reasons are much more serious: the student does not understand the order of operations, the meaning of some mathematical expression, or the nature of some expression manipulation operation/rule. For example, some students understand $-3(2x+3)$ like addition between -3, $2x$ and 3, as if it would be written $-3 + (2x + 3)$. This mistake is actually not a mistake in moving terms to other side, but a mistake in opening parentheses. However, in T-algebra this mistake was discovered during the selection of the parts for the rule *Move terms to other side* (Fig. 4). In case of pure-input interface conversion of irrelevant

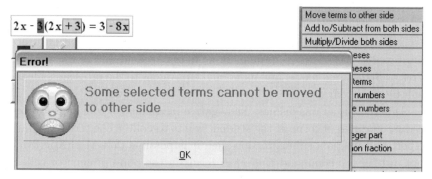

Fig. 4. Student mistake and T-algebra error message in moving terms to other side of equation.

operands usually gives an expression that will be qualified as not equivalent to the previous line. Yet even a very intelligent program could hardly give a more precise diagnosis. Diagnosing the mistake already before the input of the result tells the student where the error really is and prevents meaningless input work.

Some error situations are caused by the student's poor knowledge of precise terminology or underestimation precise use of terms. Sometimes they try to apply the rule called *Multiply monomials* to polynomials or the rule *Add numbers* to the terms containing variables. On the one hand we hope that demanding from the students use of correct names combined with their need to understand the help texts and error messages leads to better use of mathematical terms. On the other hand we understand that there is yet a long way to standardization and the menus of the existing programs are only starting-points. A possibility of dialogue simplification would be to put in the menu only one item *Multiply* while applying different rules depending on the marked expressions.

A second long-term standardization problem is the extent of allowed/supposed preprocessing. When the student performs the conversions on paper, our usual practice does not prohibit making some small conversions before the "main" operation of the step. For example, in case of collection of like terms the student can convert the monomials to normal form without doing this operation in writing. While we have never seen any exact regulations what preprocessing is allowed for a particular operation and what is not, any rule-based system should implement some decision procedure for this. There exists a trivial solution to the approval problem where the operations are just formal rewrite rules. In order to avoid long chains of trivial steps we have tried to permit some reasonable preprocessing. For example, interactive learning environment T-algebra allows application of *Combine like terms* to $2xyx$, $3x^2y$ and $-yxx$. Automated solution procedure writes the result in normal form. If the student enters the result in Free or Structured mode, any monomial equivalent to the program's answer will be accepted.

Different programs display the negative judgments of rule approval procedure in different form. If the student wants to collect like terms in MathXpert and marks a subexpression then it is possible that MathXpert does not display the command *Collect $\pm$ terms* in the pop-up menu or collects only a part of expected terms. Then the student can rethink whether the terms can be collected after some preprocessing by means of other rules or they cannot be collected at all. If T-algebra diagnoses that the rule cannot be applied to (some part of) the marked subexpression then the feedback is a bit more precipitous: an error message (usually explaining what form the argument(s) of this rule should have) and increasing of the corresponding error type counter. Therefore it is desirable to separate as clearly as possible the real mathematical mistakes from the breaches of some provisory preprocessing conventions in the program.

Today we still need some time for experiments on both: making the conventions more accurate and making the diagnosis more distinguishing. We do not claim that our counters of mistakes can be used safely for assessment purposes. At the current stage the program also saves the error situations and the teacher has the possibility to weight the mistakes.

4.3. *Checking Entered Result of Conversion*

Knowing the actual operation and the actual operands enables to analyze the input at the third stage much better. In many cases the correct input is now uniquely or almost uniquely defined by known data. If the entered result is not correct then the error messages can be formulated in terms of a specific rule and its operands/results.

T-algebra diagnoses the following errors after input of a conversion result:

(1) Entered term is not a syntactically correct expression;
(2) Entered subexpression should be preceded by a sign;
(3) Entered subexpression should be put in parentheses (order of operations);
(4) Entered subexpression does not have the required structure (is not a proper fraction, is not a monomial, has wrong number of members, *etc.*);
(5) Entered subexpression is not equivalent with marked part;
(6) Concrete parts of input (sign, coefficient, variables, exponents, denominator, *etc.*) do not have right value;
(7) Selected operation with marked terms is not performed (nothing reduced, terms are not moved to other side, *etc.*).

The first issue concerns only the entered expression. Issues 2 and 3 consider the syntactical compatibility of entered term(s) with unchanged part of the expression. Error 3 can occur when the main operation of the result has lower priority than the main operation of the marked part. For example, $(a+b)(c+d) = ac+ad+bc+bd$ but $3(a+b)(c+d) \neq 3ac+ad+bc+bd$ and thus in such context the parentheses should be put around the result of multiplication. Following our didactic principles we do not want to prevent this mistake automatically because this error is very frequent even for university students.

Issue 4 is checked by T-algebra before issue 5 (equivalence). For example, the result of multiplication of monomial with polynomial should be the sum of monomials and the result of combining like monomials should be one monomial. In case of structured and partial input modes such requirements or part of them can be fulfilled automatically. The program allows the order of the members of sums and products to be changed. Although the boxes in structured and partial modes prescribe the structure of expression, it is allowed to leave some boxes empty (unary plus, the coefficient or exponent that equals 1, the monomial with coefficient 0, *etc.*).

The message about mere non-equivalence is issued by T-algebra in cases when the program is unable to give more detailed diagnosis of category 6. At the current stage in free input mode T-algebra checks for equivalence or non-equivalence (issue 5) of the entered expression with the correct one. In simplest cases (for example, when the result is a single monomial) T-algebra checks also the correctness of specific parts of the result (issue 6). In structured and partial input modes the result is of a required structure and T-algebra is able to check for correctness of different parts (Fig. 5).

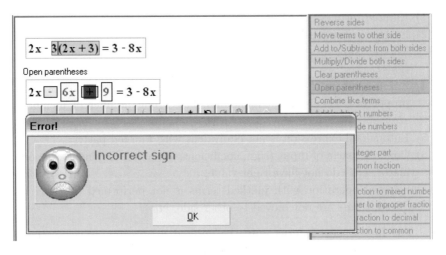

Fig. 5. Student mistake and T-algebra error message in opening parentheses.

For some rules the right syntactic structure and equivalence with previous line do not guarantee that the selected operation is really performed. In such cases T-algebra checks this issue additionally. For example, T-algebra does not accept reducing 6/12 to 60/120 or 5/10 or 6/12.

Issue 4 (right structure, number of members, *etc.*) is associated with problems of allowed or prohibited postprocessing of the result of "main" operation of the step. Working with paper and pencil, we try to economize the steps. Strong students want to combine like terms already within the step of multiplication of two polynomials or within moving the terms to other side of equation.

Some additional information about error diagnosis in T-algebra can be found in Ref. 23 and Ref. 24.

5. Conclusions

Developing a three-component expression manipulation interface, we have created a solution dialogue that

(1) Is intuitively understandable for the students;
(2) Requires generally the same amount of keyboard/mouse work as a pure input interface;
(3) Allows students to make practically all expression manipulation mistakes;
(4) Allows the program to locate the substep of solution step (choice of operation, choice of operands, execution of operation) where the student has made a mistake;
(5) Allows to point in error messages to the actual location of mistakes;
(6) Gives the teacher (in the future also the program) the possibility to choose such input mode that supports the student's actions.

Our project seems to be the first attempt to implement detailed and substep-oriented error diagnostics for expression manipulation exercises. Diagnostics in T-algebra is based on purely syntactic analysis of entered information. We check the rule, operands and result separately, pair-wise, and all together. Experiments with students demonstrate that this enables formulating helpful feedback. A natural expectation would be to use this automated detailed error diagnostics for assessment (assigning to each error type some penalty and multiplying penalties by the counters of mistakes). For this purpose we should learn to detect the cases when some error message is caused not by real mathematical mistake but by missing knowledge about the restrictions established in the program (for example, prohibition to collect two groups of like terms in one step).

Obviously our decisions and ideas need some years of practical classroom work before they can be finally confirmed. In addition, experiments are needed to solve some problems concerning standardization (for example, standardization of nomenclature of rules). Starting from the school year 2006–2007 tens of teachers in Estonian schools use T-algebra for practicing. The results of school trials and teacher experiences will contribute to and support further development of T-algebra.

Acknowledgments

Programming of T-algebra is financed by the Estonian School Computerization Foundation "Tiger Leap". The authors are financed also by Targeted Financing grant SF0182712s06 of the Estonian Ministry of Education and Research and by Estonian Doctoral School in Information and Communication Technologies.

References

1. M. Beeson, Design principles of Mathpert: Software to support education in algebra and calculus, in *Computer-Human Interaction in Symbolic Computation*, ed. N. Kajler (Springer, 1998) pp. 89–115.
2. R. Ravaglia, T. Alper, M. Rozenfeld and P. Suppes, Successful pedagogical applications of symbolic computation, in *Computer-Human Interaction in Symbolic Computation*, ed. N. Kajler (Springer, 1998) pp. 61–88.
3. Cognitive Tutor by Carnegie Learning, Inc. http://www.carnegielearning.com.
4. S. R. Alpert, M. K. Singley and P. G. Fairweather, Deploying intelligent tutors on the web: An architecture and an example. *International Journal of Artificial Intelligence in Education* 10, 2 (1999) pp. 183–197.
5. WIRIS, http://www.wiris.com/.
6. J. Nicaud, D. Bouhineau and H. Chaachoua, Mixing microworld and cas features in building computer systems that help students learn algebra, *International Journal of Computers for Mathematical Learning* 5, 2 (2004) pp. 169–211.
7. MATH-TEACHER, http://www.mathkalusa.com/.
8. J. R. Anderson, C. F. Boyle, A. Corbett and M. W. Lewis, Cognitive modeling and intelligent tutoring, *Artificial Intelligence* 42, 1 (1990) pp. 7–49.
9. D. Sleeman and J. S. Brown (eds.), *Intelligent Tutoring Systems* (Academic Press, 1982).
10. M. Quigley, A simple algebra tutor, *Journal of Artificial Intelligence in Education* 1, 1 (1989) pp. 41–52.
11. H. U. Hoppe, Deductive error diagnosis and inductive error generalisation for intelligent tutoring systems, *Journal of Artificial Intelligence in Education* 5, 1, (1994) pp. 27–49.
12. J. Nicaud, H. Chaachoua and M. Bittar, Automatic calculation of students' conceptions in elementary algebra from Aplusix log files, in *ITS 2006 Proceedings*, LNCS 4053 (2006) pp. 433–442.

13. C. Zinn, Supporting tutorial feedback to student help requests and errors in symbolic differentiation, in *ITS 2006 Proceedings*, LNCS **4053** (2006) pp. 349–359.
14. WIMS server, `http://wims.unice.fr/wims/en_home.html`.
15. C. J. Sangwin, Assessing mathematics automatically using computer algebra and the internet, *Teaching Mathematics and its Applications* **23**, 1 (2004) pp. 1–14.
16. C. J. Sangwin, Assessing elementary algebra with STACK. *International Journal of Mathematical Education in Science and Technology* (forthcoming).
17. R. Prank, Using computerised exercises on mathematical logic, *Informatik-Fachberichte* **292**, (Springer-Verlag, 1991) pp. 34–38.
18. R. Prank and H. Viira, Algebraic manipulation assistant for propositional logic, *Computerised Logic Teaching Bulletin* **4**, 1 (St Andrews Univ, 1991) pp. 13–18.
19. R. Prank, M. Issakova, D. Lepp and V. Vaiksaar, Designing next-generation training and testing environment for expression manipulation, *ICCS 2006, Part I*, LNCS **3991** (2006) pp. 928–931.
20. D. Lepp, Program for exercises on operations with polynomials, *6th International Conference on Technology in Mathematics Teaching* (2003) pp. 365–369.
21. M. Issakova, D. Lepp and R. Prank, Input design in interactive learning environment T-algebra, in *Proceedings 5th IEEE International Conference on Advanced Learning Technologies* (IEEE, 2005) pp. 489–491.
22. M. Issakova, D. Lepp and R. Prank, T-algebra: Adding input stage to rule-based interface for expression manipulation, *International Journal for Technology in Mathematics Education* **13**, 2 (2006) pp. 89–96.
23. M. Issakova, Comparison of student errors made during linear equation solving on paper and in interactive learning environment, in *Proceedings DES-TIME-2006: Dresden International Symposium on Technology and its Integration into Mathematics Education* (2006).
24. D. Lepp, Error diagnosis in problem solving environment using action-object-input scheme, in *ITS 2006 Proceedings*, LNCS **4053** (2006) pp. 769–771.

AUTOMATED GENERATION OF READABLE PROOFS FOR A CLASS OF LIMITS OF SEQUENCES AND FUNCTIONS*

JING RUAN[1, 2, a] and ZHENGYI LU[1, b]

[1] *Department of Mathematics, Wenzhou University, Wenzhou 325003, China*
[2] *Wenzhou Vocational & Technical College, Wenzhou 325003, China*
[a] *E-mail: ruanjing1979@yahoo.com.cn*
[b] *E-mail: zhengyilu@hotmail.com*

In this paper, two symbolic algorithms are given to generate readable proofs automatically for a class of limits of sequences and functions by definition. The algorithms have been implemented in the computer algebra system Maple and work effectively for a number of examples.

Keywords: Readable proof, limit of sequences, limit of functions, proof by definition.

1. Introduction

It is a well-known fact that in elementary real analysis, where the notion of limits plays a central role, "$\varepsilon - N$" ("$\varepsilon - \delta$") proofs are hard to deal with due to the difficulty of finding a suitable N (δ) for any given $\varepsilon > 0$. As a result, students often find it difficult to grasp such a fundamental concept, on which much of modern analysis rests.

Computer algebra systems have been widely used for symbolic and numeric computation. It plays a significant role in the computation of differentials, integrals, limits, etc.

Erica Melis[1-3] invented the ComplexEstimate method for proof planning that is based on a general computation which shows under an assumption $|A| < e$ (e.g. x converges to x_0) the conjecture $|B| < \varepsilon$ (e.g. $f(x)$ converges to $f(x_0)$) can be shown if B can be decomposed into $B = k \cdot A + l$ (where k and l can be functional expressions) and certain subgoals that are satisfied

*Partially supported by the National Natural Science Foundation of China (Grant no. 10371090), a National Key Basic Research Project of China (Grant no. 2004CB318000) and Zhejiang Province Natural Science Foundation (Grant no. M1030343).

in the paper's case namely $|k| < V$ (real number) $|l| < \varepsilon/2$ and $0 < V$.

In this paper, we present other algorithmic proofs for a class of limits of sequences and functions by using a computer algebra system. For any given $\varepsilon > 0$, how to find a corresponding positive number N (δ or M) for the proofs of limits of sequences (functions) is a key point in our proofs. By using the functions `limsp` and `limfp` that implement our algorithms in Maple, readable proofs of limits may be obtained automatically. Eight examples are presented to illustrate our algorithms and their implementation.

2. Algorithms for Proofs of Limits

2.1. *Proofs for Limits of Sequences*

Definition 2.1[4] A sequence $\{A_n\}$ has the limit A and we write
$$\lim_{n\to\infty} A_n = A \quad \text{or} \quad A_n \to A \quad \text{as} \quad n \to \infty$$
if for every $\varepsilon > 0$, there is a corresponding positive integer N such that if $n > N$, then $|A_n - A| < \varepsilon$.

Consider a sequence $\{A_n\}$,
$$A_n = \frac{f(n)}{g(n)} = \frac{a_p n^p + a_{p-1} n^{p-1} + \cdots + a_1 n + a_0}{b_q n^q + b_{q-1} n^{q-1} + \cdots + b_1 n + b_0}, \tag{1}$$

where a_i $(i = 1, 2, \ldots, p)$ and b_j $(j = 1, 2, \ldots, q)$ are real numbers, p and q are natural numbers. If $\lim_{n\to\infty} A_n = A$ (A is a constant), for every $\varepsilon > 0$, we hope to find a corresponding positive integer N such that if $n > N$, then $|A_n - A| < \varepsilon$.

Theorem 2.1 $F(x)$ is a polynomial function as follows
$$F(x) = a_0 x^n + a_1 x^{n-1} + a_2 x^{n-2} + \cdots + a_{n-1} x + a_n \quad (a_0 > 0).$$

When $x > x_{\max}$ (here $x_{\max}$ is the maximum of the real roots of $F(x)$), we have $F(x) > 0$.

Let
$$\frac{F(n)}{G(n)} = \frac{f(n)}{g(n)} - A.$$

If the leading coefficient of $F(n)$ is negative, let $F(n) = -F(n)$, so does $G(n)$. Let $H(n)$ be the numerator of $\frac{B}{n} - \frac{F(n)}{G(n)}$. Here $B = 1$ if the leading coefficient of $H(n)$ is positive. Otherwise, let $B = B + 1$ until the leading coefficient of $H(n)$ is positive. According to Theorem 2.1 we can find out the greatest integer N_1 that is less than or equal to r_{max} (here r_{max} is the maximum of the real roots of $H(n)$). When $n > N_1$, we have $H(n) > 0$, so $\frac{B}{n} - \frac{F(n)}{G(n)} > 0$. Therefore, we have

$$\left| \frac{f(n)}{g(n)} - A \right| = \left| \frac{F(n)}{G(n)} \right| < \frac{B}{n} \qquad (n > N_1).$$

Let $N = \max\left\{ N_1, \dfrac{B}{\varepsilon} \right\}$. For every given $\varepsilon > 0$, when $n > N$ we have

$$\left| \frac{f(n)}{g(n)} - A \right| < \varepsilon.$$

By the method we mentioned above, we can find out the positive integer N which is the key point in our readable proof of limits of sequences.

Table 1. Explanation of some Maple functions[5]

Command	Explanation
lcoeff(F)	leading coefficient of multivariate polynomial F
numer(H)	return the numerator of H
floor(K)	greatest integer less than or equal to K
ceil(K)	smallest integer greater than or equal to K
abs(K)	return the absolute value of the expression K
minimize(F(x), x=a..b)	return the infimum of F(x) over the given range [a, b]
maximize(F(x), x=a..b)	return the supremum of F(x) over the given range [a, b]

Now we describe the algorithm to find out the N and generate readable proofs for limits of sequences (see Appendix A for the corresponding program):

input $f(n)$, $g(n)$, A
output proof
begin
$\quad \dfrac{F(n)}{G(n)} = \dfrac{f(n)}{g(n)} - A$
$\quad$ **if** lcoeff $(F(n)) < 0$ **then**
$\quad\quad F(n) = -F(n)$

endif
if lcoeff $(G(n)) < 0$ **then**
$\quad G(n) = -G(n)$
endif
$B = 1; N_1 = 1; H(n)=$ numer $(\dfrac{B}{n} - \dfrac{F(n)}{G(n)})$
while lcoeff $(H(n)) < 0$ **do**
$\quad B = B+1; H(n)=$ numer $(\dfrac{B}{n} - \dfrac{F(n)}{G(n)})$
do
rmax $= \max \{$ solve $(H(n)=0) \}$
if rmax> 0 **then**
$\quad N_1=$ floor (rmax)
endif
$N= \max\{ N_1,$ floor $(\dfrac{B}{\varepsilon})\}$
print proof
end

First, we consider the case in which a_i $(i = 1, 2, \ldots, p)$ and b_j $(j = 1, 2, \ldots, q)$ are rational numbers. Without loss of generality, we can suppose that a_i $(i = 1, 2, \ldots, p)$ and b_j $(j = 1, 2, \ldots, q)$ are integers.

Now we present some examples for the cases $p = q$ and $p < q$.

Example 1 $(p = q)$ Use Definition 2.1 to prove that

$$\lim_{n \to \infty} \frac{2n^4 - 3n^3 - 2n^2 + n - 1}{n^4 + 5n^3 - 3n^2 - 2n - 4} = 2 .$$

Solution   In Maple, one just needs to input the following command

```
limsp(2*n^4-3*n^3-2*n^2+n-1, n^4+5*n^3-3*n^2-2*n-4, 2);
```

then the readable proof is obtained as follows:

Given any $\varepsilon > 0$, let N=max$\{2, [13/\varepsilon]\}$, such that if $n > N$, then

$$\left| \frac{2n^4 - 3n^3 - 2n^2 + n - 1}{n^4 + 5n^3 - 3n^2 - 2n - 4} - 2 \right| = \left| \frac{13n^3 - 4n^2 - 5n - 7}{n^4 + 5n^3 - 3n^2 - 2n - 4} \right|$$

(When $n > 2$)
$< 13/n < 13/N < \varepsilon$ $\square$

Example 2 $(p < q)$ Use Definition 2.1 to prove that

$$\lim_{n \to \infty} \frac{-3n^3 - 2n^2 + n - 1}{n^4 + 5n^3 - 3n^2 - 2n - 4} = 0 \ .$$

Solution   Use the following command

`limsp(-3*n^ 3-2*n^ 2+n-1, n^ 4+5*n^ 3-3*n^ 2-2*n-4, 0);`

then the readable proof is obtained as follows:

Given any $\varepsilon > 0$, let N=max$\{2, \ [3/\varepsilon]\}$, such that if $n > N$, then

$$\left| \frac{-3n^3 - 2n^2 + n - 1}{n^4 + 5n^3 - 3n^2 - 2n - 4} - 0 \right| = \left| \frac{3n^3 + 2n^2 - n + 1}{n^4 + 5n^3 - 3n^2 - 2n - 4} \right|$$

(When $n > 2$)
$< 3/n < 3/N < \varepsilon$ □

When a_i $(i = 1, 2, \ldots, p)$ and b_j $(j = 1, 2, \ldots, q)$ are irrational numbers, we can also use the algorithm described above to obtain the proofs.

Example 3   Use Definition 2.1 to prove that

$$\lim_{n \to \infty} \frac{\sqrt{2}n^2 - 1}{2n^2 - 5n + 1} = \frac{\sqrt{2}}{2} \ .$$

Solution   Use the command

`limsp(sqrt(2)*n^ 2-1, 2*n^ 2-5*n, sqrt(2)/2);`

we have the following readable proof:

Given any $\varepsilon > 0$, let N=max$\{18, \ [2/\varepsilon]\}$, such that if $n > N$, then

$$\left| \frac{\sqrt{2}n^2 - 1}{2n^2 - 5n + 1} - \frac{\sqrt{2}}{2} \right| = \left| \frac{-2 + 5\sqrt{2}n - \sqrt{2}}{4n^2 - 10n + 2} \right|$$

(When $n > 18$)
$< 2/n < 2/N < \varepsilon$ □

Example 4   Use Definition 2.1 to prove that

$$\lim_{n \to \infty} \frac{\ln 2 \cdot n^2 - 2}{-\pi n^2 + \sqrt{3}n + 2} = -\frac{\ln 2}{\pi} \ .$$

Solution   Use the command

```
limsp(log(2)*n^ 2-2, -Pi*n^ 2+sqrt(3)*n+2, -log(2)/Pi);
```

we have the following readable proof:

Given any $\varepsilon > 0$, let N=max$\{1, [1/\varepsilon]\}$, such that if $n > N$, then

$$\left| \frac{\ln 2 \cdot n^2 - 2}{-\pi n^2 + \sqrt{3}n + 2} - (-\frac{\ln 2}{\pi}) \right| = \left| \frac{-2\pi + \ln 2 \cdot \sqrt{3}n + 2\ln 2}{\pi(\pi n^2 - \sqrt{3}n - 2)} \right|$$

(When $n > 1$)
$< 1/n < 1/N < \varepsilon$ □

Hence, for limits of sequences like

$$\lim_{n \to \infty} A_n = \lim_{n \to \infty} \frac{f(n)}{g(n)} = \lim_{n \to \infty} \frac{a_p n^p + a_{p-1} n^{p-1} + \cdots + a_1 n + a_0}{b_q n^q + b_{q-1} n^{q-1} + \cdots + b_1 n + b_0},$$

the algorithm can also generate readable proofs.

2.2. *Proofs for Limits of Functions*

Definition 2.2.1[4]   Let f be a function defined on some open interval containing x_0, except possibly at x_0 itself, and let A be a real number. We say that the limit of $f(x)$ as x approaches x_0 is A, and write

$$\lim_{x \to x_0} f(x) = A$$

if for every number $\varepsilon > 0$, there is a number $\delta > 0$ such that

$$\text{if } 0 <| x - x_0 |< \delta, \text{ then } | f(x) - A |< \varepsilon.$$

Definition 2.2.2[4]   Let f be a function defined on an infinite interval $(-\infty, c) \cup (d, +\infty)$ for real numbers c and d, and let A be a real number. We say that the limit of $f(x)$ as x approaches ∞ is A, and write

$$\lim_{x \to \infty} f(x) = A$$

if for every number $\varepsilon > 0$, there is a number $M > 0$ such that

$$\text{if } | x |> M, \text{ then } | f(x) - A |< \varepsilon.$$

Consider the function $f(x)$, where

$$f(x) = \frac{g(x)}{h(x)} = \frac{a_p x^p + a_{p-1} x^{p-1} + \cdots + a_1 x + a_0}{b_q x^q + b_{q-1} x^{q-1} + \cdots + b_1 x + b_0}, \tag{2}$$

a_i $(i = 1, 2, \ldots, p)$ and b_j $(j = 1, 2, \ldots, q)$ are real numbers, p and q are natural numbers.

If $\lim\limits_{x \to \infty} f(x) = A$ ($\lim\limits_{x \to x_0} f(x) = A$), for every $\varepsilon > 0$, we hope to find $M > 0$ $(\delta > 0)$ such that if $\mid x \mid > M$ ($\mid x - x_0 \mid < \delta$), then $|f(x) - A| < \varepsilon$.

In the case of $\lim\limits_{x \to \infty} f(x) = A$, the method for finding a positive number M is similar to the one we have presented above for finding a positive number N of limits of sequences.

In the case of $\lim\limits_{x \to x_0} f(x) = A$, let

$$\frac{G(x)}{H(x)} = (\frac{g(x)}{h(x)} - A)/(x - x_0).$$

Let $t = t + 1$ until the minimum of $|H(x)|$ is positive in the interval $[x_0 - \frac{1}{2^t}, x_0 + \frac{1}{2^t}]$ $(t = 0, 1, 2, \ldots)$. Let m_2 (> 0) be the minimum of $|H(x)|$ in the interval $[x_0 - s, x_0 + s]$ and m_1 be the maximum of $|G(x)|$ in the same interval. Then

$$\left| \frac{g(x)}{h(x)} - A \right| = \left| \frac{G(x)}{H(x)} \right| \cdot |x - x_0| \le \frac{m_1}{m_2} \cdot |x - x_0|.$$

Let $\delta_1 = \varepsilon \cdot \dfrac{m_2}{m_1}$, $\delta = \min\{s, \delta_1\}$. When $|x - x_0| < \delta$, we have

$$\left| \frac{g(x)}{h(x)} - A \right| \le \frac{m_1}{m_2} \cdot |x - x_0| < \varepsilon.$$

In this way, we find out the positive number δ which is the key point in our readable proof of limits of functions in the form (2) when $x \to x_0$.

Now we present the algorithm to find out δ or M and generate readable proofs for limits of functions (see Appendix B for the corresponding program):

input $g(x)$, $h(x)$, x_0, A
output proof
begin
    $s = 1$; $t = 1$
    if $x_0 = \infty$ **then**
        $\dfrac{F(x)}{G(x)} = \dfrac{f(x)}{g(x)} - A$
        if lcoeff $(F(x)) < 0$ **then**
            $F(x) = -F(x)$

endif
if lcoeff $(G(x)) < 0$ **then**
    $G(x) = -G(x)$
endif
$B = 1; M_1 = 1; H(x) =$ numer $\left(\dfrac{B}{x} - \dfrac{F(x)}{G(x)}\right)$
while lcoeff $(H(x)) < 0$ **do**
    $B = B + 1; H(x) =$ numer$\left(\dfrac{B}{x} - \dfrac{F(x)}{G(x)}\right)$
enddo
rmax $=$ max $\{$ solve $(H(x) = 0)$ $\}$
if rmax> 0 **then**
    $M_1 =$ floor (rmax)
endif
$M =$ max$\{ M_1,$ floor $\left(\dfrac{B}{\varepsilon}\right)\}$
printf proof
else
$\dfrac{G(x)}{H(x)} = \left(\dfrac{g(x)}{h(x)} - A\right)/(x - x_0)$
$m_1 =$ceil(maximize(abs $(G(x)), x = -s + x_0 \;..\; s + x_0))$
$m_2 =$floor(minimize(abs $(H(x)), x = -s + x_0 \;..\; s + x_0))$
while $m_2 = 0$ **do**
    $t = t + 1; \quad s = \dfrac{1}{2^{t-1}}$
    $m_1 =$ceil(maximize(abs $(G(x)), x = -s + x_0 \;..\; s + x_0))$
    $m_2 =$floor(minimize(abs $(H(x)), x = -s + x_0 \;..\; s + x_0))$
enddo
$M = \dfrac{m_1}{m_2}; \; \delta_1 = \dfrac{\varepsilon}{M}; \; \delta =min\{s, \delta_1\}$
print proof
endif
end

Example 5   Use Definition 2.2.2 to prove that

$$\lim_{x \to \infty} \frac{\sqrt{2}x^2 - 1}{2x^2 - 5x} = \frac{\sqrt{2}}{2} \;.$$

Solution   Use the command

```
limfp(sqrt(2)*x^ 2-1, 2*x^ 2-5*x, infinity, sqrt(2)/2);
```

we have the following readable proof:

Given any $\varepsilon > 0$, let $M =\max\{ 20, \ [\frac{2}{\varepsilon}] \}$, such that if $|x| > M$, then

$$\left| \frac{\sqrt{2x^2 - 1}}{2x^2 - 5x} - \frac{\sqrt{2}}{2} \right| = \left| \frac{-2 + 5\sqrt{2}x}{2\,(x^2 - 5x)} \right| \qquad \text{(When } |x| > 20\text{)}$$

$$< 2/|x| < 2/M < \varepsilon \quad \square$$

Example 6 Use Definition 2.2.1 to prove that

$$\lim_{x \to 2} \frac{x^4 - 3x^3 + x - 1}{x^3 - 5x - 7} = \frac{7}{9} .$$

Solution Use the command

limfp(x^ 4−3*x^ 3+x−1, x^ 3−5*x−7, 2, 7/9);

we have the following readable proof:

Given any $\varepsilon > 0$, let $\delta =\min\{ \ \frac{1}{2}, \ \frac{1}{3}\varepsilon \ \}$, such that if $|x - 2| \le \delta$, then

$$\left| \frac{x^4 - 3x^3 + x - 1}{x^3 - 5x - 7} - \frac{7}{9} \right| = \left| \frac{9x^4 - 34x^3 + 44x + 40}{9\,(x^3 - 5x - 7)} \right|$$

$$= \left| \frac{9x^3 - 16x^2 - 32x - 20}{9\,(x^3 - 5x - 7)} \right| \cdot |x - 2|$$

$$\le \frac{77}{34}\,\delta \le 3\,\delta < \varepsilon \quad \square$$

Example 7 Use Definition 2.2.1 to prove that

$$\lim_{x \to 1} \frac{x^2 - 2x - 3}{x^2 - 3x + 2} = -4 .$$

Solution Use the command

limfp(x^ 2−2*x−3, x^ 2−3*x+2, 1, −4);

we have the following readable proof:

Given any $\varepsilon > 0$, let $\delta =\min\{ \ \frac{1}{2147483648}, \ \frac{1}{5}\varepsilon \ \}$, such that if $|x - 1| \le \delta$, then

$$\left| \frac{x + 3}{x - 2} - 4 \right| = \left| 5 \cdot \frac{x - 1}{x - 2} \right|$$

$$= \left| \frac{5}{x-2} \right| \cdot |x-1|$$

$$\leq \frac{5}{1} \, \delta \leq 5 \, \delta < \varepsilon \quad \square$$

Example 8 Use Definition 2.2.1 to prove that

$$\lim_{x \to 2} \frac{x^2 - \pi x - 1}{\sqrt{2}\, x^2 + 2} = \frac{-2\pi + 3}{4\sqrt{2} + 2}.$$

Solution Use the command

```
limfp(x^ 2-Pi*x-1, sqrt(2)*x^ 2+2, 2, (-2*Pi+3)/ (4*
sqrt(2)+2));
```

we have the following readable proof:

Given any $\varepsilon > 0$, let $\delta = \min\{\, 1,\; \frac{1}{2}\varepsilon \,\}$, such that if $|x - 2| \leq \delta$, then

$$\left| \frac{x^2 - \pi x - 1}{\sqrt{2}x^2 + 2} - \frac{-2\pi + 3}{4\sqrt{2} + 2} \right|$$

$$= \left| \frac{\sqrt{2}x^2 + 2x^2 - 4\pi x \sqrt{2} - 2\pi x - 4\sqrt{2} - 8 + 2\pi \sqrt{2}x^2 + 4\pi}{2\, (\sqrt{2}x^2 + 2)(2\sqrt{2} + 1)} \right|$$

$$= \left| \frac{\sqrt{2}x + 2x + 2\pi x \sqrt{2} - 2\pi + 2\sqrt{2} + 4}{2\, (\sqrt{2}x^2 + 2)(2\sqrt{2} + 1)} \right| \cdot |x - 2|$$

$$\leq \frac{38}{26} \, \delta \leq 2 \, \delta < \varepsilon \quad \square$$

Hence, for all limits of functions like

$$\lim_{x \to x_0} f(x) = \lim_{x \to x_0} \frac{g(x)}{h(x)} = \lim_{x \to x_0} \frac{a_p x^p + a_{p-1} x^{p-1} + \cdots + a_1 x + a_0}{b_q x^q + b_{q-1} x^{q-1} + \cdots + b_1 x + b_0},$$

the algorithm can generate the readable proofs.

3. Future Work

In this paper, we have provided algorithms for generating readable proofs automatically for limits of the forms (1) and (2). How to propose algorithmic proofs for other cases such as $\lim\limits_{n\to\infty} \sqrt[n]{n} = 1$, $\lim\limits_{n\to\infty} \dfrac{1}{\sqrt[n]{n!}} = 0$ and $\lim\limits_{n\to\infty} \sqrt[n]{a} = 1$ is our future work.

Appendix A. (Program of Proofs for Limits of Sequence)

```
limsp:=proc(f, g, A)
local u, u1, F, G, B, v, H, r, m, s, rmax, N1, i:
u1:=f/g:
u:=simplify(f/g-A): F:=numer(u): G:=denom(u):
if evalf(lcoeff(F))<0 then F:=-F: fi:
if evalf(lcoeff(G))<0 then G:=-G: fi:
B:=1: v:=simplify(B/n-F/G): H:=numer(v):
while evalf(lcoeff(H))<0 do
    B:=B+1: v:=simplify(B/n-F/G): H:=numer(v):
od:
if has(H, n) then
    r:=[fsolve(H, n)]: m:=nops(r): s:=[ ]:
    if m>0 then
        for i from 1 to m do
            if is(r[i]>0) then s:=[op(s), r[i]]: fi:
        od:
        if is(nops(s)>0) then rmax:=ceil(max(op(s))):
        else rmax:=1:
        fi:
    else rmax:=1:
    fi:
    N1:=rmax:
else N1:=1:
fi:
if evalf(A)>=0 then
    printf(" Given any ε > 0,
    let N=max{%a, [%a/ε]}, such that if n>N, then \ n

    |%a-%a| \n=|%a| (When n>%a) \ n
    <%a/n<%a/N< ε", N1, B, u1, A, F/G, N1, B, B):
else
    printf(" Given any ε > 0,
    let N=max{%a, [%a/ε]}, such that if n>N, then \ n
```

```
      |%a-(%a)| \n=|%a| (When n>%a) \ n
      <%a/n<%a/N< ε", N1, B, u1, A, F/G, N1, B, B):
  fi:
  end:
```

Appendix B. (Program of Proofs for Limits of Functions)

```
  with(numtheory):
  limfp:=proc(f, g, x0, A)
  local u1, u2, u3, B, F, G, M, m1, m2, s, t, i, v, r,
m, H,
  rmax, N1:
  u1:=simplify(f/g): u2:=simplify(f/g-A):
  if has(x0, infinity) then
      F:=numer(u2): G:=denom(u2):
      if evalf(lcoeff(F))<0 then F:=-F: fi:
      if evalf(lcoeff(G))<0 then G:=-G: fi:
      B:=1: v:=simplify(B/x-F/G): H:=numer(v):
      while evalf(lcoeff(H))<0 do
          B:=B+1: v:=simplify(B/x-F/G): H:=numer(v):
      od:
      if has(H, x) then
          r:=[fsolve(H, x)]: m:=nops(r): s:=[ ]:
          if m>0 then
              for i from 1 to m do
                  if is(r[i]>0) then s:=[op(s), r[i]]:
fi:
              od:
              if is(nops(s)>0) then
rmax:=ceil(max(op(s))):
              else rmax:=1:
              fi:
          else rmax:=1:
          fi:
          N1:=rmax:
      else N1:=1:
      fi:
      if is(evalf(A)>= 0) then
          printf(" Given any ε > 0,
          let M=max{%a, [%a/ε]}, such that if |x|>M,
```

```
then \n
        |%a-%a| \n=|%a|    (When |x|>%a) \ n
        <%a/|x|<%a/M< ε", N1, B, u1, A, F/G, N1, B,
B):
    else
        printf(" Given any ε > 0,
        let M=max{%a, [%a/ε]}, such that if |x|>M,
then \n
        |%a-(%a) | \n=|%a|    (When |x|>%a) \ n
        <%a/|x|<%a/M< ε", N1, B, u1, A, F/G, N1, B,
B):
    fi:
  else
    u3:=factor(u2/(x-x0)): F:=numer(u3): G:=denom(u3):
    t:=1: s:=1:
    m1:=ceil(evalf(maximize(abs(collect(F, x)),
      x=-1+evalf(x0, 10)..1+evalf(x0, 10)), 10)):
    m2:=floor(evalf(minimize(abs(collect(G, x)),
      x=-1+evalf(x0, 10)..1+evalf(x0, 10)), 10)):
    while m2=0 do
        t:=t+1: s:=1/2 ^ (t-1):
        m1:=ceil(evalf(maximize(abs(collect(F, x)),
          x=-s+evalf(x0, 10)..s+evalf(x0, 10)), 10)):
        m2:=floor(evalf(minimize(abs(collect(G, x)),
          x=-s+evalf(x0, 10)..s+evalf(x0, 10)), 10)):
    od:
    M:=ceil(m1/m2):
    if sign(evalf(A))>=0 and type(A, '+')=false then
        printf(" Given any ε > 0, let δ=min{%a, %a*ε},
        such that if | x-%a|≤ δ, then \n
        |%a-%a| \n=|%a| \n=|%a |*|x-%a| \n
        ≤%a/%a*δ ≤%a*δ < ε",
        s, 1/M, x0, u1, A, u2, u3, x0, m1, m2, M):
    else
        printf(" Given any ε > 0, let δ=min{%a, %a*ε},
        such that if | x-(%a)|≤ δ, then \n
        |%a-%a| \n=|%a| \n= |%a|*|x-%a| \n
        ≤%a/%a*δ ≤%a*δ < ε",
        s, 1/M, x0, u1, A, u2, u3, x0, m1, m2, M):
```

```
      fi:
   fi:
   end:
```

References

1. E. Melis, The Limit Domain, *Proceedings of the Fourth International Conference on Artificial Intelligence Planning Systems*, 199–207, AAAI (1998).
2. E. Melis, AI-Techniques in Proof Planning, *Proceedings of the 13th European Conference on Artificial Intelligence*, 494–498, John Wiley and Sons, Chichester (1998).
3. E. Melis, J. Siekmann, Knowledge-Based Proof Planning, *Artif. Intell.* 115(1): 65–105 (1999).
4. F. L. Zhang, M. X. Yao, Y. H. Zhang, *Limits and Continuity, Calculus with Space Analytic Geometry*, Tianjin University Press (2003).
5. X. X. Chen, *Maple Instruction Reference*, National Defence Industry Press (2002).

COMPUTER ALGEBRA MEETS AN ANCIENT EGYPTIAN PROBLEM

YIU-KWONG MAN

Department of Mathematics, Science, Social Science and Technology
The Hong Kong Institute of Education
10 Lo Ping Road, Tai Po, Hong Kong
E-mail: ykman@ied.edu.hk

An improved Fibonacci-Sylvester algorithm for computing unit fraction expansions is presented. In general, the maximal denominators computed by this new algorithm are comparatively smaller than those obtained by the original algorithm. Discussions of its implementation in computer algebra systems, comparison of tested results, ideas for further research and its applications in undergraduate teaching are included.

Keywords: Unit fraction, improved Fibonacci-Sylvester algorithm, computer algebra.

1. Introduction

The problem of decomposing a proper fraction into a sum of distinct unit fractions (reciprocals of positive integers) originated in ancient Egypt.[6] In the famous Rhind Mathematical Papyrus,[14] there is a table showing how to decompose fractions $2/n$ into sums of distinct unit fractions, where $5 \leq n \leq 101$ and n is odd. For example, $2/7$ is written as $1/4 + 1/28$. The Egyptians probably knew that $2/(2n + 1) = 1/(n + 1) + 1/(n + 1)(2n + 1)$ since one can rediscover most of the results in the papyrus by this identity. However, they might not know a general approach for decomposing fractions m/n with $2 < m < n$. It was not until 1202 that Fibonacci (1180–1250) made a breakthrough by proposing a general algorithm for computing unit fraction expansions for arbitrary fractions. The correctness of the algorithm was first proved by J. J. Sylvester (1814–1897) in 1880. Thus, it is called the Fibonacci-Sylvester algorithm (or the Greedy Algorithm) nowadays. Since then, some number theorists are interested in studying the quantitative aspects of unit fraction expansions. For instance, there are new algorithms that improve upon the Fibonacci-Sylvester algorithm in various ways, bounding the size of the maximal denominator or limiting the number of terms in the expansions.[3] In Section 2, we describe the Fibonacci-Sylvester algorithm and analyse its basic properties, together with some examples. In Section 3, we present a new improved Fibonacci-Sylvester algorithm. In general, it has the advantage that the maximal denominators obtained are comparatively smaller than those computed by the original algorithm. In fact, the differences bewteen the maximal denominators could be very large, as illustrated in the examples. In Section 4, discussion of its implementation in computer algebra systems and some tested results are described. Using the examples in [1,4], further tested results obtained by the improved Fibonacci-Sylvester algorithm are compared with those found by the Continued Fraction algorithm, the Bleicher–Erdős algorithm and the Golomb algorithm (see [1,3,9,11,12]). Finally, we conclude with some ideas for further research and its applications in undergraduate teaching.

2. The Fibonacci-Sylvester Algorithm

The original Fibonacci-Sylvester algorithm is described below. A simple proof of its correctness is also provided.

Theorem 2.1 (Fibonacci-Sylvester algorithm). *If a, b are co-prime integers and $1 < a < b$, then a/b can be expressed as a sum of distinct unit fractions in the following way.*

Decompose a/b via the division algorithm to obtain

$$\frac{a}{b} = \frac{1}{q+1} + \frac{a-r}{b(q+1)}, \quad where\ b = aq + r;\ 0 \le r < a.$$

If the residual fraction $(a - r)/b(q + 1)$ is a unit fraction, then the process terminates. Otherwise, the same step is applied to the residual fraction(s) repeatedly until a unit fraction expansion is obtained.

Proof. First,

$$\frac{a}{b} = \frac{a(q+1)}{b(q+1)} = \frac{(aq+r)+(a-r)}{b(q+1)} = \frac{b+(a-r)}{b(q+1)} = \frac{1}{q+1} + \frac{a-r}{b(q+1)}.$$

Second,

$$\frac{1}{q+1} - \frac{a-r}{b(q+1)} = \frac{b-a+r}{b(q+1)} > 0.$$

Hence, $(a-r)/b(q+1) < 1/(q+1) < a/b$, which implies the unit fractions obtained are all distinct. Third, $0 < a - r \leq a$, which implies the whole process will terminate in at most a steps. □

The following results describe the basic properties of this algorithm.

Corollary 2.1. *Let a, b be co-prime integers and $1 < a < b$. If a/b is decomposed via the Fibonacci-Sylvester algorithm as*

$$\frac{a}{b} = \frac{1}{n_1} + \frac{1}{n_2} + \cdots + \frac{1}{n_k},$$

where $n_1 < n_2 < \cdots < n_k$ and $k > 1$, then
(a) $k \leq a$;
(b) $n_i(n_i - 1) < n_{i+1}$, where $1 \leq i \leq k - 1$, and
(c) $n_1 \prod_{i=1}^{k-1}(n_i - 1) < n_k \leq bn_1 n_2 \cdots n_{k-1}$.

Proof. (a) It follows from the proof of Theorem 2.1. (b) Let $a/b = p_0/q_0$ and p_i/q_i be the ith residual fraction generated, where $1 \leq i \leq k - 1$. Based on the division property, we have $p_{i-1}(n_i - 1) \leq q_{i-1} < p_{i-1}n_i$, and so $1/n_i < p_{i-1}/q_{i-1} \leq 1/(n_i - 1)$. Since $1/n_{i+1} < p_{i-1}/q_{i-1} - 1/n_i \leq 1/(n_i - 1) - 1/n_i = 1/n_i(n_i - 1)$, so $n_i(n_i - 1) < n_{i+1}$. (c) By Theorem 2.1, we have $n_2 < q_1 \leq bn_1$, $n_3 < q_2 \leq q_1 n_2$, $n_4 < q_3 \leq q_2 n_3$, ..., and $n_k < q_{k-1} \leq q_{k-2}n_{k-1}$, so $n_k \leq bn_1 n_2 \cdots n_{k-1}$. By (b), $n_1 - 1 < n_2/n_1$, $n_2 - 1 < n_3/n_2$, ..., and $n_{k-1} - 1 < n_k/n_{k-1}$, so $n_1 \prod_{i=1}^{k-1}(n_i - 1) < n_k$. Hence, $n_1 \prod_{i=1}^{k-1}(n_i - 1) < n_k \leq bn_1 n_2 \cdots n_{k-1}$. □

Corollary 2.2. *Let a, b be co-prime integers and $1 < a < b$. If a/b is decomposed via the Fibonacci-Sylvester algorithm into a unit fraction expansion and n_k $(k > 1)$ is the maximal denominator, then $\log n_k < 2^{a-2} \log(bc)$, where c is the ceiling of b/a.*

Proof. From the proof of Corollary 2.1, we have $n_2 < bn_1$, $n_3 < bn_1 n_2 < (bn_1)^2$, $n_4 < bn_1 n_2 n_3 < (bn_1)^4$ and so on. Hence,

$$n_k \leq bn_1 n_2 \ldots n_{k-1} < (bn_1)^{2^{k-2}} \leq (bn_1)^{2^{a-2}}.$$

Since n_1 is equal to the ceiling of b/a, so the result follows after taking logarithm. □

The following examples illustrate how the Fibonacci-Sylvester algorithm works. We can see that the exponential growth of the denominators is rather significant. The same notations used in the proof of Corollary 2.1 are adopted.

Example 2.1. By the Fibonacci-Sylvester algorithm, we obtain $3/7 = 1/3 + 1/11 + 1/231$, as shown in Table 1. (Note: $n_3 = bn_1n_2$.)

Table 1.

i	n_i	p_i	q_i
0	-	3	7
1	3	2	21
2	11	1	231
3	231	-	-

Example 2.2. By the Fibonacci-Sylvester algorithm, we obtain

$$\frac{5}{91} = \frac{1}{19} + \frac{1}{433} + \frac{1}{249553} + \frac{1}{93414800161} + \frac{1}{17452649778145716451681},$$

as shown in Table 2. (Note: $n_5 = bn_1n_2n_3n_4$.)

Table 2.

i	n_i	p_i	q_i
0	-	5	91
1	19	4	1729
2	433	3	748657
3	249553	2	186829600321
4	93414800161	1	17452649778145716451681
5	17452649778145716451681	-	-

The next example appeared in the original 1969 edition of Beck et al, which was then cited in [1,8]. Unfortunately due to typo, the answer provided is wrong. The correct answer is shown below.

Example 2.3. By the Fibonacci-Sylvester algorithm, we obtain

$$\frac{5}{121} = \frac{1}{25} + \frac{1}{757} + \frac{1}{763309} + \frac{1}{873960180913} + \frac{1}{1527612795642093418846225},$$

as shown in Table 3. (Note: $n_5 = bn_1n_2n_3n_4$.)

Comparing with the results in [1,4], namely

$$\frac{5}{121} = \frac{1}{42} + \frac{1}{70} + \frac{1}{726} + \frac{1}{770} + \frac{1}{1815} \quad \text{and}$$

$$\frac{5}{121} = \frac{1}{25} + \frac{1}{759} + \frac{1}{208725},$$

210

Table 3.

i	n_i	p_i	q_i
0	-	5	121
1	25	4	3025
2	757	3	2289925
3	763309	2	1747920361825
4	873960180913	1	1527612795642093418846225
5	1527612795642093418846225	-	-

we can see that the Fibonacci-Sylvester algorithm yields neither the shortest expansion nor the expansion with the smallest maximal denominator. As what Beck et al (2000) said, this algorithm attempts to find the best possible unit fraction at each step, but the overall effect is not optimal, as illustrated in the above examples.

3. A New Improved Fibonacci-Sylvester Algorithm

The Fibonacci-Sylvester algorithm is greedy in the sense that the largest unit fraction less than a non-unit fraction concerned is chosen at each step of decomposition. By modifying this *greedy* step slightly, we can obtain an improved version of the algorithm below.

Theorem 3.1 (Improved Fibonacci-Sylvester algorithm). *If a and b are co-prime integers and $1 < a < b$, then a/b can be expressed as a sum of distinct unit fractions in the following way.*

S1: Choose the smallest divisor of b, say c, such that $a < c \le b$ and $b = mc$.
S2: Decompose a/b via the division algorithm to obtain

$$\frac{a}{b} = \frac{1}{m(q+1)} + \frac{a-r}{b(q+1)}, \quad where \ c = aq + r; \ 0 \le r < a.$$

If the residual fraction $(a-r)/b(q+1)$ is a unit fraction, then the process terminates. Otherwise, the steps S1 and S2 are applied to the residual fraction(s) repeatedly until a unit fraction expansion is obtained.

Proof. First,

$$\frac{a}{b} = \frac{a(q+1)}{b(q+1)} = \frac{(aq+r)+(a-r)}{b(q+1)} = \frac{c+(a-r)}{b(q+1)} = \frac{1}{m(q+1)} + \frac{a-r}{b(q+1)}.$$

Second,

$$\frac{1}{m(q+1)} - \frac{a-r}{b(q+1)} = \frac{c-a+r}{b(q+1)} > 0.$$

Hence, $(a-r)/b(q+1) < 1/m(q+1) < a/b$, which implies the unit fractions obtained are all distinct. Third, $0 < a - r \leq a$, which implies the whole process will terminate in at most a steps. $\qquad\square$

The following results describe the basic properties of this new algorithm.

Corollary 3.1. *Let a, b be co-prime integers and $1 < a < b$. If a/b is decomposed via the Improved Fibonacci-Sylvester algorithm as*

$$\frac{a}{b} = \frac{1}{n_1} + \frac{1}{n_2} + \cdots + \frac{1}{n_k},$$

where $n_1 < n_2 < \cdots < n_k$, $k > 1$ and c_i, m_i are positive integers defined in Theorem 3.1, then
(a) $k \leq a$;
(b) $n_i(n_i/m_i - 1) < n_{i+1}$, where $1 \leq i \leq k - 1$, and
(c) $n_1 \prod_{i=1}^{k-1}(n_i/m_i - 1) < n_k \leq c_1 c_2 \cdots c_{k-1} n_1$.

Proof. (a) It follows from the proof of Theorem 3.1. (b) Let $a/b = p_0/q_0$ and p_i/q_i be the ith residual fraction generated, where $1 \leq i \leq k - 1$. By the division algorithm, $c_i = p_{i-1} d_i + r_i$, where d_i, r_i are integers and $0 \leq r_i < p_{i-1}$. Since $q_{i-1} = c_i m_i$ and $p_{i-1} d_i \leq c_i < p_{i-1}(d_i + 1)$, so $p_{i-1} d_i m_i \leq q_{i-1} < p_{i-1}(d_i + 1)m_i$. By Theorem 3.1, $n_i = q_i(d_i + 1)/c_i = m_i(d_i + 1)$. Hence, $p_{i-1}(n_i - m_i) \leq q_{i-1} < p_{i-1} n_i$, and $1/n_i < p_{i-1}/q_{i-1} \leq 1/(n_i - m_i)$. Since $1/n_{i+1} < p_{i-1}/q_{i-1} - 1/n_i \leq 1/(n_i - m_i) - 1/n_i = m_i/n_i(n_i - m_i)$, so $n_i(n_i - m_i) < m_i n_{i+1}$. (c) By Theorem 3.1, $n_2 < q_1 \leq c_1 n_1$, $n_3 < q_2 \leq c_2 n_2$, $n_4 < q_3 \leq c_3 n_3$, ..., and $n_k < q_{k-1} \leq c_{k-1} n_{k-1}$, so $n_k \leq c_1 c_2 \cdots c_{k-1} n_1$. By (b), $(n_1/m_1 - 1) < n_2/n_1$, $(n_2/m_2 - 1) < n_3/n_2$, ..., and $(n_{k-1}/m_{k-1} - 1) < n_k/n_{k-1}$, so $n_1 \prod_{i=1}^{k-1}(n_i/m_i - 1) < n_k$. Hence, $n_1 \prod_{i=1}^{k-1}(n_i/m_i - 1) < n_k \leq c_1 c_2 \cdots c_{k-1} n_1$. $\qquad\square$

Comparing Corollary 2.1(b) with Corollary 3.1(b), we see that the growth rate of the successive denominators, n_{i+1}/n_i, of the original Fibonacci-Sylvester algorithm is compartively faster than that of the Improved Fibonacci-Sylvester algorithm. It means that if both algorithms are used to compute an expansion for a given fraction and the expansions obtained are of equal length, then the maximal denominator generated by the original algorithm would be most likely larger than that of the improved algorithm. In fact, the examples described below support this argument.

Corollary 3.2. *Let a, b be co-prime integers and $1 < a < b$. If a/b is decomposed via the Improved Fibonacci-Sylvester algorithm into a unit* *fraction expansion and n_k is the maximal denominator, then $\log n_k <$ $2^{a-2} \log(bw)$, where w is the ceiling of c_1/a.*

Proof. From the proof of Corollary 3.1, we have $c_2 \le q_1 \le c_1 n_1$, $c_3 \le q_2 \le c_2 n_2 < c_1 c_2 n_1 \le (c_1 n_1)^2$, $c_4 \le q_3 \le c_3 n_3 < c_1 c_2 c_3 n_1 \le (c_1 n_1)^4$ and so on. Hence,

$$n_k < c_1 c_2 \cdots c_{k-1} n_1 < (c_1 n_1)^{2^{k-2}} \le (c_1 n_1)^{2^{a-2}}.$$

Since $w = d_1 + 1$ is equal to the ceiling of c_1/a and $c_1 n_1 = c_1 m_1 (d_1 + 1) = b(d_1 + 1)$, so the result follows after taking logarithm. □

Corollary 3.3. *The upper bound of the maximal denominator given in Corollary 3.2 is not greater than the upper bound given in Corollary 2.2.*

Proof. In Corollary 2.2, we have $bn_1 = b\lceil b/a \rceil$. On the other hand, in Corollary 3.2, we have $c_1 n_1 = c_1 (b/c_1) \lceil c_1/b \rceil = b \lceil c_1/a \rceil$. Since $\lceil c_1/a \rceil \le \lceil b/a \rceil$, so the result follows. □

The following examples illustrate how the Improved Fibonacci-Sylvester algorithm works. The same notations used in the proof of Corollary 3.1 are adopted.

Example 3.1. By the Improved Fibonacci-Sylvester algorithm, we obtain $3/7 = 1/3 + 1/14 + 1/42$, as shown in Table 4. (Note: $n_3 < c_1 c_2 n_1$.)

Table 4.

i	c_i	m_i	n_i	p_i	q_i
0	-	-	-	3	7
1	7	1	3	2	21
2	3	7	14	1	42
3	-	-	42	-	-

Example 3.2. By the Improved Fibonacci-Sylvester algorithm, we obtain $5/91 = 1/26 + 1/78 + 1/273$, as shown in Table 5. (Note: $n_3 < c_1 c_2 n_1$.)

Example 3.3. By the Improved Fibonacci-Sylvester algorithm, we obtain $5/121 = 1/33 + 1/99 + 1/1089$, as shown in Table 6. (Note: $n_3 < c_1 c_2 n_1$.)

From these examples, we can see that the maximum denominators obtained by the Improved Fibonacci-Sylvester algorithm are much less than

Table 5.

i	c_i	m_i	n_i	p_i	q_i
0	-	-	-	5	91
1	7	13	26	3	182
2	7	26	78	1	273
3	-	-	273	-	-

Table 6.

i	c_i	m_i	n_i	p_i	q_i
0	-	-	-	5	121
1	11	11	33	4	363
2	11	33	99	1	1089
3	-	-	1089	-	-

that obtained by the original algorithm. Gardner[8] mentioned that Bleicher did not know whether or not a three term expansion for 5/121 can have a maximal denominator less than 208725. The result of Example 3.3 provides a positive answer for it. In fact, the size of the maximal denominator has been reduced significantly by the new algorithm. The choice of c_i in each division step is crucial to account for such an improvement.

4. Implementation in Computer Algebra Systems

We have seen that the growth of the denominators in the unit fraction expansions could be quite significant. To automate the calculations involved, it will be convenient to implement the algorithm in computer algebra systems (CAS) and let CAS compute the denominators for the unit fraction expansions.

The pseudo-codes below are self-explanatory. They can be implemented in MAPLE or other CAS easily. The names **Fibo1** and **Fibo2** refer to the Fibonacci-Sylvester algorithm and the Improved Fibonacci-Sylvester algorithm, respectively.

Fibo1(a,b)
Input: co-prime integers a, b such that $1 < a < b$.
Output: the denominators of the unit fraction expansion of a/b.
if $a = 1$ **then return** $\{b\}$
$\quad c \leftarrow$ **ceil**(b/a)

$q \leftarrow$ **simplify**((ac-b)/(bc))
return $\{c\} \cup$ **Fibo1**(num(q), den(q)).

Fibo2(a,b)
Input: co-prime integers a, b such that $1 < a < b$.
Output: the denominators of the unit fraction expansion of a/b.
if $a = 1$ **then return** $\{b\}$
   $s \leftarrow$ **divisors**(b)
   $i \leftarrow 1$
   while $s[i] < a$ **do** $i \leftarrow i + 1$
   $c \leftarrow s[i]$
   $d \leftarrow$ **ceil**(c/a)
   $q \leftarrow$ **simplify**((ad-c)/(bd))
return $\{bd/c\} \cup$ **Fibo2**(num(q), den(q)).

Using the implemented programs, we can compare the effectiveness of **Fibo1** and **Fibo2** in computing unit fraction expansions. The tested results are summarized in the following two tables.

Table 7.   Comparison of the effectiveness of **Fibo1** and **Fibo2**.

Value of b	No. of a which are co-prime with b	No. of cases that they have equal max deno.	No. of cases that **Fibo2** has larger max deno.	No. of cases that **Fibo2** has smaller max deno.
10	3	3 (100.00%)	0 (0.00%)	0 (0.00%)
100	39	7 (17.95%)	2 (5.12%)	30 (76.92%)
1000	399	13 (3.26%)	6 (1.50%)	380 (95.23%)
10000	3999	31 (0.78%)	28 (0.70%)	3940 (98.52%)
100000	39999	45 (0.11%)	120 (0.30%)	39834 (99.59%)

The above results suggest that if the value of b is sufficiently large, then **Fibo2** has a larger chance to generate a unit fraction expansion with smaller maximal denominator than that of **Fibo1**. Also, if their expansions are of equal length, it is unlikely that **Fibo2** will generate a larger maximal denominator than **Fibo1**. The latter observation agrees very well with the theoretical analysis provided in Corollary 2.1 and Corollary 3.1.

The next table summarizes a few more tested results based on the examples given in [1,3,4]. The purpose is to provide a preliminary study the effectiveness of **Fibo2** in comparison with the Continued Fraction algo-

Table 8. Comparison of **Fibo1** and **Fibo2** when their expansions have equal lengths.

Value of b	No. of such cases	No. of cases that they have equal max deno.	No. of cases that **Fibo2** has larger max deno.	No. of cases that **Fibo2** has smaller max deno.
10	3	3 (100.00%)	0 (0.00%)	0 (0.00%)
100	29	7 (24.13%)	0 (0.00%)	22 (75.86%)
1000	99	7 (7.07%)	0 (0.00%)	92 (92.93%)
10000	333	3 (0.90%)	0 (0.00%)	330 (99.10%)
100000	1119	3 (0.27%)	0 (0.00%)	1116 (99.73%)

rithm,[3] the Bleicher-Erdős algorithm,[4] the Farey-Series algorithm[1] and the Golomb algorithm.[9]

For convenience, we use the following abbreviations to name the algorithms concerned,

- C.F. — the Continued Fraction algorithm;
- B & E — the Bleicher and Erdős algorithm;
- Farey — the Farey-Series algorithm; and
- Golomb — the Golomb algorithm.

From the above results, we can see that the Improved Fibonacci-Sylvester algorithm can generate unit fraction expansions with smallest maximal denominators for the tested examples. However, we do not claim that it is already an optimal algorithm, in the sense that it can always generate unit fraction expansions with smallest maximum denominators and shortest length. As far as we know, the optimal algorithm does not exist yet. Thus, it has room for further research. For those who are interested in studying the asymptotic bounds for the maximal denominators and the length of unit fraction expansions, please refer to [2,4,10,13,15,16].

5. Final Remarks

In this paper, we have presented an Improved Fibonacci-Sylvester algorithm for computing unit fraction expansions, by modifying the *greedy* step of the original algorithm. Tested examples suggest this new algorithm can generate unit fraction expansions with smaller maximal denominators than the original algorithm in most cases. In fact, this merit is very significant when we are comparing examples whose expansions are of equal lengths. However, there still has room for further improvements. For instance, there may be more than one divisor of b which is greater than a,

Table 9. Effectiveness of the Improved Fibonacci-Sylvester algorithm compared with some existing algorithms for computing unit fraction expansions.

a/b	Name of algorithm	maximal denominator in the expansion	no. of terms in the expansion
$\frac{5}{121}$	C.F.	11737	5
	B & E	87120	7
	Farey	11737	5
	Golomb	11737	5
	Fibo1	$> 1.5 \times 10^{24}$	5
	Fibo2	1089	3
$\frac{19}{123}$	C.F.	1599	3
	B & E	14760	6
	Farey	8323	3
	Golomb	1599	3
	Fibo1	8323	3
	Fibo2	1107	5
$\frac{59}{121}$	C.F.	9680	5
	B & E	87190	6
	Farey	20328	4
	Golomb	9680	21
	Fibo1	20328	4
	Fibo2	363	5
$\frac{21}{23}$	C.F.	253	6
	B & E	552	6
	Farey	230734	6
	Golomb	253	11
	Fibo1	644046	5
	Fibo2	184	6

it may be worthwhile to use all such candidates to obtain unit fraction expansions and then choose the optimal one as the final answer. It will be an interesting experimental research. Another research direction would be to compare the effectiveness of the existing algorithms via implementations and testings using a large tested pool of proper fractions. It would perhaps give us insight on the weaknesses of existing algorithms and ideas for their further improvements. Also, there is apparently lack of research on finding a lower bound for the number of terms involved in unit fraction expansions, so it is another good research direction to pursue. In his book, Guy[10] mentioned quite a lot of interesting unsolved number theory problems related to unit fractions. They are often simple to understand but yet challenging, which could arouse even the junior undergraduate students to study.

Therefore, it opens up educational ideas for us to incorporate the topic of unit fractions in undergraduate mathematics courses, such as elementary number theory, history of mathematics or mathematics in computer science, etc. For instance, asking the students to implement and explore the existing algorithms for unit fraction expansions could be a very interesting and meaningful individual or small group project. Relevant examples for teaching purposes can be found in [2,7,12].

References

1. A. Beck, M. N. Bleicher, D. W. Crowe, *Excursions into Mathematics* (A. K. Peters, Massachusetts, 2000).
2. L. Beeckmans, *J. Num. Theory* **43**, 173–185 (1993).
3. M. N. Bleicher, *J. Num. Theory* **4**, 342–382 (1972).
4. M. N. Bleicher, P. Erdős, *J. Num. Theory* **8**, 157–168 (1976).
5. D. E. Dobbs, A. J. Hetzel, *Int.J. Math. Educ. Sci. Technol.* **34**(5), 742–751 (2003).
6. H. Eves, *An Introduction to the History of Mathematics (6th edition)* (Saunders College Publishing, London, 1990).
7. P. Ernest, in *Mathematics in School* (Longman, London, 1989).
8. M. Gardner, *Scientific American* **23**(4), 22–26 (1978).
9. S. W. Golomb, *American Math. Month.* **69**, 785–786 (1962).
10. R. Guy, *Unsolved Problems in Number Theory (2nd edition)* (Springer-Verlag, New York, 1994).
11. Y. K. Man, *Mathmedia* **26**(4), 52–59 (2002).
12. Y. K. Man, *Int.J. Math. Educ. Sci. Technol.* **35**(4), 612–617 (2004).
13. G. Martin, *Trans. Amer. Math. Soc.* **351**(9), 3641–3657 (1999).
14. G. Robins, C. Shulte, *The Rhind Mathematical Papyrus* (Dover, New York, 1987).
15. H. Yokota, *J. Num. Theory* **28**, 258–271 (1988).
16. H. Yokota, *J. Num. Theory* **28**, 272–282 (1988).

FINITE SERIES EXPANSIONS FOR POWERS OF SINE AND COSINE FUNCTIONS VIA *MATHEMATICA*

TILAK DE ALWIS

Mathematics Department, Southeastern Louisiana University
Hammond, LA 70403, USA
E-mail: talwis@selu.edu

In this paper, we obtain finite series expansions for positive integer powers of sine and cosine functions. The terms of the expansions consist of trigonometric functions of multiple angles. Such formulas do exist in the literature. However, more than the final results themselves, we are interested in the actual method of obtaining them. We use the method of successive differences of sequences and the computer algebra system (CAS) Mathematica to obtain our results.

Keywords: Double angle formula, Mathematica, mathematical induction, Pascal triangle, binomial coefficient.

1. Introduction

Let n be a positive integer. One of the main goals of this paper is to obtain finite series expansions for $\text{Sin}^n x$ and $\text{Cos}^n x$. The terms of expansions will consist of sines and cosines of multiple angles, namely terms such as $\text{Sin}(mx)$ and $\text{Cos}(mx)$ where m represents an even or odd positive integer. Such expansions do exist in the literature.[1] What is unique in this paper, more than the final results themselves, is the method used to obtain them:

We first consider two cases, n is odd, or n is even. For example, for the case n is even, suppose we want to obtain an expansion for $\text{Cos}^n x$. For smaller values of n such as 2 or 4, it is not difficult to perform the calculation by hand, using the following Double Angle Formula from trigonometry:[2]

$$\text{Cos}\, 2x = 2\text{Cos}^2 x - 1 \tag{1}$$

The above Eq. (1) implies the following formula:

$$\text{Cos}^2 x = \frac{1}{2}(1 + \text{Cos}\, 2x) \tag{2}$$

The above Eq. (2) provides a formula for $\text{Cos}^n x$ for $n = 2$. To obtain a corresponding formula for $n = 4$, one can square both sides of Eq. (2) as follows:

$$\text{Cos}^4 x = \frac{1}{4}[1 + 2\text{Cos}(2x) + \text{Cox}^2(2x)] = \frac{1}{4}\left[1 + 2\text{Cos}(2x) + \frac{1 + \text{Cos}(4x)}{2}\right]$$

$$(3)$$

By simplifying the Eq. (3), we obtain the following expression for $\text{Cos}^4 x$:

$$\text{Cos}^4 x = \frac{1}{8}[3 + 4\text{Cos}(2x) + \text{Cox}(4x)] \tag{4}$$

However, for larger even values of n, the above calculations are somewhat tedious to perform by hand. Therefore, one can use a CAS such as *Mathematica*[3] to help with the task.

We will use the following procedure: Using *Mathematica*, we first obtain expressions for $\text{Cos}^n x$, for some sample even values such as $n = 2, 4, 6, \ldots$. Then we will arrange the coefficients of these expressions in a certain array, similar to Pascal's Triangle of Binomial Coefficients.[4] By inspecting certain diagonal sequences in this array, one can consider their successive differences. Using these successive differences, one can conjecture certain formulas for the sequences, with the aid of Mathematica. In this way, one can proceed to find a general closed-form formula to describe any entry in our array of coefficients. This leads to a closed-form formula for $\text{Cos}^n x$ for the case n is even. The formula we will obtain is a finite series expansion for $\text{Cos}^n x$ in terms of cosines of even multiples of x, such as $\text{Cos}\,2x, \text{Cos}\,4x, \text{Cos}\,6x, \ldots$. *Mathematica* can be used to check the accuracy of the conjectured formula for any specific even value of n. However, such verification does not qualify as a mathematical proof. One can use methods such as mathematical induction[5] to prove the conjectured formula mathematically. Similarly, one can also obtain a formula for $\text{Cos}^n x$, where n is a positive odd integer. Using the finite series expansions for $\text{Cos}^n x$ one can deduce similar expansions for $\text{Sin}^n x$ as well.

The above described method of obtaining finite series expansions for $\text{Cos}^n x$ uses only very basic mathematical techniques. Therefore it is even accessible to the very beginner. Our method is quite valuable, because it promotes the pattern recognition skills, and also the usage of a CAS as a conjecture-forming tool. For another approach using Fast Discrete Fourier Transform, the reader is encouraged to see the reference.[6]

In the next section, we will show the specific details of the method described in the introductory section.

2. Finite Series Expansions for $\text{Cos}^n x$ Where n Is a Positive Even Integer

In this section, we will obtain a finite series expansion for $\text{Cos}^n x$, where n is any positive even integer. Since n is a positive even integer, one can write $n = 2k$, where k is some positive integer.

For any given n, one can use the **"TrigReduce"** command of *Mathematica*[3] to obtain an expression for $\text{Cos}^n x$ in terms of cosines of multiple angles. For example, to obtain an expression for $\text{Cos}^8 x$, one can use the following *Mathematica* command:

Input: TrigReduce [Cos[x]^8]

In order to execute the above command, press **"Shift-Enter"**. The output is given below:

Output:

$$\frac{1}{128}(35 + 56\text{Cos}[2x] + 28\text{Cos}[4x] + 8\text{Cos}[6x] + \text{Cos}[8x])$$

Rather than performing the above calculation for various even n values one at a time, the **"Table"** command of *Mathematica*[3] enables one to perform a series of calculations at once. For example, in order to obtain expressions for $\text{Cos}^{2k} x$ for $k = 1, 2, \ldots, 8$ one can use the following single command:

Input: TableForm[Table[TrigReduce[Cos[x]^(2k)],{k, 1, 8}]]

The output is given in the following table.

Table 2.1.   Expansions for $(\text{Cos x})\hat{\ }(2k)$ for $k = 1, 2, \ldots, 8$

$[1 + \text{Cos}(2x)]/2$

$[3 + 4\text{Cos}(2x) + \text{Cos}(4x)]/8$

$[10 + 15\text{Cos}(2x) + 6\text{Cos}(4x) + \text{Cos}(6x)]/32$

$[35 + 56\text{Cos}(2x) + 28\text{Cos}(4x) + 8\text{Cos}(6x) + \text{Cos}(8x)]/128$

$[126 + 210\text{Cos}(2x) + 120\text{Cos}(4x) + 45\text{Cos}(6x) + 10\text{Cos}(8x)$
$\qquad\qquad\qquad\qquad\qquad\qquad\qquad\qquad +\text{Cos}(10x)]/512$

$[462 + 792\text{Cos}(2x) + 495\text{Cos}(4x) + 220\text{Cos}(6x) + 66\text{Cos}(8x)$
$\qquad\qquad\qquad\qquad\qquad\qquad +12\text{Cos}(10x) + \text{Cos}(12x)]/2048$

$[1716 + 3003\text{Cos}(2x) + 2002\text{Cos}(4x) + 1001\text{Cos}(6x)$
$\qquad\qquad +364\text{Cos}(8x) + 91\text{Cos}(10x) + 14\text{Cos}(12x) + \text{Cos}(14x)]/8192$

$[6435 + 11440\text{Cos}(2x) + 8008\text{Cos}(4x) + 4368\text{Cos}(6x)$
$\qquad\qquad +1820\text{Cos}(8x) + 560\text{Cos}(10x) + 120\text{Cos}(12x)$
$\qquad\qquad\qquad\qquad +16\text{Cos}(14x) + \text{Cos}(16x)]/32768$

Our task is to find a pattern for the coefficients in the above Table 2.1. The fractional coefficients of the rows are given by 1/2, 1/8, 1/32, 1/128, ... These clearly exhibit a pattern, given by the sequence $1/2^{2k-1}$, where $k = 1, 2, \ldots$. Therefore, by forgetting these fractional coefficients, let us arrange the integer coefficients of each row in the following Table 2.2.

Table 2.2. The integer coefficients of rows of Table 2.1.

1	1							
3	4	1						
10	15	6	1					
35	56	28	8	1				
126	210	120	45	10	1			
462	792	495	220	66	12	1		
1716	3003	2002	1001	364	91	14	1	
6435	11440	8008	4368	1820	560	120	16	1

We now want to find a single formula to describe the entries of the above array. For the moment, let us ignore the first row and the first column of the above array. Define the diagonal sequence $1, 1, 1, \ldots$ by $v_1(m)$, the diagonal sequence $4, 6, 8, 10, 12, \ldots$ by $v_2(m)$, the diagonal sequence $15, 28, 45, 66, 91, \ldots$ by $v_3(m)$, etc., where $m = 1, 2, \ldots$. The patterns for $v_1(m)$ and $v_2(m)$ are clear, so our immediate task is to analyze the other sequences starting with $v_3(m)$. Since we are about to take the successive differences of $v_3(m)$, let us define $v_3(m)$ to be the same as the sequence $v_{3,0}(m)$, which is given by $15, 28, 45, 66, 91, \ldots$. The successive differences of this sequence, denoted by $v_{3,1}(m)$ are given by $13, 17, 21, 25, \ldots$. Now form the successive differences of $v_{3,1}(m)$. In this way, we obtain the sequence $v_{3,2}(m)$ given by $4, 4, 4, \ldots$ where all the terms are equal to a constant, which is 2^2. Note that $v_{3,2}(m)$ is just the second successive differences of the original sequence $v_{3,0}(m)$ or $v_3(m)$. What this means is that starting from the constant sequence $v_{3,2}(m)$ and using a suitable addition process twice, one can arrive back at the original sequence $v_3(m)$, as given by the following equations:

$$v_{3,0}(1) = 15; \; v_{3,1}(1) = 13; \; v_{3,2}(m) = 4 \tag{5}$$

$$v_{3,1}(m) = v_{3,1}(m-1) + v_{3,2}(m-1) \text{ for } m \geq 2 \tag{6}$$

$$v_{3,0}(m) = v_{3,0}(m-1) + v_{3,1}(m-1) \text{ for } m \geq 2 \tag{7}$$

The Eq. (6) and (7) imply the following equation for $i = 0, 1$:

$$v_{3,i}(m) = v_{3,i}(1) + \sum_{j=1}^{m-1} v_{3,i+1}(j) \tag{8}$$

Therefore, one can use Eq. (8) together with Eq. (5) to find a formula for the sequence $v_3(m)$. *Mathematica* is an ideal tool to perform such calculations efficiently. For this purpose, one can use the "**Sum**" command of *Mathematica*[3] as shown below:

Program 2.1:
```
Clear[v];
v[3,2][m_]:=4;
v[3,1][1]=13;
v[3,0][1]=15;
v[3,i_][m_]:=v[3,i][1]+Sum[v[3,i+1][j],{j,1,m-1}];
Factor[Simplify[v[3,0][m]]]
```

Press "**Shift-Enter**" to execute the program. As the output, one obtains $(2 + m)(3 + 2m)$, which means that we have obtained the following formula for the sequence $v_3(m)$, where $m = 1, 2, \ldots$:

$$v_3(m) = (m + 2)(2m + 3) \tag{9}$$

Now consider the next sequence $v_4(m) = v_{4,0}(m)$ given by $56, 120, 220, \ldots$. The first successive differences yield $v_{4,1}(m)$, given by the terms $64, 100, 144, 196, 256, \ldots$. The successive differences of $v_{4,1}(m)$ yield the sequence $v_{4,2}(m)$, whose terms are given by $36, 44, 52, 60, \ldots$. Finally, the successive differences of $v_{4,2}(m)$ yield the sequence $v_{4,3}(m)$, whose terms are $8, 8, 8, 8, \ldots$. Note that $v_{4,3}(m)$ is a constant sequence, whose terms are all equal to 2^3. Therefore, as done before, starting from this constant sequence, one can go back and recover the original sequence $v_4(m)$ by a suitable addition process. See the following equations:

$$v_{4,0}(1) = 56; \ v_{4,1}(1) = 64; \ v_{4,2}(1) = 36; \ v_{4,3}(m) = 8 \tag{10}$$

$$v_{4,i}(m) = v_{4,i}(1) + \sum_{j=1}^{m-1} v_{4,i+1}(j) \tag{11}$$

One can use Eqs. (10) and (11) to write the following *Mathematica* program to find a formula for $v_4(m)$:

Program 2.2:
```
v[4,3][m_]:=8;
v[4,2][1]=36;
v[4,1][1]=64;
v[4,0][1]=56;
v[4,i_][m_]:=v[4,i][1]+Sum[v[4,i+1][j],{j,1,m-1}];
Factor[Simplify[v[4,0][m]]]
```

When the program is executed, one gets $(2/3)(2 + m)(3 + m)(5 + 2m)$ as the output. This means we have the following formula for $v_4(m)$:

$$v_4(m) = \frac{2}{3}(m + 2)(m + 3)(2m + 5) \qquad (12)$$

One can similarly analyze the sequences $v_5(m) = v_{5,0}(m)$ given by $210, 495, 1001, \ldots$. The fourth differences of this sequence turn out to be a constant sequence $v_{5,4}(m)$, where the constant is equal to 2^4. Therefore, one can use a *Mathematica* program similar to Program 2.1 or 2.2 to obtain the following result:

$$v_5(m) = \frac{1}{6}(m + 3)(m + 4)(2m + 5)(2m + 7) \qquad (13)$$

Similarly, one can obtain the following formula for the sequence $v_6(m)$:

$$v_6(m) = \frac{1}{15}(m + 3)(m + 4)(m + 5)(2m + 7)(2m + 9) \qquad (14)$$

Looking back, the Eqs. (9), (12), (13), and (14) provide formulas for the sequences $v_3(m)$, $v_4(m)$, $v_5(m)$ and $v_6(m)$ respectively. We want to find a common pattern for these sequences, but as of right now, the pattern does not seem to be very clear. Observe that some of the terms in Eqs. (9), (12), (13), and (14) are of the form $(m + k)$, while the others are of the form $(2m + k)$, where k is some positive integer. Therefore, let us rewrite these four equations as follows, so that all the terms are of the form $(2m + k)$:

$$v_3(m) = \frac{1}{2}(2m + 3)(2m + 4) = \frac{1}{2!}(2m + 3)(2m + 4) \qquad (15)$$

$$v_4(m) = \frac{2}{3}\frac{(2m + 4)(2m + 6)(2m + 5)}{2^2} = \frac{1}{3!}(2m+4)(2m+5)(2m+6) \qquad (16)$$

$$v_5(m) = \frac{1}{6}\frac{(2m + 6)(2m + 8)(2m + 5)(2m + 7)}{2^2}$$
$$= \frac{1}{4!}(2m + 5)(2m + 6)(2m + 7)(2m + 8) \qquad (17)$$

$$v_6(m) = \frac{1}{15} \frac{(2m+6)(2m+8)(2m+10)(2m+7)(2m+9)}{2^3}$$

$$= \frac{1}{5!}(2m+6)(2m+7)(2m+8)(2m+9)(2m+10)$$

(18)

The Eqs. (15)–(18) clearly reveal a certain pattern. Thus, we were able to conjecture the following formula for the sequence $v_k(m)$ where m and k are positive integers with $k \geq 3$:

$$v_k(m) = \binom{2m+2k-2}{k-1}$$

(19)

As can be verified directly, Eq. (19) is also true for $k = 1$ and $k = 2$, where m is any positive integer.

We now want to find a formula to describe an arbitrary entry in any row or column of Table 2.2. In order to do this, we need an additional notation. Recall that the kth row of Table 2.2 corresponds to the integer coefficients of the expansion of $\mathrm{Cos}^{2k}x$, where k is any positive integer. Therefore, let us denote the sequence of elements of the kth row of Table 2.2 by $a_{k,0}$, $a_{k,1}$, $a_{k,2}, \ldots$, $a_{k,k}$, where k is any positive integer. It is clear that $a_{k,k}=1$ for any positive integer k and $a_{k,k-1}=2k$ for any positive integer $k > 1$. On the other hand, it is not hard to see that $a_{k,1} = v_k(1)$, $a_{k,2} = v_{k-1}(1),\ldots$, etc, where k is any positive integer. So using Eq. (19) one can in general write the following, where k and i are any positive integers such that $0 < i \leq k$:

$$a_{k,i} = v_{k-i-1}(i) = \binom{2k}{k-i}$$

(20)

However, the above Eq. (20) is not valid for $i = 0$. This is so because, when $i = 0$, the right-hand side of Eq. (20) yields $\binom{2k}{k}$, producing the sequence $2, 6, 20, 70, 252, \ldots$ for different positive integers k. However, the actual sequence $a_{k,0}$ is just the first column of Table 2.2, consisting of the entries $1, 3, 10, 35, 126, \ldots$. This motivates the following formula for $a_{k,0}$, where k is any positive integer:

$$a_{k,0} = \frac{1}{2}\binom{2k}{k}$$

(21)

We are finally in a position to conjecture a general closed-form formula for $\mathrm{Cos}^{2k}(x)$ where k is any positive integer. Recall that for any positive integer k, the kth row of Table 2.1 gives the formula for $\mathrm{Cos}^{2k}(x)$, and the fractional coefficient of this row is just $1/2^{2k-1}$. All the integer coefficients of Table 2.1 are given in Table 2.2. Moreover, the coefficients of the kth row of Table 2.2

are given by $a_{k,i}$ where i is an integer such that $0 \le i \le k$. Combining these remarks with Eqs. (20) and (21), we finally have the following conjecture:

$$\text{Cos}^{2k}(x) = \frac{1}{2^{2k-1}} \left[\frac{1}{2} \binom{2k}{k} + \sum_{i=1}^{k} \binom{2k}{k-i} \text{Cos}(2ix) \right] \qquad (22)$$

The Eq. (22) expresses an even power of a cosine function as a finite series whose terms are a linear combination of cosines of even multiples of angles. *Mathematica* can be used to verify the accuracy of the equation for any specific value of k as follows:

Program 2.3
```
k=Random[Integer,{1,100}] (*This selects a random integer
                                    between 1 and 100*);
expr1=TrigReduce[Cos[x]^(2k)];
expr2=(1/2^(2k-1))((1/2)Binomial[2k,k]+
                Sum[Binomial[2k,k-i]*Cos[2i*x],{i,1,k}]);
Simplify[expr1-expr2]
```

The above program chooses as k any random integer between 1 and 100, and calculates two expressions: The first expression "expr1" is a direct calculation of $\text{Cos}^{2k}(x)$ using the **"TrigReduce"** command of *Mathematica*. The second expression "expr2" is the same as Eq. (22). The last line of the program calculates and simplifies the difference between these two expressions. When the program is executed, one gets zero as the output, which means that "expr1" is equal to "expr2". Therefore, the program checks the accuracy of Eq. (22) for the chosen value of k. However, this is not a mathematical proof, but merely a verification of the formula for a specific value of k.

Although excluded here due to space limitations, one can use mathematical induction[5] to prove Eq. (22). for any positive integer k, and any real number x.

In the next section, we will obtain a formula for $\text{Cos}^n x$ where n is a positive odd integer.

3. Finite Series Expansions for $\text{Cos}^n x$ Where n Is a Positive Odd Integer

Suppose n is a positive odd integer. Without loss of generality, one can assume that $n > 1$. Then write $n = 2k + 1$ for some positive integer k. The goal in this section is to obtain a finite series expansion for $\text{Cos}^{2k+1}(x)$.

One way of doing this is to use a procedure very similar to that of the previous section. However, another method is to use Eq. (22) obtained in the previous section to our advantage. For example, let us multiply both sides of Eq. (22) by $\text{Cos}\,x$ to obtain the following:

$$\text{Cos}^{2k+1}x = \frac{1}{2^{2k-1}}\left\{\frac{1}{2}\binom{2k}{k}\text{Cos}\,x + \sum_{i=1}^{k}\binom{2k}{k-i}\text{Cos}(2ix)\text{Cos}\,x\right\} \quad (23)$$

The product formula for cosine, $\text{Cos}\,A\text{Cos}\,B = (1/2)[\text{Cos}(A+B)+\text{Cos}(A-B)]$ enables one to rewrite the product terms $\text{Cos}(2ix)\text{Cos}\,x$ in Eq. (23) as a sum of cosine terms.[2] See below:

$$\text{Cos}^{2k+1}x = \frac{1}{2^k}\left\{\binom{2k}{k}\text{Cos}\,x + \sum_{i=1}^{k}\binom{2k}{k-i}[\text{Cos}[(2i+1)x]+\text{Cos}[(2i-1)x]]\right\}$$

$$= \frac{1}{2^k}\left\{\binom{2k}{k}\text{Cos}\,x + \sum_{i=1}^{k}\binom{2k}{k-i}\text{Cos}[(2i+1)x]+\sum_{j=0}^{k-1}\binom{2k}{k-j-1}\text{Cos}[(2j+1)x]\right\}$$

$$= \frac{1}{2^k}\left\{\binom{2k}{k}\text{Cos}\,x + \sum_{i=1}^{k-1}\left[\binom{2k}{k-i}+\binom{2k}{k-i-1}\right]\text{Cos}[(2i+1)x]\right.$$

$$\left. + \binom{2k}{0}\text{Cos}[(2k+1)x]+\binom{2k}{k-1}\text{Cos}\,x\right\}$$

$$= \frac{1}{2^{2k}}\left\{\text{Cos}\,x\left[\binom{2k}{k-1}+\binom{2k}{k}\right]+\sum_{i=1}^{k-1}\binom{2k+1}{k-i}\text{Cos}[(2i+1)x]+\binom{2k}{0}\text{Cos}[(2k+1)x]\right\}$$

$$= \frac{1}{2^{2k}}\left\{\binom{2k+1}{k}\text{Cos}\,x+\sum_{i=1}^{k}\binom{2k+1}{k-i}\text{Cos}[(2i+1)x]\right\}$$

$$= \frac{1}{2^{2k}}\sum_{i=0}^{k}\binom{2k+1}{k-i}\text{Cos}[(2i+1)x]$$

Therefore, one obtains the following formula for $\text{Cos}^{2k+1}x$:

$$\text{Cos}^{2k+1}x = \frac{1}{2^{2k}}\sum_{i=0}^{k}\binom{2k+1}{k-i}\text{Cos}[(2i+1)x] \quad (24)$$

The above Eq. (24) is valid for any integer $k \geq 0$, and for any real number x. One can also prove Eq. (24) independently from Eq. (22), using mathematical induction.

We are now also in a position to find finite series expansions for powers of sine functions. One method is to set up and analyze an array similar to the previous section with the help of *Mathematica*. Another method is to deduce them directly from Eqs. (22) and (24). We will follow the latter approach:

The Eq. (22) is valid for any positive integer k and for any real number x. Therefore, replace x by $\pi/2 - x$ to obtain the following equation:

$$\text{Cos}^{2k}(\pi/2 - x) = \frac{1}{2^{2k-1}} \left[\frac{1}{2} \binom{2k}{k} + \sum_{i=1}^{k} \binom{2k}{k-i} \text{Cos}[(2i(\pi/2 - x)] \right]$$
(25)

Since $\text{Cos}(\pi/2 - x) = \text{Sin}\,x$ and $\text{Cos}[(2i(\pi/2 - x)] = (-1)^i\text{Cos}(2ix)$, Eq. (25) simplifies to the following:

$$\text{Sin}^{2k}x = \frac{1}{2^{2k-1}} \left[\frac{1}{2} \binom{2k}{k} + \sum_{i=1}^{k} (-1)^i \binom{2k}{k-i} \text{Cos}(2ix) \right]$$
(26)

Similarly, one can replace x by $\pi/2 - x$ in Eq. (24) and simplify to obtain the following:

$$\text{Sin}^{2k+1}(x) = \frac{1}{2^{2k}} \sum_{i=0}^{k} (-1)^i \binom{2k+1}{k-i} \text{Sin}[(2i+1)x]$$
(27)

The Eqs. (26) and (27) provide finite series expansions for positive integer powers of $\text{Sin}\,x$ in terms of trigonometric functions of multiple angles.

4. Pascal Type Properties for the Coefficients in the Expansion of $\text{Cos}^{2k}x$

In this section we will investigate an interesting property of the coefficients given in Table 2.2, arising from the expansion of $\text{Cos}^{2k}x$, for positive integer values of k. The properties we will observe are very similar to the one exhibited by Pascal's Triangle consisting of Binomial Coefficients.[4]

Again, recall the notation that we have been using. For any positive integer k, the coefficients in the kth row of Table 2.2 are denoted by $a_{k,0}$, $a_{k,1},\ldots, a_{k,k}$. It is not hard to make the following observations for Table 2.2:

(a) Consider the first two elements of say, row 3. They are $a_{3,0} = 10$ and $a_{3,1} = 15$. Note that the first element of the next row, i.e. $a_{4,0}$ can be obtained as a linear combination of those two elements $a_{3,0}$ and $a_{3,1}$. Specifically, $a_{4,0} = 35 = 2(10)+15 = 2a_{3,0}+a_{3,1}$. The same relationship holds between any two consecutive rows. In general, we can write this property as follows:

$$2a_{k,0} + a_{k,1} = a_{k+1,0} \quad k \geq 1$$
(28)

(b) Consider the first three elements of say, row 3. They are $a_{3,0} = 10$, $a_{3,1} = 15$ and $a_{3,2} = 6$. Observe that the second element of the next row, i.e. $a_{4,1}$ can be obtained as a specific linear combination of those three elements. Specifically, $a_{4,1} = 56 = 2(10+15)+6 = 2(a_{3,0}+a_{3,1})+a_{3,2}$. The same relationship holds between any two rows. More accurately, we can write this relationship as follows:

$$2(a_{k,0} + a_{k,1}) + a_{k,2} = a_{k+1,1} \text{ for } k \geq 1 \tag{29}$$

In the above Eq. (29), for $k = 1$ the entry $a_{k,2}$ is interpreted as zero.

(c) For any row, consider any three consecutive elements, other than the first three consecutive elements. For example, for row 3, consider the three consecutive elements $a_{3,1} = 15$, $a_{3,2} = 6$ and $a_{3,3} = 1$. Then the entry $a_{4,2}$ can be obtained as a linear combination of those three entries. Namely, $a_{4,2} = 28 = 15 + 2(6) + 1 = a_{3,1} + 2a_{3,2} + a_{3,3}$. In general, we have the following relationship, valid for $i \geq 2$, $k \geq 3$ and $i \leq k$:

$$a_{k,i-1} + 2a_{k,i} + a_{k,i+1} = a_{k+1,i} \tag{30}$$

In the above Eq. (30), $a_{k,k+1}$ entry is interpreted as zero. The Eqs. (28), (29), and (30) serve an important purpose. Using these three relationships, given any row of Table 2.2, one can build the next row! This idea is quite similar to the corresponding property for Pascal's Triangle consisting of Binomial Coefficients.[4]

5. Conclusion

In this paper, we used a computer algebra system to conjecture certain types of trigonometric formulas, namely finite series expansions for powers of sine and cosine functions. Most of these formulas are available in literature, but the novelty of the paper is the particular method used to obtain them. With the aid of a CAS, even the beginning student is in a position to conjecture many other formulas in trigonometry. Also of interest are the relationships between the elements of the array given in the paper. These are similar to the relationships in Pascal's Triangle consisting of the Binomial Coefficients, and the reader is encouraged to discover more such connections!

References

1. I. S. Gradshetyn and I. M. Ryzhik, *Tables of Integrals, Series, and Products* (Academic Press, San Diego, 1980).

2. M. L. Lial, J. Hornsby, and D. I. Schneider, *Trigonometry*, 7th ed. (Addison-Wesley, Boston, 2001).

3. S. Wolfram, *The Mathematica Book*, 5th ed. (Cambridge University Press, Cambridge, 2003).

4. D. M. Burton, *Elementary Number Theory*, 3rd ed. (Wm. C. Brown, Dubuque, Iowa, 1989).

5. S. S. Epp, *Discrete Mathematics with Applications*, 2nd ed. (PWS Publishing, Boston, 1995).

6. A. Akritas, J. Uhl, P. Vikglas, On Some Applications of the (Fast) Discrete Fourier Transform, to appear in *The Mathematica Journal*.

SOLVING THE HEAT AND WAVE EQUATIONS WITH THE (FAST) DISCRETE FOURIER TRANSFORM

ALKIVIADIS G. AKRITAS and PANAGIOTIS S. VIGKLAS

Department of Computer and Communication Engineering, University of Thessaly
Volos, GR-38221, Greece
E-mail: {akritas, pviglas}@uth.gr
www.uth.gr

J. JERRY UHL

Department of Mathematics, University of Illinois at Urbana-Champaign
Urbana, IL 61801, USA
E-mail: juhl@cm.math.uiuc.edu

In this paper, we present in detail a little known application of the fast Discrete Fourier Transform (DFT), also known as FFT. Namely, we first examine the use of FFT in approximating polynomials with sines and cosines (also known as Fast Fourier Fit or FFF) and then derive and solve the heat and wave equations.

Keywords: Fast discrete Fourier transform, FFT, fast Fourier fit, heat and wave equations.

1. Introduction

We begin with a review of the basic definition needed. Let $\mathcal{R}$ be a ring, $n \in \mathbb{Z}_{\geq 1}$, and $\omega \in \mathcal{R}$ be a primitive nth root of unity; that is, $\omega^n = 1$ and $\omega^{n/t} - 1$ is not a zero divisor (or, $\omega^{n/t} - 1 \neq 0$) for any prime divisor t of n. We represent the polynomial $f = \sum_{i=0}^{n-1} f_i x^i \in \mathcal{R}[x]$, of degree $< n$ by the coefficient list, in reverse order, $\{f_0, \ldots, f_{n-1}\} \in \mathcal{R}^n$.

Definition 1.1 (DFT). The R-linear map $DFT_\omega : \mathcal{R}^n \to \mathcal{R}^n$, which evaluates a polynomial at the powers of ω, i.e. $DFT_\omega : \{f_0, \ldots, f_{n-1}\} \to \frac{1}{\sqrt{n}}\{f(1), f(\omega), \ldots, f(\omega^{n-1})\}$, is called the `Discrete Fourier Transform` (DFT).

In other words, the Discrete Fourier Transform is a special multipoint evaluation at the powers $1, \omega, \ldots, \omega^{n-1}$ of a primitive nth root of unity ω.

The fast implementation of the DFT is known as the fast DFT, or simply as FFT; it can be performed in time $O(n \log n)$. Details can be found in the literature.[1,6,7] Keeping it simple, we mention in passing that the inverse Discrete Fourier Transform is defined as the problem of interpolation at the powers of ω and is easily solved.

In *Mathematica* the map DFT_ω and its inverse are implemented–for the complex numbers–by the functions `Fourier[]`, and `InverseFourier[]`. The fast Fourier transform is implemented in `Fourier[]`. So, for example, the definition is verified by

```
f[x_]  :=  x³ - 7x + 7;
{Fourier[CoefficientList[f[x], x]]} ==
    {n = 4; ω = e^((2 π I)/n) ; 1/√n {f[1], f[ω], f[ω²], f[ω³]}}
```

True

2. FFT Is the Basis of Fast Fourier Fit (FFF)

We next turn our attention to the problem of Fast Fourier Fit or FFF, i.e. the problem of approximating functions with sines and/or cosines.

Definition 2.1. Periodic functions $f : \mathbb{R} \to \mathbb{C}$, in one real variable and with values in the complex plane, can be approximated (or fitted) by complex trigonometric polynomials of the form

$$f(t) = \sum_{k=-n}^{n} c_k e^{k\omega i t} = \frac{\alpha_0}{2} + \sum_{k=1}^{n}(\alpha_k \cos(k\omega t) + \beta_k \sin(k\omega t))$$

where c_k are the Fourier fit coefficients satisfying

$$c_0 = \frac{\alpha_0}{2}, \quad c_k = \frac{\alpha_k - i\beta_k}{2}, \quad c_{-k} = \frac{\alpha_k + i\beta_k}{2}$$

and $\alpha_0 = 2c_0$, $\alpha_k = c_k + c_{-k}$, $\beta_k = i(c_k - c_{-k})$ for $k = 1,\ldots,n$, and $\omega = \frac{2\pi}{L}$ with $L > 0$, see [5].

The problem of fast Fourier fit has attracted the attention of some of the best scientific minds of all times. Gauss came up with a fast Fourier fit algorithm in 1866. The modern version of the fast Fourier fit is due to John Tukey and his cohorts at IBM and Princeton.[3]

We will be using the function `FastFourierFit[]` found in the literature,[2] to compute the approximating complex trigonometric polynomials mentioned in Definition 2.1 above.

```
jump[n_]  := jump[n] = 1/(2 n);
Fvalues[F_, L_, n_]  :=
   N[Table[F[L t], {t, 0, 1 - jump[n], jump[n]}]];


numtab[n_]  := numtab[n] = Table[k, {k, 1, n}];


FourierFitters[L_, n_, t_]  :=
   Table[E^((2 π I k t)/L), {k, -n + 1, n - 1}];


coeffs[n_, list_]  :=
   Join[Reverse[Part[Fourier[list], numtab[n]]],
      Part[InverseFourier[list], Drop[numtab[n], 1]]] /
      N[Sqrt[Length[list]]]


FastFourierFit[F_, L_, n_, t_]  :=
   Chop[FourierFitters[L, n, t] .
      coeffs[n, Fvalues[F, L, n]]];
```

The code works as follows: the functions `jump[]` and `Fvalues[]` produce a list of $2n - 1$ equally spaced data points off the plot of the function $f(t)$ between $t = 0$ and $t = L$. Then, the function `numtab[]` creates a list of integers from 1 to n, which is used by `coeffs[]` to concatenate two lists. The first of these lists is the Fourier transform (taken in *reversed* order) of the first n points, while the second list is the inverse Fourier transform (with the first element removed) of the same n points. To wit, the list generated by `coeffs[]` has a total of $2n - 1$ points.

Finally, the function `FastFourierFit[]` takes the dot product of the list $\left\{e^{(-n+1)2\pi it/L}, \ldots, 1, \ldots, e^{(n-1)2\pi it/L}\right\}$ generated by `FourierFitters[]` and the list concatenated by `coeffs[]`. (All numbers in the list with magnitude less than 10^{-10} are rounded to 0.)

`FastFourierFit[]` takes four arguments; the first one is the periodic function or in general the list of data points which we want to fit; the second argument is the period L of the function; the third argument is the number n for the equally spaced $2n - 1$ data points and the last argument is the variable we want to use. Note that `FastFourierFit[]` uses the built-in functions `Fourier[]` and `InverseFourier[]`, with computational cost $n \log n$.

Example 2.1. To see how the function `FastFourierFit[]` is used, consider the periodic function $f(x) = \cos(2\pi x) \sin(1 - \cos(3\pi x))$ with period

$L = 2$. A plot is given in Fig. 1.

```
f[x_] :=Cos[2π x]Sin[1-Cos[3π x]];
L=2;
cycles=2;
Plot[f[x],{x,0,cycles L},
    AxesLabel→{"x","f(x)"},
    PlotStyle→{{Thickness[0.007],RGBColor[0,0,1]}},
    PlotLabel→"cycles" cycles,
    Epilog→{{RGBColor[1,0,0],
    Thickness[0.007],Line[{{0,0},{L,0}}]},
    {Text["One Period",{L/2,0.1}]}}];
```

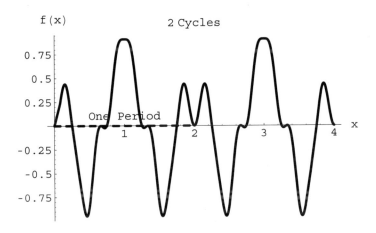

Fig. 1.   Approximating $f(x)$ with $n = 4$.

```
L=2; n=4;
fApproximation[t_] = FastFourierFit[f,L,n,t]
```

$-0.0967056 - 0.113662\ e^{-I\pi t} -$
$0.113662\ e^{I\pi t} + 0.32403\ e^{-2\ I\pi t} + 0.32403\ e^{2\ I\pi t} -$
$0.113662\ e^{-3\ I\pi t} - 0.113662\ e^{3\ I\pi t}$

or its real (non-complex) version

```
fApproximationReal[t_] =
  Chop[ComplexExpand[fApproximation[t]]]
```

$$-0.0967056 - 0.227324\ Cos[\pi\ t] +$$
$$0.64806\ Cos[2\ \pi\ t] - 0.227324\ Cos[3\ \pi\ t]$$

Note that the coefficients of $fApproximation(t)$ and $fApproximation\text{-}Real(t)$ satisfy the *relations* mentioned in Definition 2.1. Moreover, $f(x)$ has pure cosine fit. This was expected because the function $f(x) = \cos(2\pi x)\sin(1 - \cos(3\pi x))$ is even; that is, for the function $evenf(x)$, defined on the extended interval $0 \le x \le 2L$, we have $evenf(x) = f(x)$, $0 \le x \le L$, and $evenf(x) = f(2L - x)$, $L \le x \le 2L$. See also its plot in Fig. 1. Later on we will meet odd functions as well; those have pure sine fits.

The functions $f(x)$ and $fApproximationReal(t)$ are plotted together in Fig. 2. As we see, what FastFourierFit[] does is to pick $2n - 1$ equally spaced data points off the plot of $f(x)$ between $x = 0$ and $x = L$; it then tries to fit these points with a combination of complex exponentials.

```
fplot = Plot[f[x], {x, 0, L},
  AxesLabel→{"x", "f(x)"},
  PlotStyle→{Thickness[0.008], RGBColor[0, 0, 1]},
  AspectRatio→ 1/GoldenRatio ,
  DisplayFunction→Identity];

fapproxPlot = Plot[fApproximationReal[t],
  {t, 0, L}, PlotStyle→{{Thickness[0.008],
  RGBColor[1, 0, 0], Dashing[{0.03, 0.03}]}},
  AspectRatio→ 1/GoldenRatio ,
  DisplayFunction→Identity];

fdata = Table[N[{x, f[x]}], {x, 0, L - L/(2 n-1), L/(2 n-1)}];
fdataplot =
  ListPlot[fdata, PlotStyle→PointSize[0.02],
  DisplayFunction→Identity];
Show[fplot, fapproxPlot, fdataplot,
  DisplayFunction→ $DisplayFunction];
```

As we mentioned before, the coefficients c_k of the approximating polynomial in Definition 2.1 are computed using the fast Fourier transform–

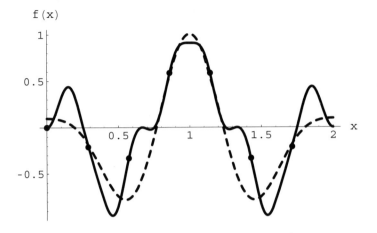

Fig. 2. The dashed plot is that of the approximating function.

incorporated in the function `FastFourierFit[]`. Another way of computing those coefficients is using the integrals

$$c_k = \frac{1}{L} \int_0^L f(t)e^{-\frac{ik(2\pi)t}{L}} dt$$

which results in the integral Fourier fit.

This formula for the coefficients is obtained if we assume that for a fixed n, the function $f(t)$ is being approximated by the function

$$complexApproximation(t) = \sum_{k=-n}^{n} c_k e^{\frac{k(2\pi)it}{L}}$$

where $L > 0$, and we set

$$f(t) = complexApproximation(t).$$

Then, we will definitely have

$$\int_0^L complexApproximation(t)e^{-\frac{j(2\pi)it}{L}} dt = \int_0^L f(t)e^{-\frac{j(2\pi)it}{L}} dt.$$

But

$$\int_0^L complexApproximation(t)e^{-\frac{j(2\pi)it}{L}} dt = Lc_j$$

and, hence, the formula for the coefficients.

The two approximations resulting from the fast Fourier fit and the integral Fourier fit are pretty close, and almost identical for large values of n.

The disadvantage of the integral Fourier fit is that the integrals that need to be computed sometimes are very hard and impractical even for numerical integration. Nonetheless, the method is useful for hand computations, whereas doing fast Fourier fit by hand is completely out of the question.

The advantage of the integral Fourier fit is that, in theoretical situations, it provides a specific formula to work with. However, after the theory is developed and calculations begin, people switch to the fast Fourier fit.

Recapping, note that `FastFourierFit[]` is a "double" approximation. It first uses sines and cosines to approximate a continuous periodic function and then uses discrete Fourier transform to approximate integrals involving these trigonometric polynomials—in effect replacing numerical integration by sampling.

3. FFF in Deriving the Heat and Wave Equations

The fast Fourier is a very useful tool and we now demonstrate its power by deriving the heat and wave equations.[2] However, some preliminaries are in order.

3.1. *Preliminaries*

As we have seen in the previous examples, using the fast Fourier fit we usually get a mixture of both sines and cosines. But sometimes we get pure sines as in

```
f[x_] = x (1-x) (2-x);
Chop[ComplexExpand[FastFourierFit[f,L=2,n=4,t]]]
```

$0.386374\ Sin[\pi\ t] + 0.046875\ Sin[2\ \pi\ t] + 0.0113738\ Sin[3\ \pi\ t]$

or pure cosines as in

```
f[x_] = x (1-x)² (2-x);
Chop[ComplexExpand[FastFourierFit[f,L=2,n=4,t]]]
```

$0.123047 + 0.0662913\ Cos[\pi\ t]\ -$
$0.09375\ Cos[2\ \pi\ t] - 0.0662913\ Cos[3\ \pi\ t]$

We will focus our attention on pure sine approximations, obtained for *odd* functions. (Even functions were mentioned earlier.)

To get a pure sine fit of $f(x)$ in the interval $0 \leq x \leq L$, two things need to be satisfied: (a) $f(0) = f(L) = 0$, and (b) for the function $oddf(x)$, defined on the extended interval $0 \leq x \leq 2L$, we have $oddf(x) = f(x)$, $0 \leq x \leq L$, and $oddf(x) = -f(2L - x)$, $L \leq x \leq 2L$.

That is, the part of the plot to the right of the center line, has to be the negative mirror image of its plot to the left of the center line.

The requirement $f(0) = f(L) = 0$, stated above, comes from the fast fourier fit of $oddf(x)$ on $0 \leq x \leq 2L$. This means the function $oddf(x)$ is approximated with the functions $\sin(k\pi t/L)$, which are all zeroed out at $t = 0$ and $t = L$. Therefore, if we want a good sines approximation of $f(x)$ on $0 \leq x \leq L$ we have to have $f(0) = f(L) = 0$.

If a given function $f(x)$ is approximated with a mixture of sines and cosines, there is a way to obtain a pure sine fit. Namely, if $f(x)$ is defined in the interval $0 \leq x \leq L$, and $f(0) = f(L) = 0$, we define a new function, $oddf(x)$ on the interval $0 \leq x \leq 2L$ as follows:

$$oddf(x) = f(x), \quad 0 \leq x \leq L,$$
$$oddf(x) = -f(2L - x), \quad L \leq x \leq 2L.$$

This new function, $odd(x)$, will clearly have a pure sine fit in the interval $0 \leq x \leq 2L$.

Example 3.1. Consider the function $f(x) = 6x(4 - x)e^{-x}$, which is approximated with a mixture of sines and cosines on $0 \leq x \leq L = 4$.

```
f[x_] = 6 x (4-x) E^-x;
Chop[ComplexExpand[FastFourierFit[f, L=4, n=3, t]]]
```

$2.94583 - 1.04677 \, Cos[\frac{\pi \, t}{2}] - 1.32181 \, Cos[\pi \, t] +$
$3.03426 \, Sin[\frac{\pi \, t}{2}] + 0.643404 \, Sin[\pi \, t]$

Since it satisfies $f(0) = f(L) = 0$, we can define the new function $oddf(x)$, which has a pure sine fit in the interval $0 \leq x \leq 2L$.

```
oddf[x_] := f[x] /; 0≤x≤L;
oddf[x_] := -f[2 L-x] /; L<x≤2 L;
Chop[ComplexExpand[FastFourierFit[oddf, 2 L, 3, t]]]
```

$4.10249 \, Sin[\frac{\pi \, t}{4}] + 2.39086 \, Sin[\frac{\pi \, t}{2}]$

238

If the condition $f(0) = f(L) = 0$ is not satisfied then the function $f(x)$ needs a bit more work before it can have a pure sine approximation. Namely, to "fix" the problem we first run a line through the endpoints $f(0)$, $f(L)$, say $line(x) = f(0) + (f(L) - f(0))x/L$, and then define the function $adjustedf(x) = f(x) - line(x)$, for which $adjustedf(0) = adjustedf(L) = 0$.

Example 3.2. Consider the function $3|0.25x - \langle 0.25x \rangle| + 1$, defined on the interval $0 \le x \le L = 3$, where $\langle 0.25x \rangle$ denotes the closest integer to $0.25x$. For this function we have $f(0) \ne f(L)$, with both being $\ne 0$. Its Fourier approximation includes both sines and cosines.

```
f[x_] = 3 Abs[0.25 x - Round[0.25 x]] + 1; {f[0], f[L = 3]}
```

$\{1, 1.75\}$

```
Chop[ComplexExpand[FastFourierFit[f, L = 3, n = 4, t]]]
```

$1.82031 - 0.446978 \; Cos\left[\frac{2\pi t}{3}\right] - 0.1875 \; Cos\left[\frac{4\pi t}{3}\right] -$
$0.115522 \; Cos[2\pi t] - 0.419519 \; Sin\left[\frac{2\pi t}{3}\right] -$
$0.046875 \; Sin\left[\frac{4\pi t}{3}\right] - 0.0445194 \; Sin[2\pi t]$

Since $f(0) \ne f(L)$ we clearly cannot, yet, apply our technique to get a pure sine approximation of this function. To "fix" the problem we first run $line(x)$ through the endpoints of the plot, and then we define the function $adjustedf(x) = f(x) - line(x)$, with $adjustedf(0) = adjustedf(L) = 0$. See Fig. 3.

We can now apply our technique to $adjustedf(t)$ and obtain a pure sine approximation of it.

```
line[x_] = (f[L] - f[0]) x / L + f[0];
adjustedf[x_] = f[x] - line[x];
Plot[adjustedf[x], {x, 0, L},
    PlotStyle→{{Thickness[0.01], RGBColor[0, 0, 1]}},
    AxesLabel→{"x", "adjustedf"}];

oddAdjustedf[x_] := adjustedf[x] /; 0≤x≤L;
oddAdjustedf[x_] := -adjustedf[2 L - x] /; L<x≤2 L;

Chop[ComplexExpand[FastFourierFit[oddAdjustedf, 2 L, n = 4, t]]]
```

$0.772748 \; Sin\left[\frac{\pi t}{3}\right] - 0.1875 \; Sin\left[\frac{2\pi t}{3}\right] + 0.0227476 \; Sin[\pi t]$

3.2. The Heat Equation $\frac{\partial^2 temp(x,t)}{\partial x^2} = \frac{\partial temp(x,t)}{\partial t}$

We can now tackle the heat equation.

Problem 3.1. Start with a heated wire L units long with the temperature allowed to vary from position to position on the wire. The function $startertemp(x)$ gives the temperature at the point x, for $0 \leq x \leq L$, of the wire at the start of the experiment. Because of the previous discussion we consider, without loss of generality, functions $startertemp(x)$ for which $startertemp(0) = startertemp(L) = 0$. That way we can easily obtain a pure sine approximation.

Think of the wire as the interval $0 \leq x \leq L$. At the start of the experiment, we instantly cool the ends at $x = 0$ and $x = L$ and maintain these ends at temperature 0; we also take pains to guarantee that the rest of the wire is perfectly insulated.

The problem is to find a formula for $temp(x,t)$, so that we can tell the temperature at a given point x, at time t after the start of the experiment.

We first give a theoretical solution, which we then compare with one obtained based on FFF.

Theoretical Solution (Based on Fourier Transforms).
Given the problem statement, the previous discussion on odd functions

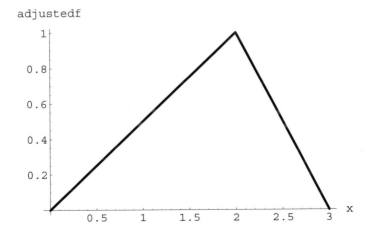

Fig. 3.   The adjusted function.

and using the integral computation of the coefficients, we have

$$\alpha_k = 0,$$

$$\beta_k = \int_0^L f(x) \sin\left(\frac{k\pi x}{L}\right) dx.$$

Specifically for the heat equation, β_k becomes

$$\beta_k = \int_0^L temp(y,t) \sin\left(\frac{k\pi y}{L}\right) dy.$$

Taking the first derivative of the expression above, we obtain

$$\frac{d\beta_k}{dt} = \beta_k^{(1)} = \int_0^L \frac{\partial temp(y,t)}{\partial t} \sin\left(\frac{k\pi y}{L}\right) dy.$$

Applying the Sine Fourier Transform on both of the heat equation, we have

$$\int_0^L \frac{\partial temp(y,t)}{\partial t} \sin\left(\frac{k\pi y}{L}\right) dy = \int_0^L \frac{\partial^2 temp(y,t)}{\partial x^2} \sin\left(\frac{k\pi y}{L}\right) dy.$$

We observe that the left-hand side above is identical to the first derivative of β_k, i.e. to $\beta_k^{(1)}$, while the right-hand side is equal to $\beta_k^{(2)}$. So we have

$$\frac{d\beta_k}{dt} = -\frac{k^2\pi^2}{L^2}\beta_k.$$

with verification being left to the reader. Solving this last differential equation, we obtain

$$\beta_k = \lambda e^{-\frac{k^2\pi^2}{L^2}t},$$

where $\lambda = \beta_k(0)$.

Similarly, from the initial condition $temp(x,0) = startertemp(x)$, we obtain

$$\beta_k(0) = \int_0^L temp(y,0) \sin\left(\frac{k\pi y}{L}\right) dy = \int_0^L startertemp(y) \sin\left(\frac{k\pi y}{L}\right) dy.$$

Hence, β_k becomes

$$\beta_k = e^{-\frac{k^2\pi^2}{L^2}t} \int_0^L startertemp(y) \sin\left(\frac{k\pi y}{L}\right) dy.$$

It easily follows that the Inverse Fourier transform gives the solution of the heat equation:

$$temp(x,t) = \frac{2}{L} \sum_{k=1}^{\infty} \beta_k \sin\left(\frac{k\pi x}{L}\right) =$$

$$\frac{2}{L} \sum_{k=1}^{\infty} e^{-\frac{k^2\pi^2}{L^2}t} \sin\left(\frac{k\pi x}{L}\right) \int_0^L startertemp(y) \sin\left(\frac{k\pi y}{L}\right) dy.$$

Indeed, we have:

```
startertemp[x_] = 0.2 Sin[2x]²(x-3)²; L=3;
temp[x_, t_] : =
```

$$\frac{2}{L}\sum_{k=1}^{8} e^{-\frac{k^2\pi^2}{L^2}t}\, \text{Sin}[\tfrac{k\ \pi\ x}{L}] \int_0^L \text{startertemp}[y]\,\text{Sin}[\tfrac{k\ \pi\ y}{L}]\,dy;$$

```
temp[2.5, 1]
```

0.0590846

Solution Based on Fast Fourier Fit. Using FFF we can easily obtain the formula for $temp(x,t)$ proceeding as follows.

(a) Adjust the function $startertemp(x)$ (that is, make $startertemp(x)$ an *odd* function) and using the fast Fourier fit obtain a sines only approximation of it, for a given accuracy n. Given the original assumptions $startertemp(0) = startertemp(L) = 0$, this step is easily done.
(b) Pick off the coefficients $A(k)$ of the $\sin(k\pi x/L)$ terms of the sines only approximation of the adjusted $startertemp(x)$.
(c) Write down the formula for $temp(x,t)$ as

$$temp(x,t) = \sum_{k=1}^{n} A_k e^{-\frac{k^2\pi^2}{L^2}t} \sin\left(\frac{k\pi x}{L}\right).$$

Note. The terms $\sin(k\pi t/L)$ in the sines only approximation of the adjusted $startertemp(x)$ are written as $\sin(k\pi x/L)$, i.e. the usual t's are replaced by x's.

The central question that needs to be answered is why were the terms $e^{-\frac{k^2\pi^2}{L^2}t}$ introduced. This is explained below.

It is well known[4] that to a first approximation, and after the appropriate unit adjustments are made, the function $temp(x,t)$ satisfies the partial differential equation $\frac{\partial^2 temp(x,t)}{\partial x^2} = \frac{\partial temp(x,t)}{\partial t}$, known as the heat equation. That is, the second derivative of $temp(x,t)$ with respect to x equals the first derivative of $temp(x,t)$ with respect to t.

The boundary conditions for this differential equation are

$$temp(x,0) = startertemp(x),$$
$$temp(0,t) = 0 \quad \text{and} \quad temp(L,t) = 0, \forall t.$$

The key boundary conditions are

242

$$temp(0,t) = 0 \quad \text{and} \quad temp(L,t) = 0, \forall t,$$

which agree with the fact that $\sin(k\pi x/L) = 0$ for $x = 0$ and $x = L$ for all positive integers k. That means that for each fixed time t, and any value of n, we can approximate $temp(x,t)$ with a sines only fit of the form

$$approxtemp(x,t) = \sum_{k=1}^{n} u(t,k) \sin\left(\frac{k\pi x}{L}\right),$$

where the Fourier fit coefficients $u(t,k)$ have to be determined. Note that these coefficients depend on t as well as k because you expect a different adjusted sine fit at different times t.

The heat equation says $\frac{\partial^2 temp(x,t)}{\partial x^2} = \frac{\partial temp(x,t)}{\partial t}$. Instead of $temp(x,t)$ we use its approximation, $approxtemp(x,t)$, into the heat equation and see that

$$\sum_{k=1}^{n} u(t,k)(\frac{k\pi}{L})^2(-\sin\left(\frac{k\pi x}{L}\right)) = \sum_{k=1}^{n} \frac{\partial u(t,k)}{\partial t} \sin\left(\frac{k\pi x}{L}\right).$$

However, the above equation is valid only if the following exponential differential equation is true:

$$\frac{\partial u(t,k)}{\partial t} = -u(t,k)(\frac{k\pi}{L})^2.$$

But we already know that the solution to this last differential equation is

$$u(t,k) = A(k)e^{-(\frac{k\pi}{L})^2 t}.$$

So, in order to compute the Fourier fit coefficients we have to determine the coefficients $A(k)$.

Substituting these $u(t,k)$ into $approxtemp(x,t)$, we obtain

$$approxtemp(x,t) = \sum_{k=1}^{n} A(k)e^{-(\frac{k\pi}{L})^2 t} \sin\left(\frac{k\pi x}{L}\right),$$

which for $t = 0$ becomes

$$approxtemp(x,0) = \sum_{k=1}^{n} A(k) \sin\left(\frac{k\pi x}{L}\right).$$

This is the approximation to the starting temperature, so we pick off the $A(k)$'s from the sine fit of the adjusted $startertemp(x)$.

Example 3.3. At the start of this particular experiment, the temperature of the wire at position x (for $0 \leq x \leq L = 3$) is given by the following function $startertemp(x) = 0.2\sin^2(2x)(x-3)$.

For the given function we have $startertemp(0) = startertemp(L) = 0$ and its plot is shown below in Fig. 4 for $t = 0$.

```
L=3;
startertemp[x_] =0.2Sin[2x]^2(x-3)^2;
{startertemp[0],startertemp[L]}
```

$\{0, 0\}$

```
Plot[startertemp[x],{x,0,L},
   PlotStyle→{{Thickness[0.007],
   RGBColor[0,0,1]}},
   AxesLabel→{"x","startertemp[x]"}];
```

We next adjust the function $startertemp(x)$ and arbitrarily setting $n = 8$ we compute its sines only approximation with FFF. That is, we have:

```
oddStartertemp[x_] :=startertemp[x]/;0≤x≤L;
oddStartertemp[x_] :=-startertemp[2 L-x]/;L<x≤2 L;

sinesOnlyfit[t_] =
Chop[ComplexExpand[
FastFourierFit[oddStartertemp,2 L,n=8,x]]]
```

$0.379996\ Sin[\frac{\pi\ x}{3}] + 0.395139\ Sin[\frac{2\ \pi\ x}{3}] + 0.298906\ Sin[\pi\ x] +$
$0.0691479\ Sin[\frac{4\ \pi\ x}{3}] - 0.0908022\ Sin[\frac{5\ \pi\ x}{3}] -$
$0.0548269\ Sin[2\ \pi\ x] - 0.0186735\ Sin[\frac{7\ \pi\ x}{3}]$

We then pick off the coefficients of the $\sin(k\pi t/L)$ terms:

```
A[k_] := Coefficient[sinesOnlyfit[t],Sin[(k π x/L)]];
Table[A[k],{k,1,n}]
```

$\{0.379996, 0.395139, 0.298906, 0.0691479,$
$-0.0908022, -0.0548269, -0.0186735, 0\}$

and the function $temp(x, t)$ is:

```
temp[x_, t_] = Σ A[k] E^-(k π/L)^2 t Sin[(k π) x/L]
              k=1
```

$$0.379996 \ e^{-\frac{\pi^2 t}{9}} \ Sin[\frac{\pi x}{3}] + 0.395139 \ e^{-\frac{4\pi^2 t}{9}} \ Sin[\frac{2\pi x}{3}] +$$
$$0.298906 \ e^{-\pi^2 t} \ Sin[\pi x] + 0.0691479 \ e^{-\frac{16\pi^2 t}{9}} \ Sin[\frac{4\pi x}{3}] -$$
$$0.0908022 \ e^{-\frac{25\pi^2 t}{9}} \ Sin[\frac{5\pi x}{3}] - 0.0548269 \ e^{-4\pi^2 t} \ Sin[2\pi x] -$$
$$0.0186735 \ e^{-\frac{49\pi^2 t}{9}} \ Sin[\frac{7\pi x}{3}]$$

```
temp[2.5, 1]
```

0.0592159

The result is pretty close to the one obtained earlier using the theoretical solution.

In Fig. 4 we show the temperature distribution, $temp[x, t]$, for various values of t.

```
g[t_] := Plot[temp[x,t], {x, 0, L},
    AxesLabel→{"x", " temp"},
    PlotStyle→{{Thickness[0.01], Black}},
    AspectRatio→0.5, PlotLabel→N[t] " = t",
PlotRange→ {0,1.5}];

timestep=1; Table[g[t],{t,0,8,timestep}]

Show[GraphicsArray[{{g[0],g[0.1],g[0.2]},
{g[0.3],g[0.4],g[0.5]}},
ImageSize→ {500,500},GraphicsSpacing→ {0,0}]];
```

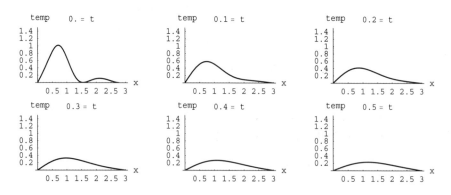

Fig. 4. The initial temperature distribution ($t = 0$) along with $temp[x, t]$ at various time steps.

3.3. The Wave Equation $\frac{\partial^2 position(x,t)}{\partial x^2} = \frac{\partial^2 position(x,t)}{\partial t^2}$

We state the wave equation problem analogously.

Problem 3.2. Start with a string fixed at 0 and L on the x-axis. The string is pulled to an initial position and then allowed to vibrate on its own, starting with initial velocity 0. The function $starterposition(x)$ gives the position of the wire at the point x, for $0 \leq x \leq L$. As in the case of the heat equation, because of the previous discussion we consider, without loss of generality, functions $starterposition(x)$ for which $starterposition(0) = starterposition(L) = 0$. That way we can easily adjust them for pure sine approximation.

The problem is to find a formula for $position(x, t)$, so that we can tell the position of the string at a given point x, at time t after the start of the experiment.

Solution. The solution of the wave equation is analogous to the heat equation presented here and can be found in [2].

4. Conclusions

Our goal has been to put together several difficult-to-access applications of FFT for educational purposes. Hopefully, the programs provided here will facilitate the understanding of these concepts and will be of help for further experimentation and development.

References

1. W. L. Briggs and V. E. Henson, *The DFT: An Owners Manual for the Discrete Fourier Transform* (SIAM, Philadelphia, 1995).
2. B. Davis and J. Uhl, *Differential Equations & Mathematica — Part of the "Calculus & Mathematica" series of books* (Math Everywhere, Inc., 1999).
3. D. Kahaner, C. Moler and S. Nash, *Numerical Methods and Software* (Prentice Hall, Englewood Cliffs, New Jersey, 1989).
4. M. Pickering, *An Introduction to Fast Fourier Transform Methods for Partial Differential Equations, with Applications* (John Wiley & Sons, New York, 1986).
5. W. Strampp, V. Ganzha and E. Vorozhtsov, *Höhere Mathematik mit Mathematica, Vieweg Lehrbuch Computeralgebra* (Braunschweig/Wiesbaden, 1997).
6. J. S. Walker, *Fast Fourier Transforms*, Second Edition (CRC Press, Boca Raton, 1996).
7. H. J. Weaver, *Applications of Discrete and Continuous Fourier Analysis* (John Wiley & Sons, New York, 1983).

AUTHOR INDEX